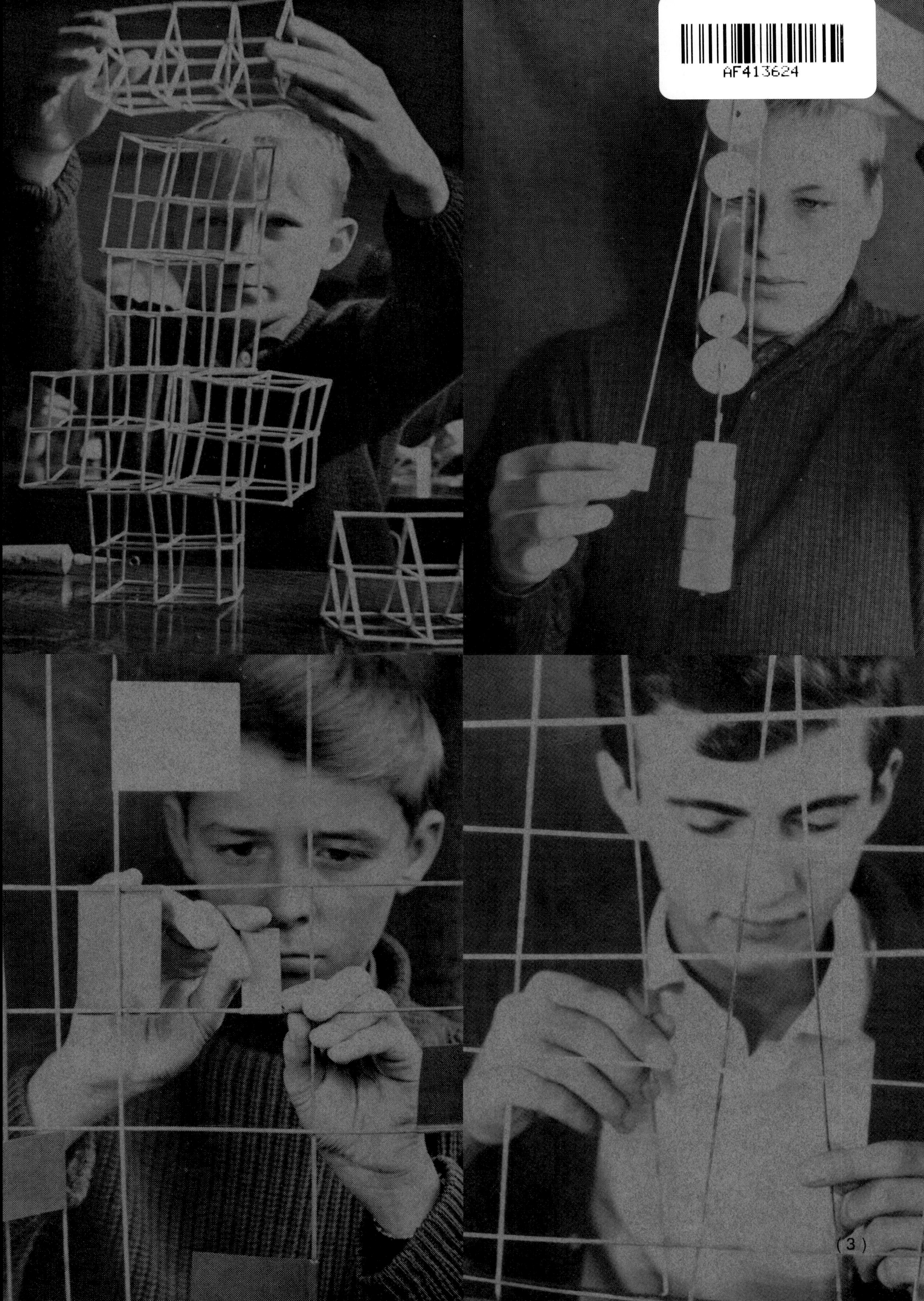
AF413624

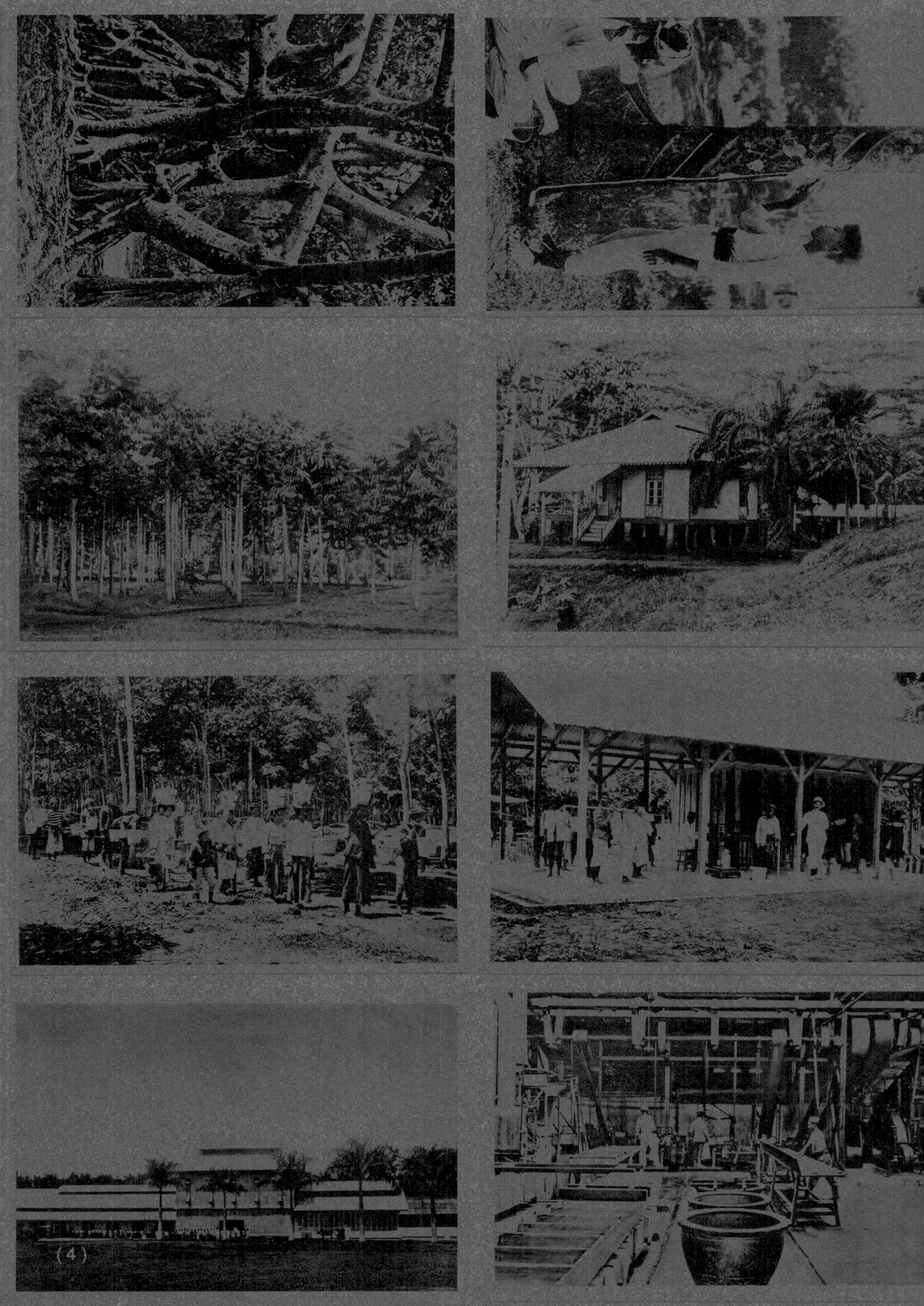

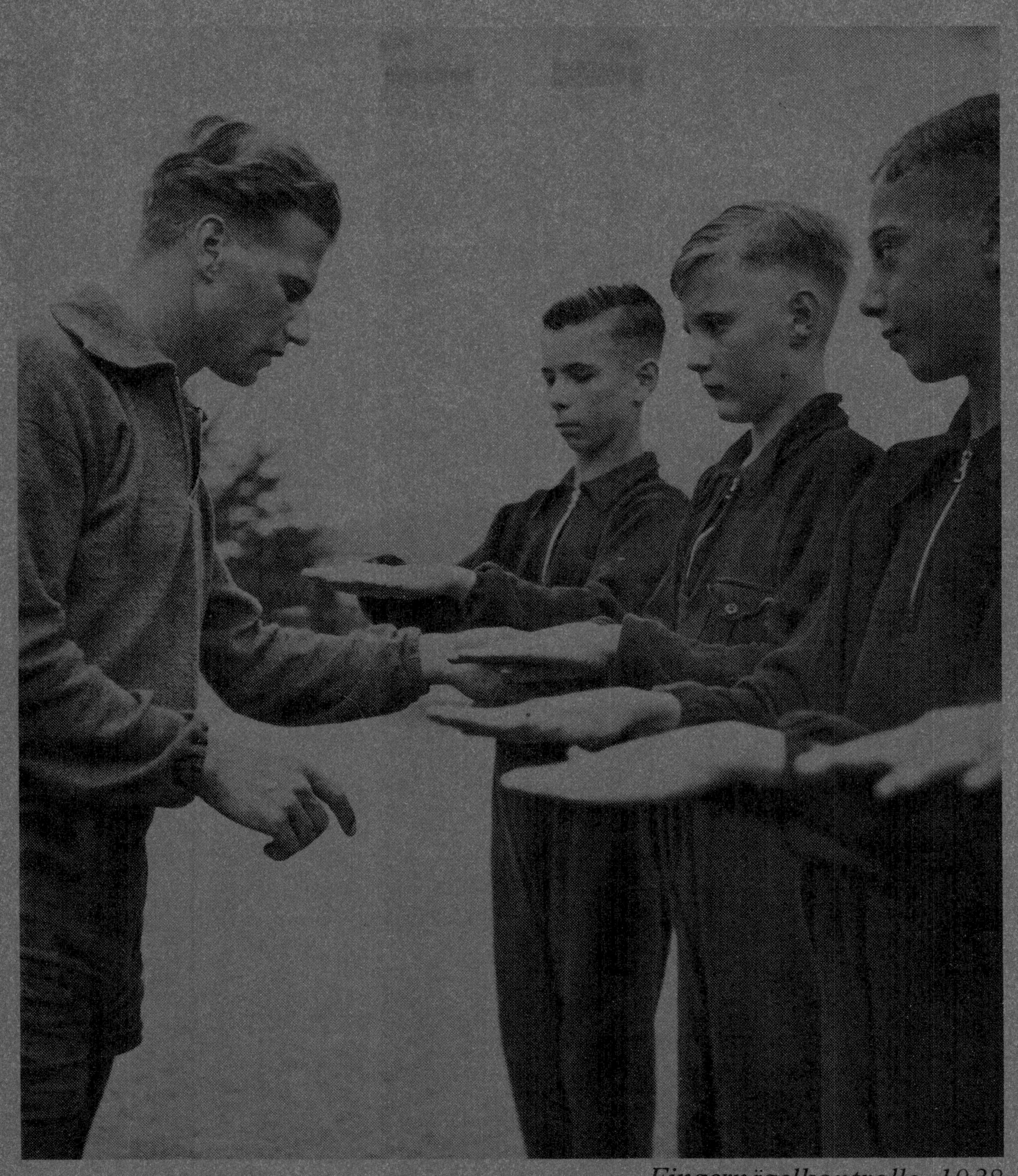

Fingernägelkontrolle, 1938

(5)

Creemos que el joven que crezca sin tener idea
de cómo se produce una mazorca de maíz, una fruta,
cómo se produce el azúcar, cómo se producen
los tejidos, cómo se produce la carne, la leche, los
alimentos, creemos que el joven que no tenga idea de
eso, sencillamente crecerá ignorando algo que es
fundamental. Sin tener una idea de eso crecerá
un joven deformado. Y no se olviden de algo: que
la aspiración de nuestra sociedad, de nuestra revolución
es que algún día trabajo manual y trabajo intelectual
sean realizados prácticamente por todos, por todos.

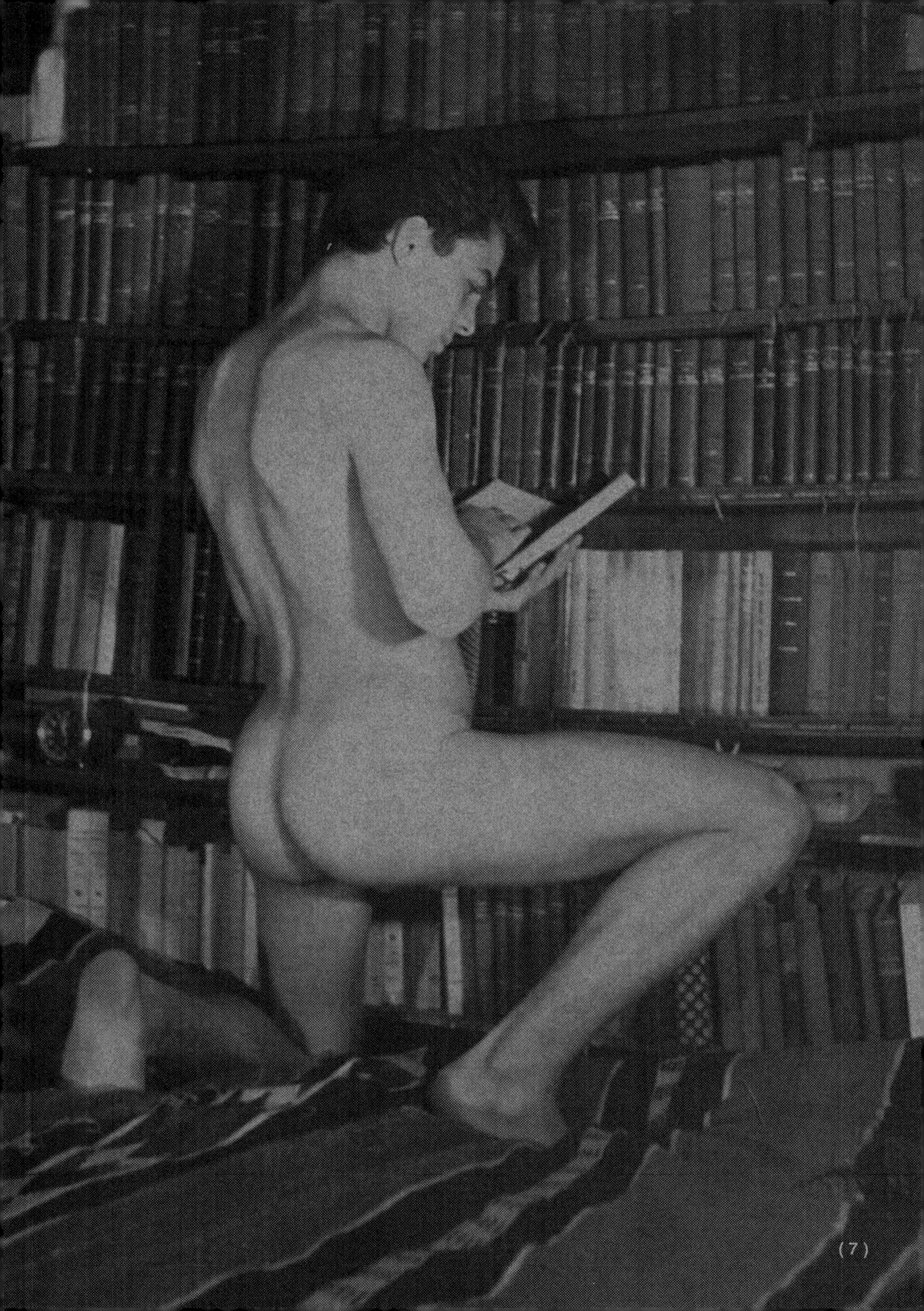

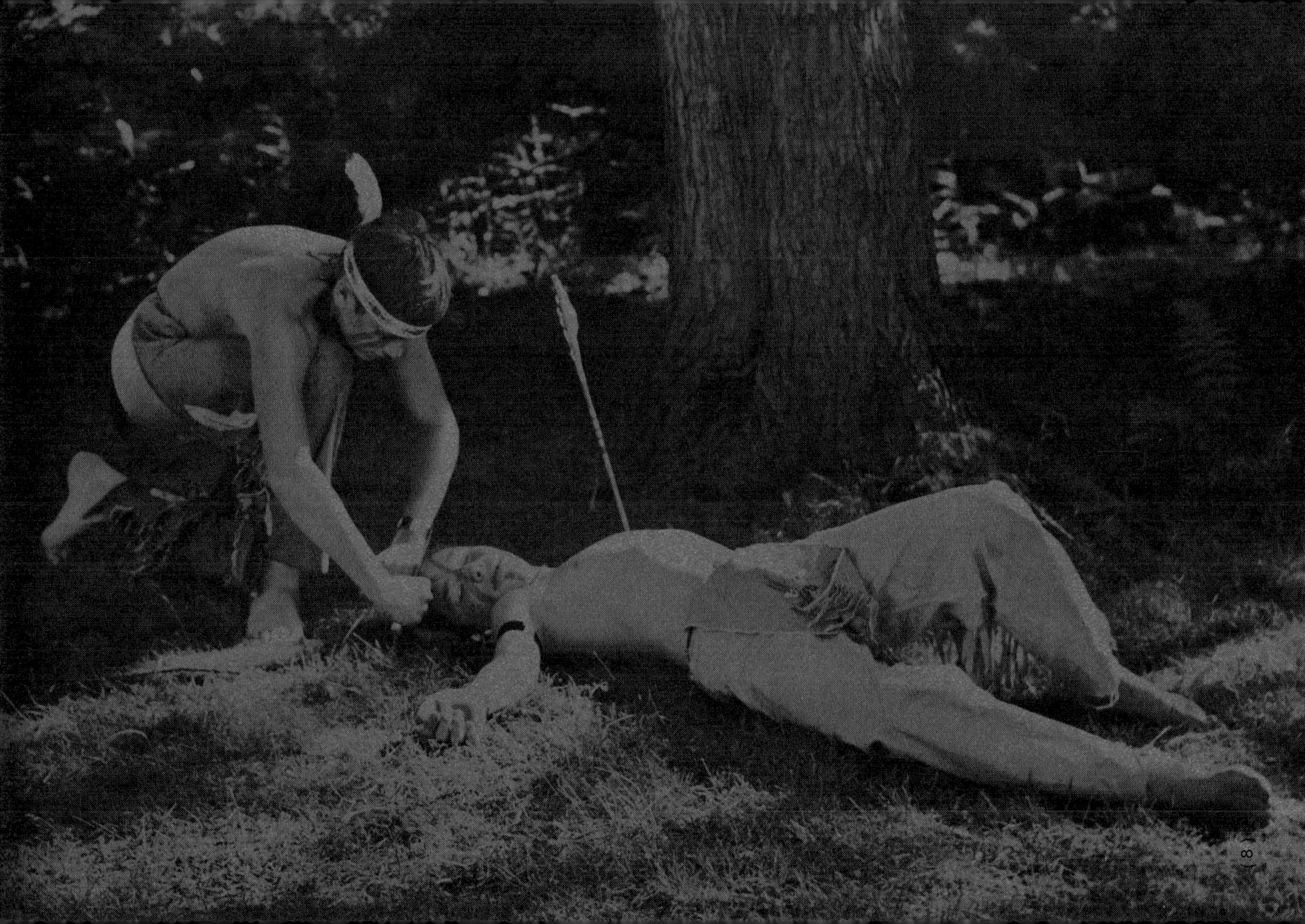

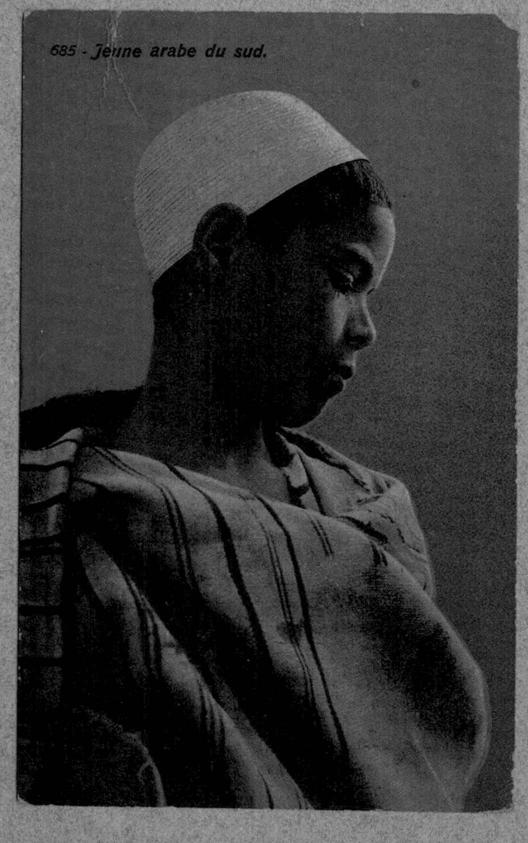

685 - Jeune arabe du sud.

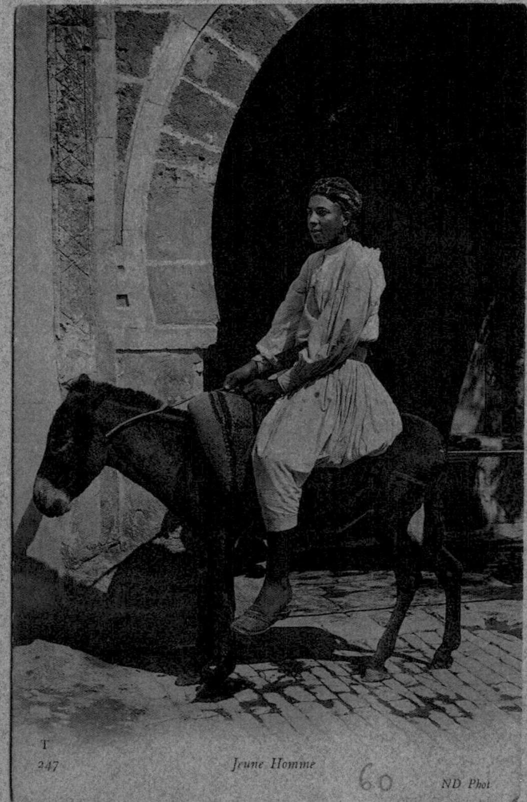

247

Jeune Homme

ND Phot

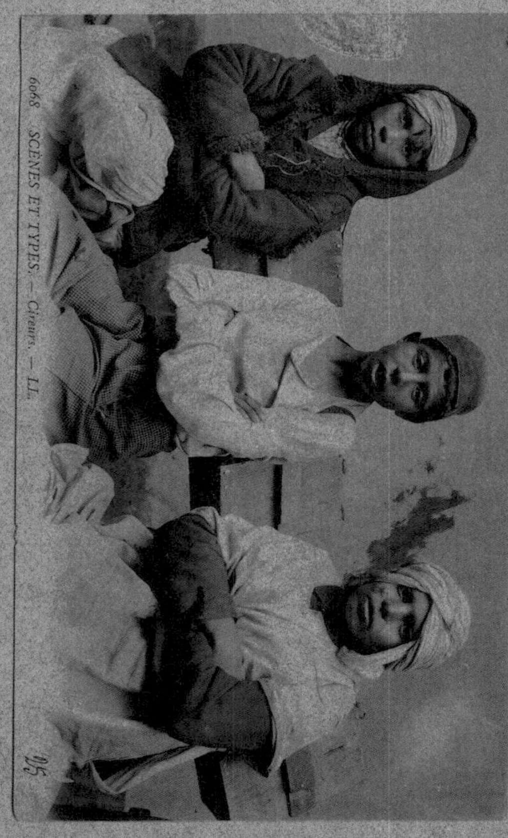

6068 SCENES ET TYPES. — Cireurs. — LL.

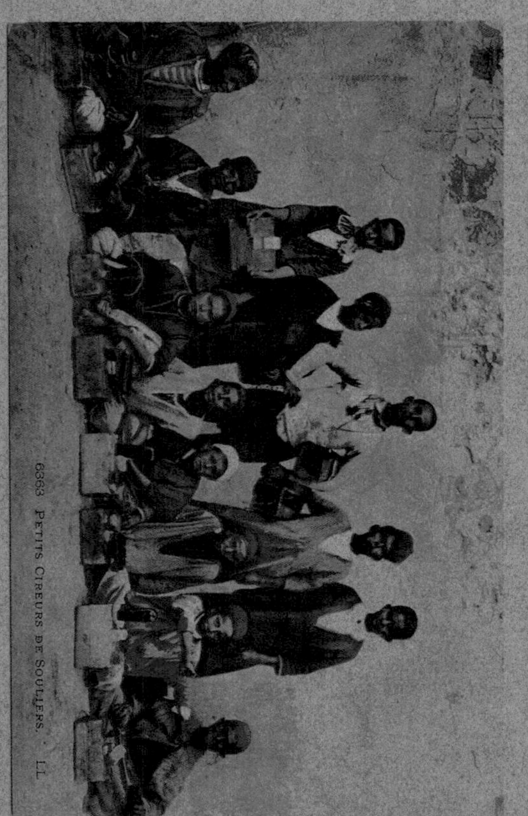

6363 Petits Cireurs de Souliers. LL.

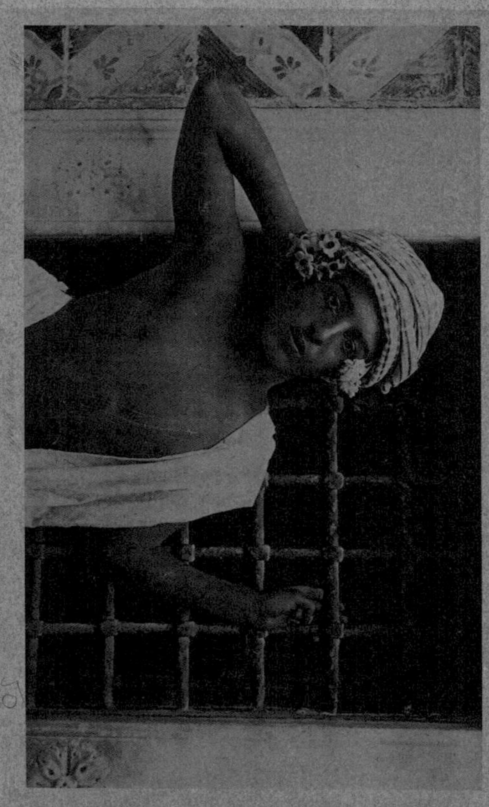

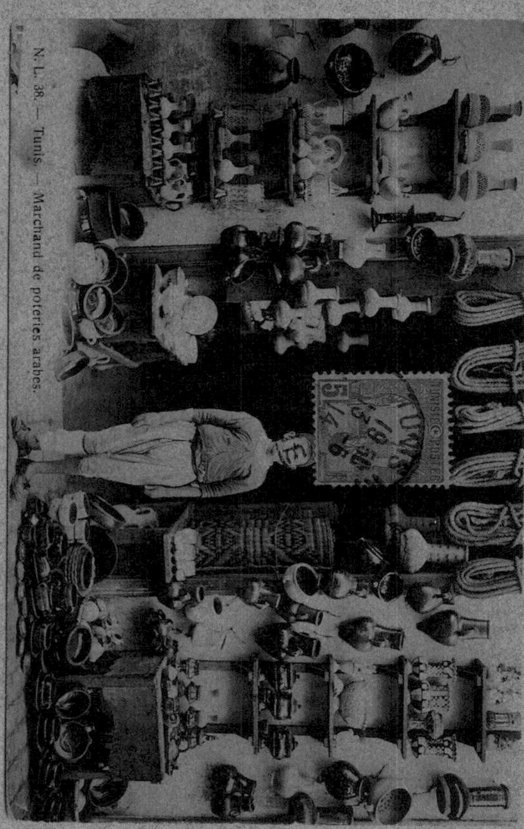

N. L. 38. — Tunis. — Marchand de poteries arabes.

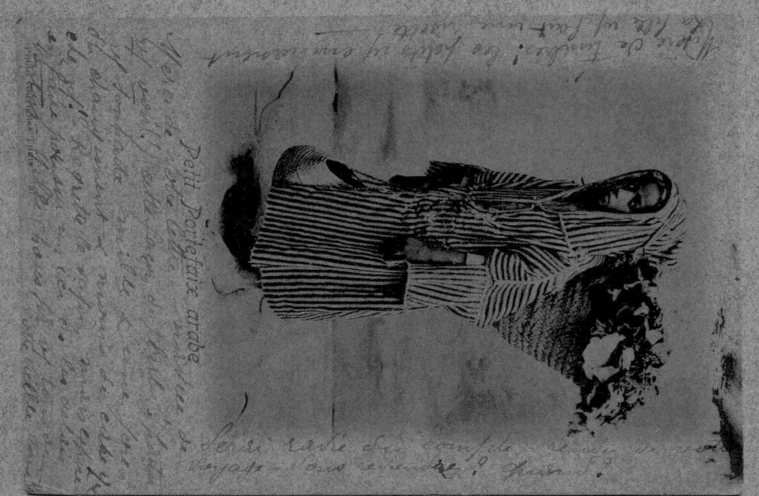

Petit Portefaix arabe

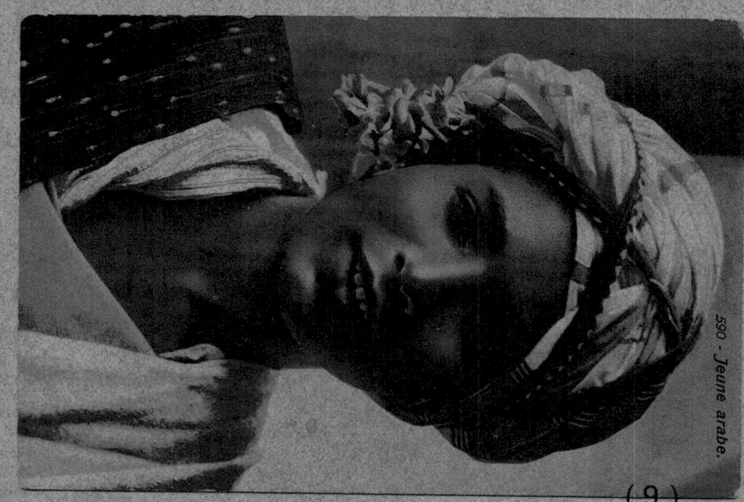

590 - Jeune arabe.

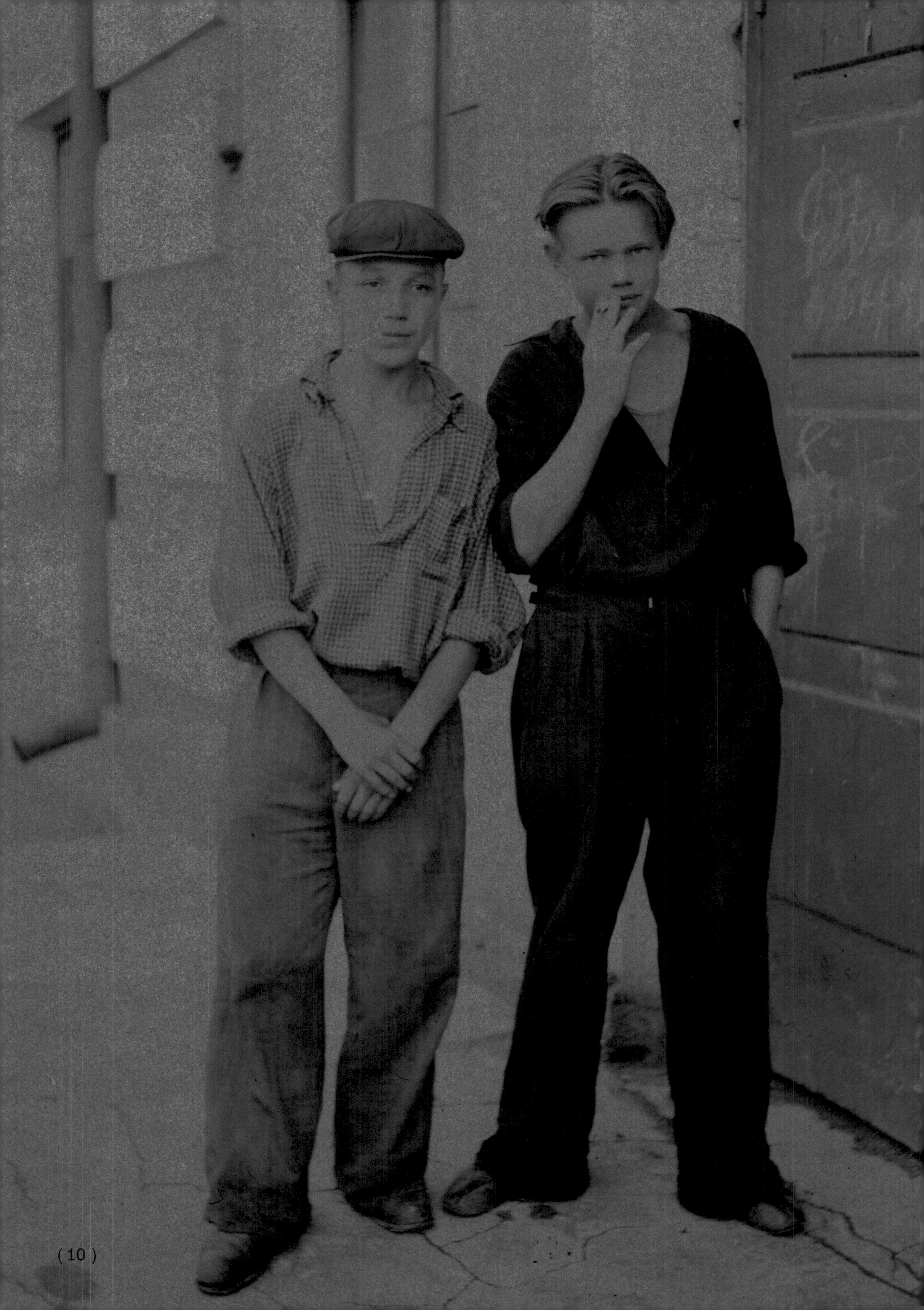

sans frontière
pour un hebdo de l'immigration
Mardi 29 Mai 1979
N° 03
4fr
Exclusif:
pétition de Longwy
Photos SE. DES
Au nom de la loi:
TAISEZ-VOUS!

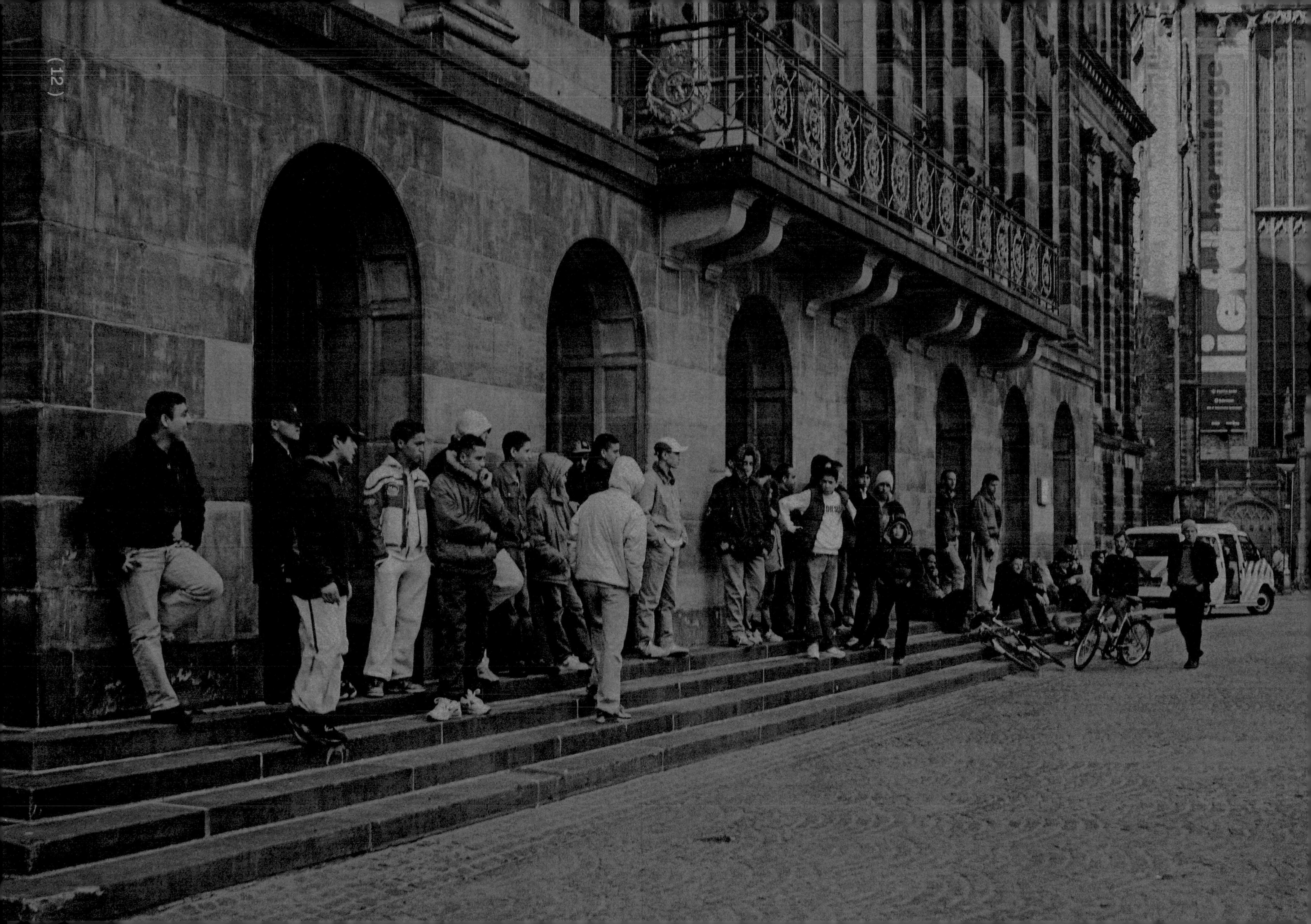

liefd hermitage

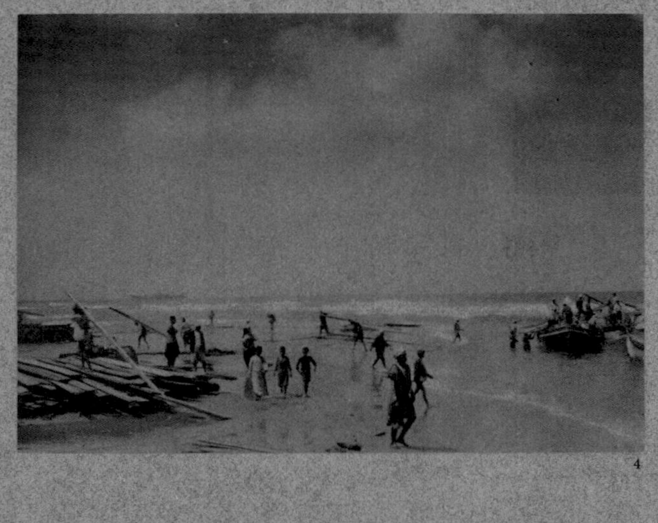

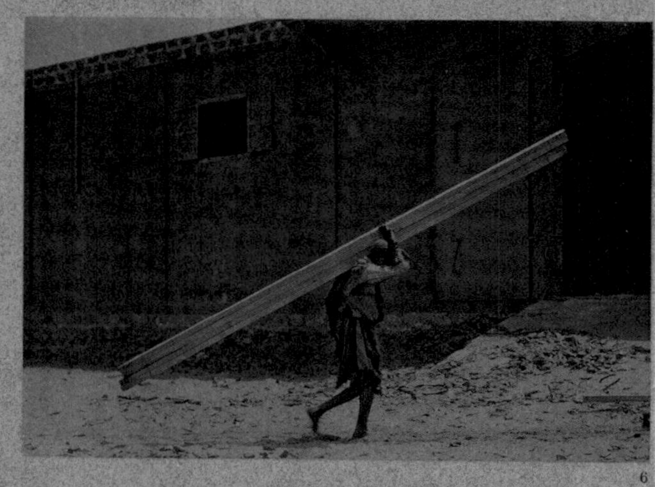

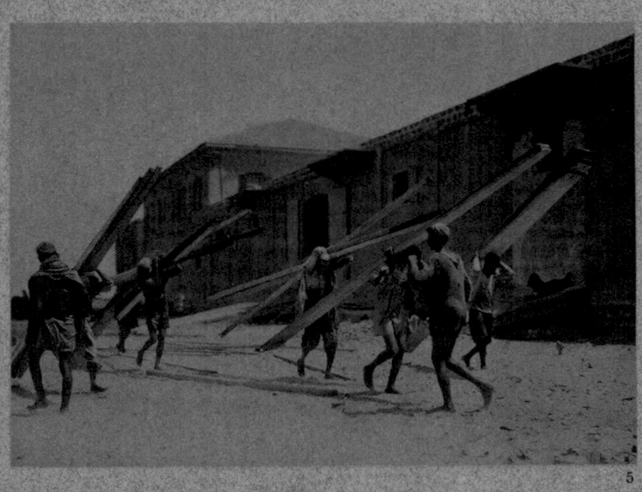

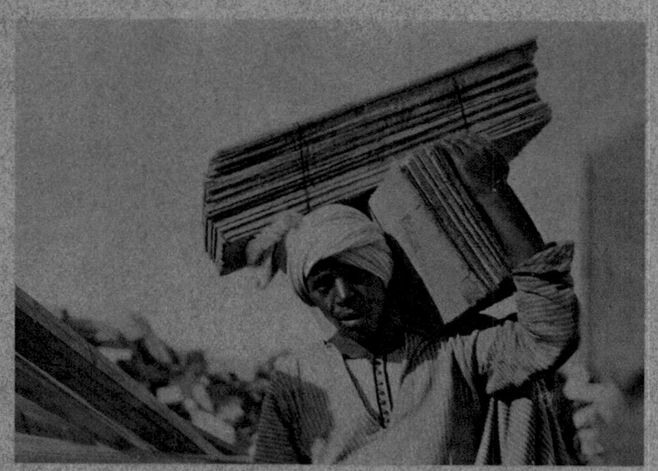

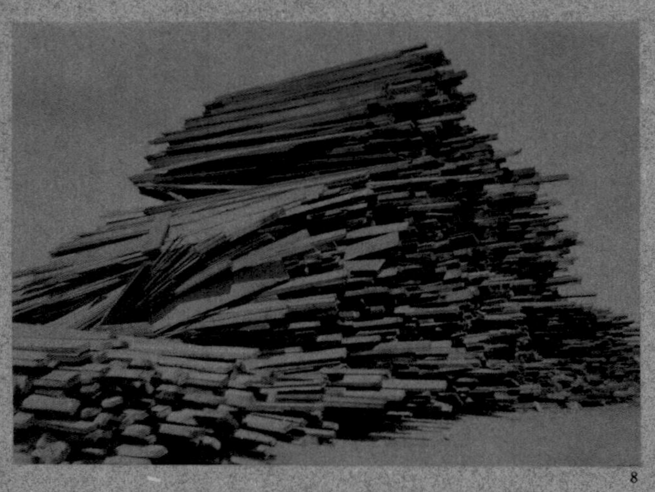

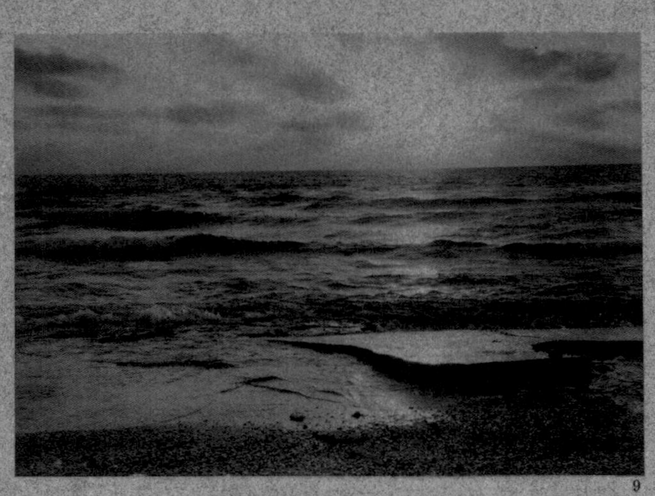

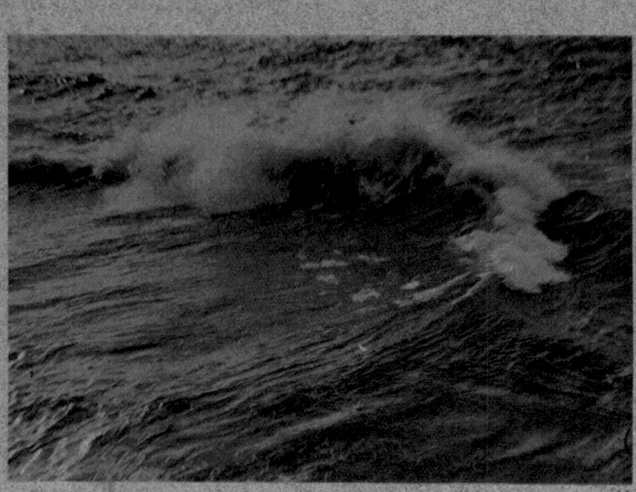

(13)

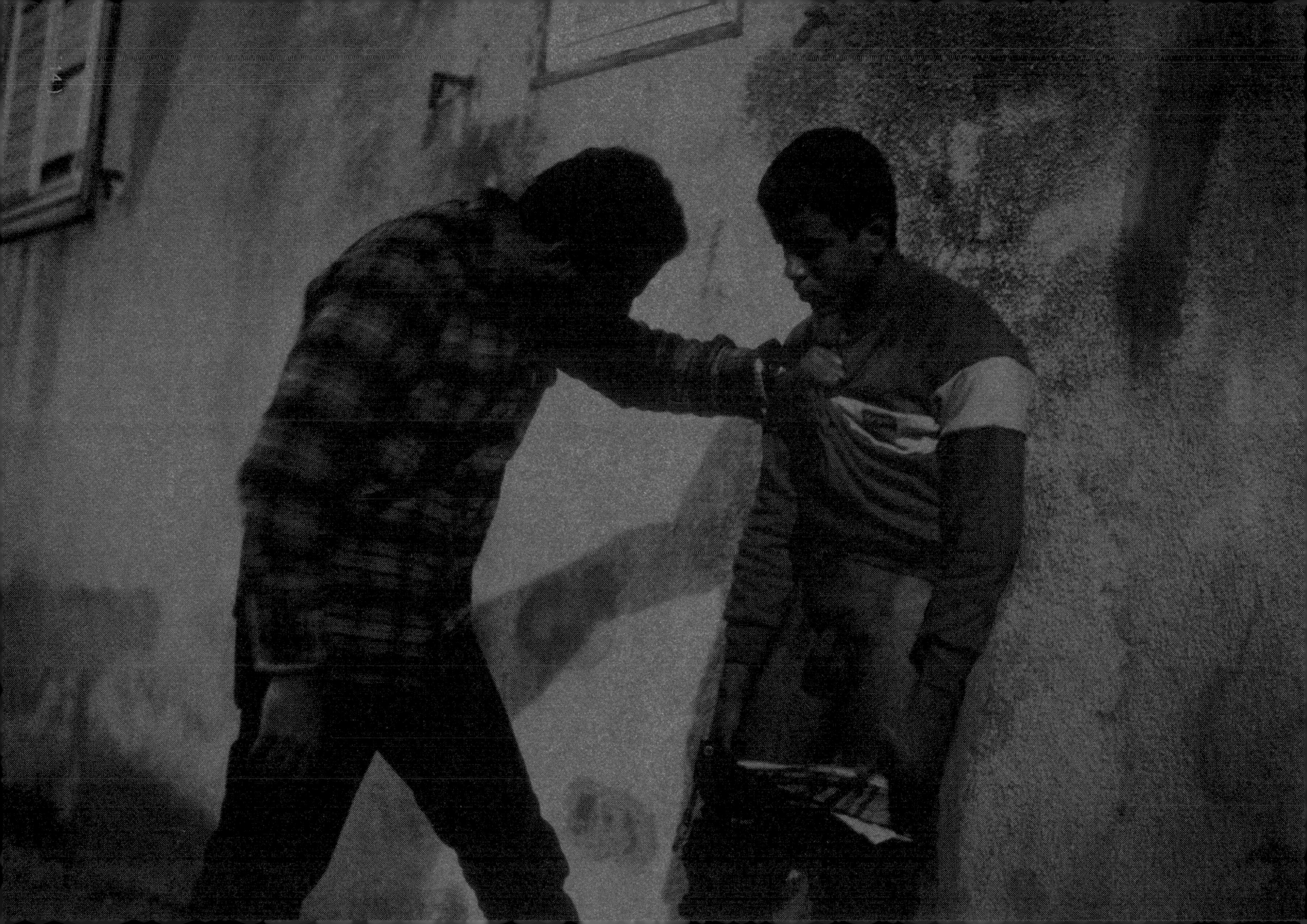

You wonder why we uprise
Politically unstabilised
Economically destabilised
People dehumanised
Youth criminalised
Mentally vandalised
Housing ghettoised
Politically unrecognised
And you wonder why we uprise.

Leroy Cooper, Liverpool 8.

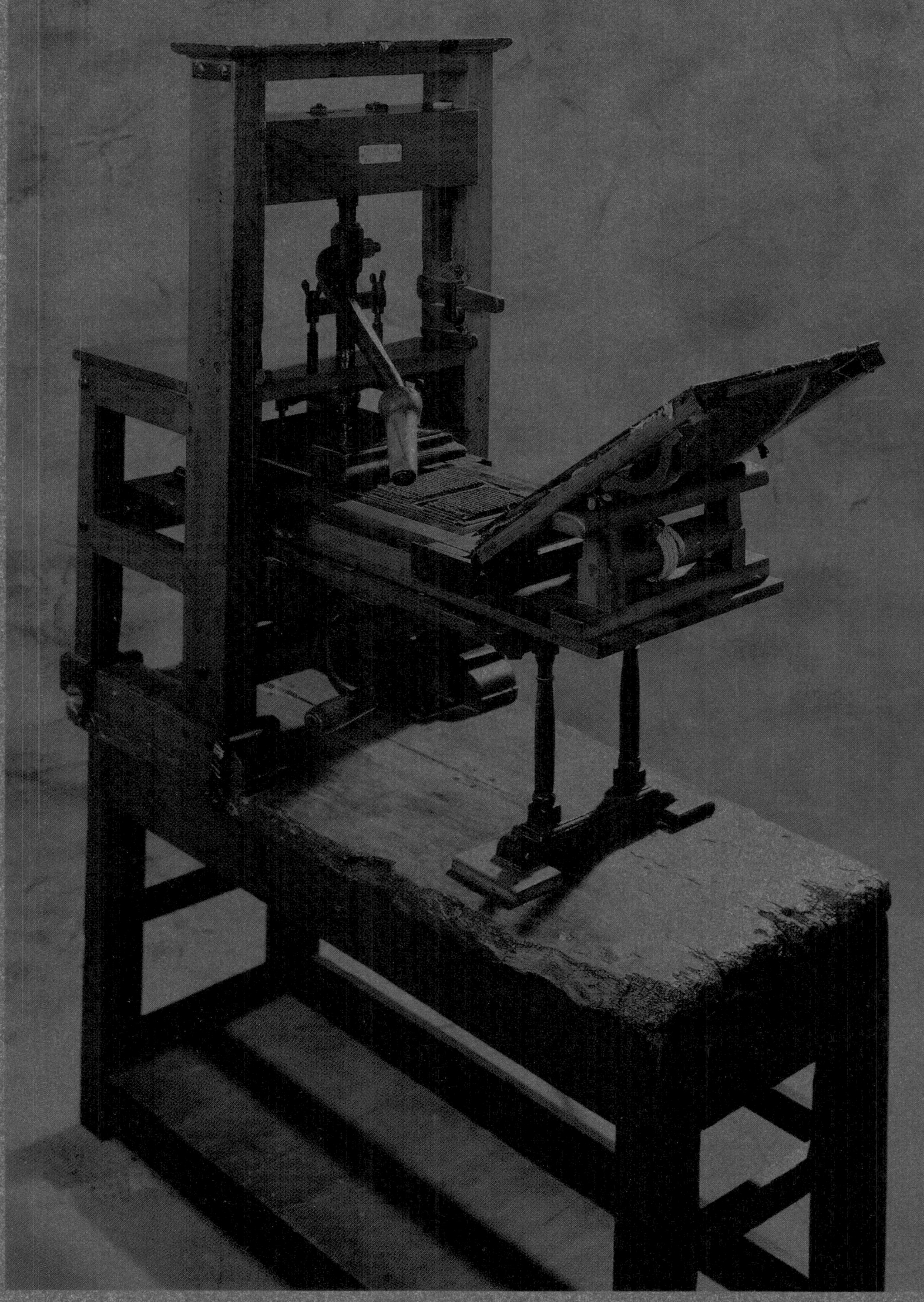

8. Clandestine Press. Eighteenth century. Musée de l'Imprimerie et de la Banque, Lyon, France (photo: Studio Dussouillez, Rutter).

(16) This small eighteenth-century "clandestine press" was designed to be stowed rapidly in a closet to evade detection by the police (cat. no. 110).

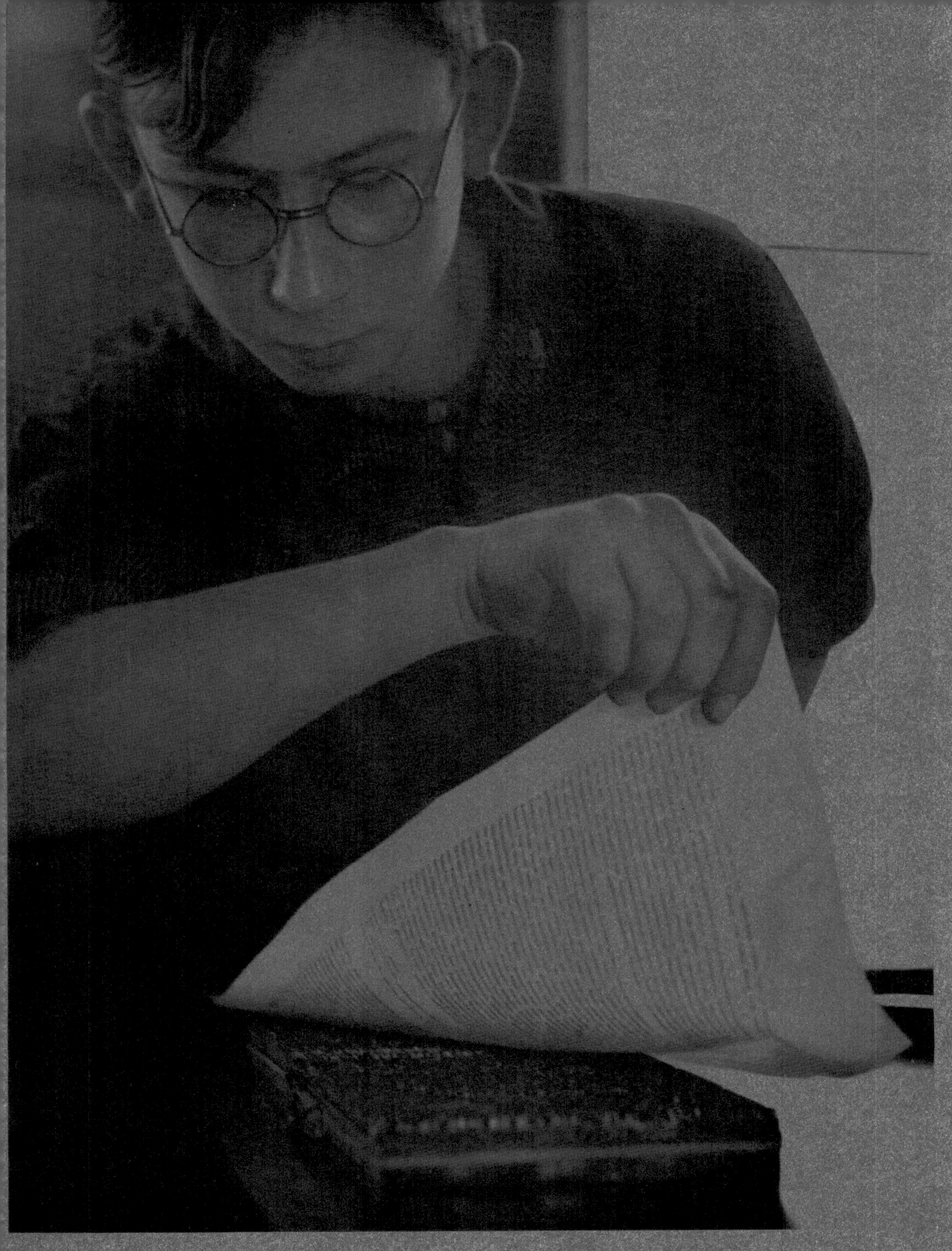

Buchdrucker

(17)

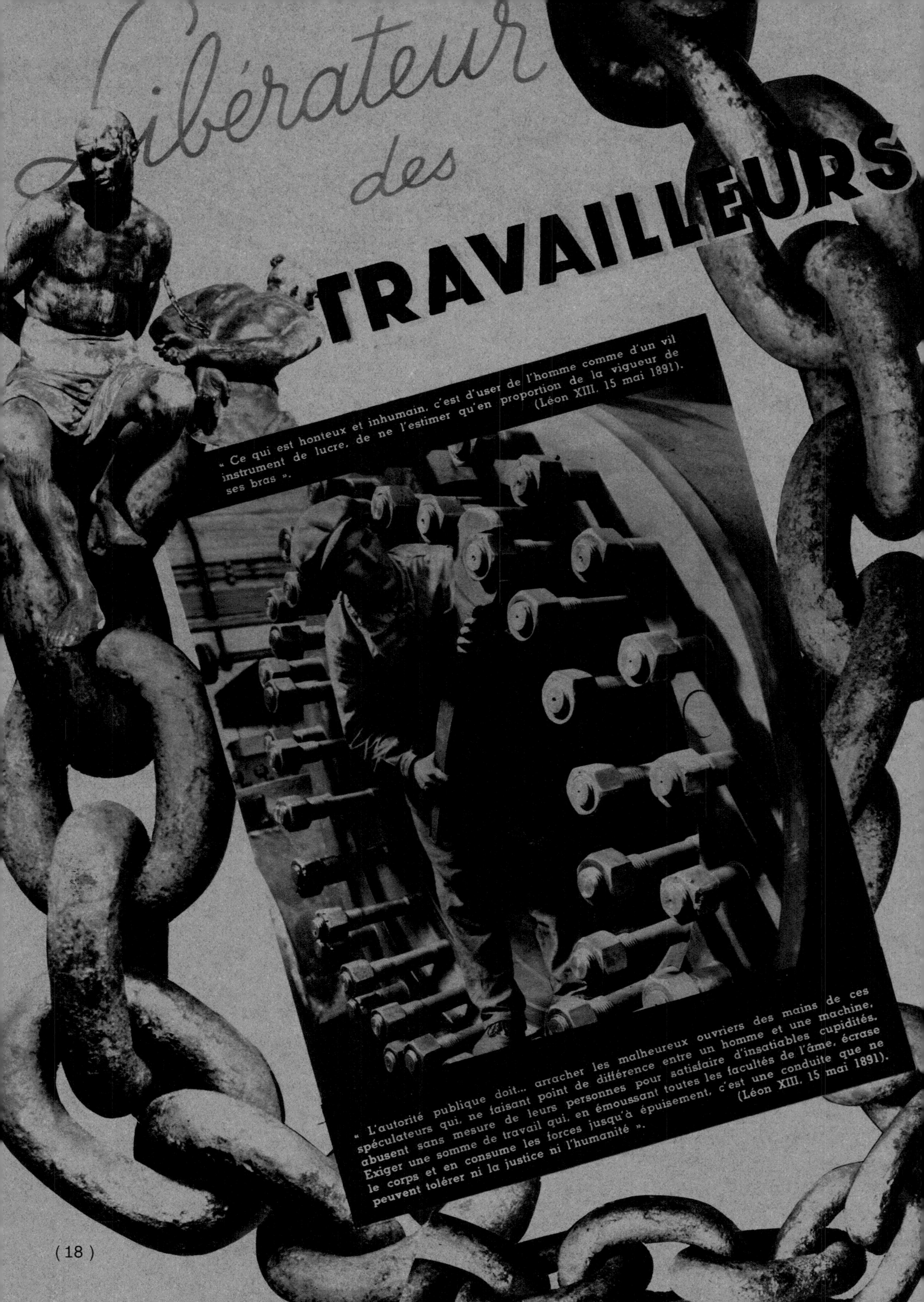

Libérateur des TRAVAILLEURS

« Ce qui est honteux et inhumain, c'est d'user de l'homme comme d'un vil instrument de lucre, de ne l'estimer qu'en proportion de la vigueur de ses bras ». (Léon XIII. 15 mai 1891).

« L'autorité publique doit... arracher les malheureux ouvriers des mains de ces spéculateurs qui, ne faisant point de différence entre un homme et une machine, abusent sans mesure de leurs personnes pour satisfaire d'insatiables cupidités. Exiger une somme de travail qui, en émoussant toutes les facultés de l'âme, écrase le corps et en consume les forces jusqu'à épuisement, c'est une conduite que ne peuvent tolérer ni la justice ni l'humanité ». (Léon XIII. 15 mai 1891).

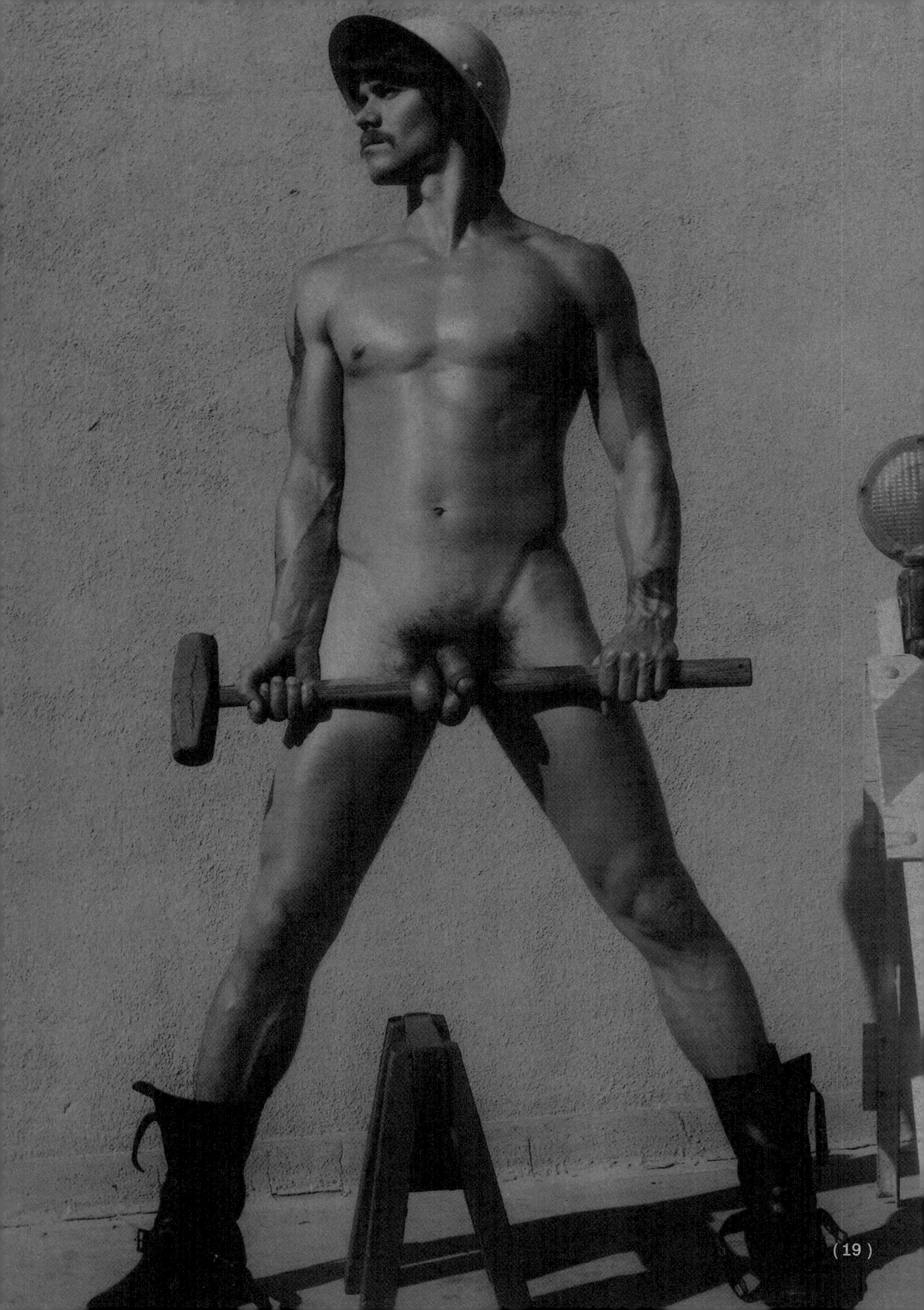

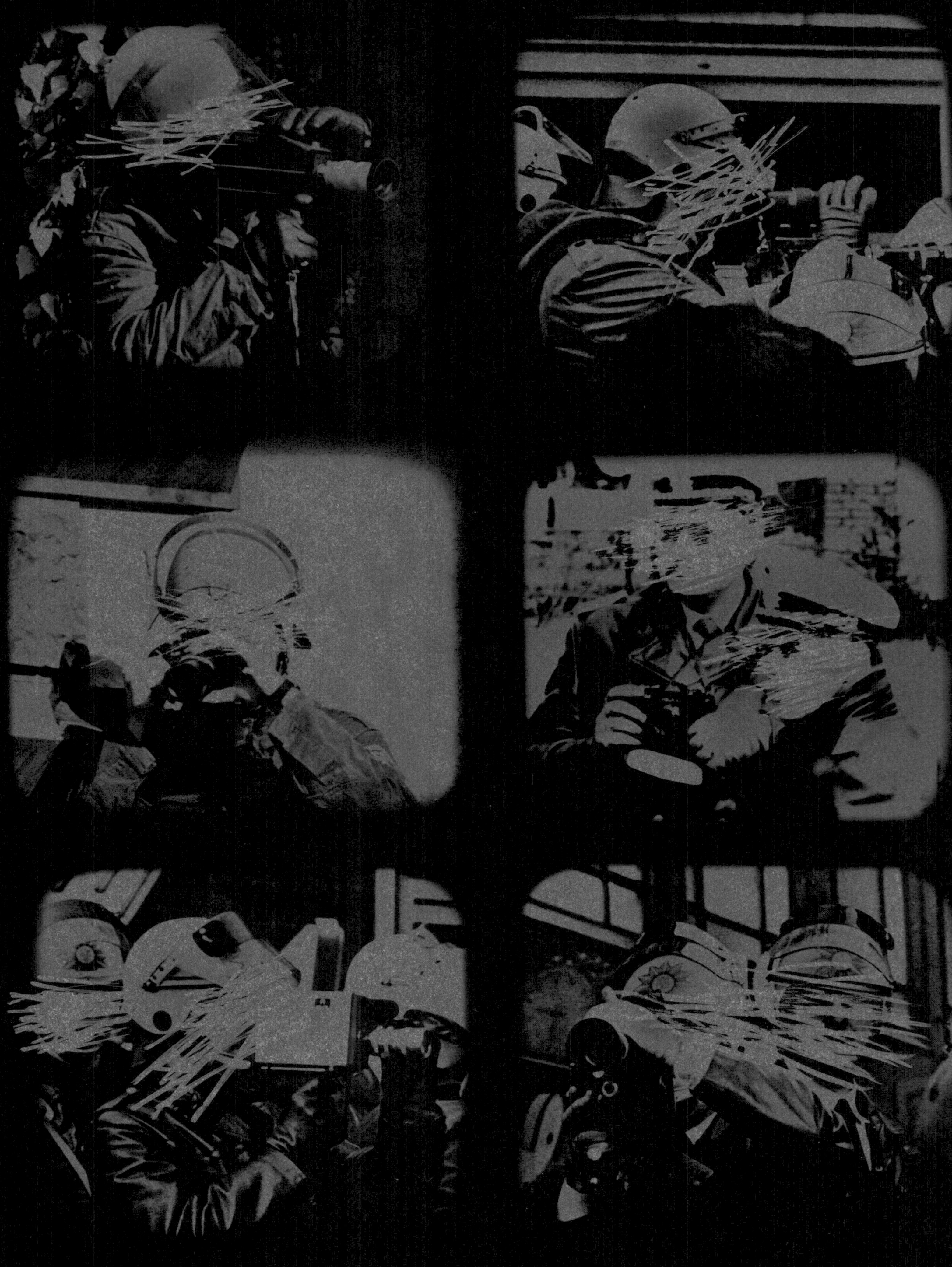

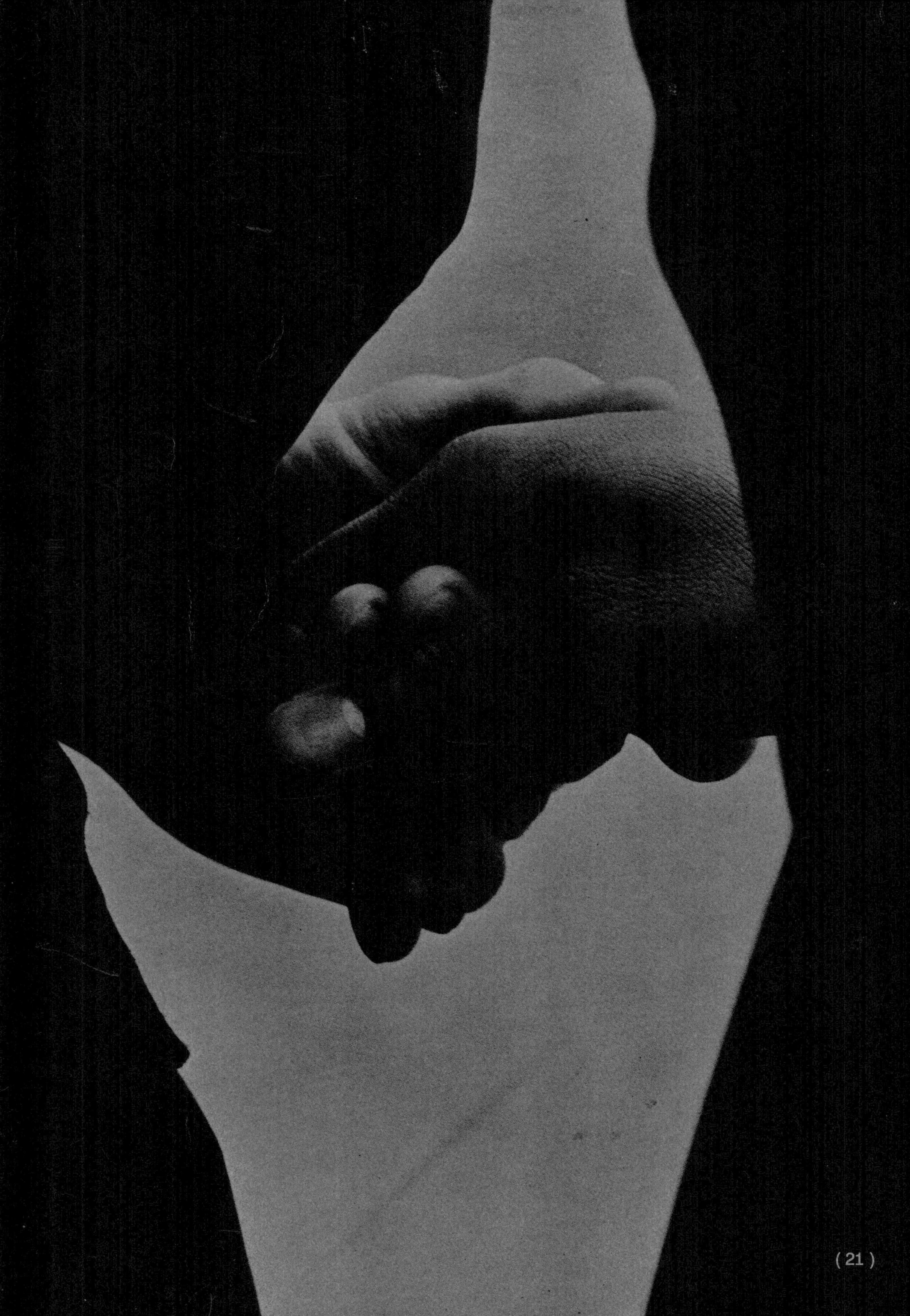

THE TORY ANSWER TO THE HOUSING CRISIS

BUY YOUR OWN HOME

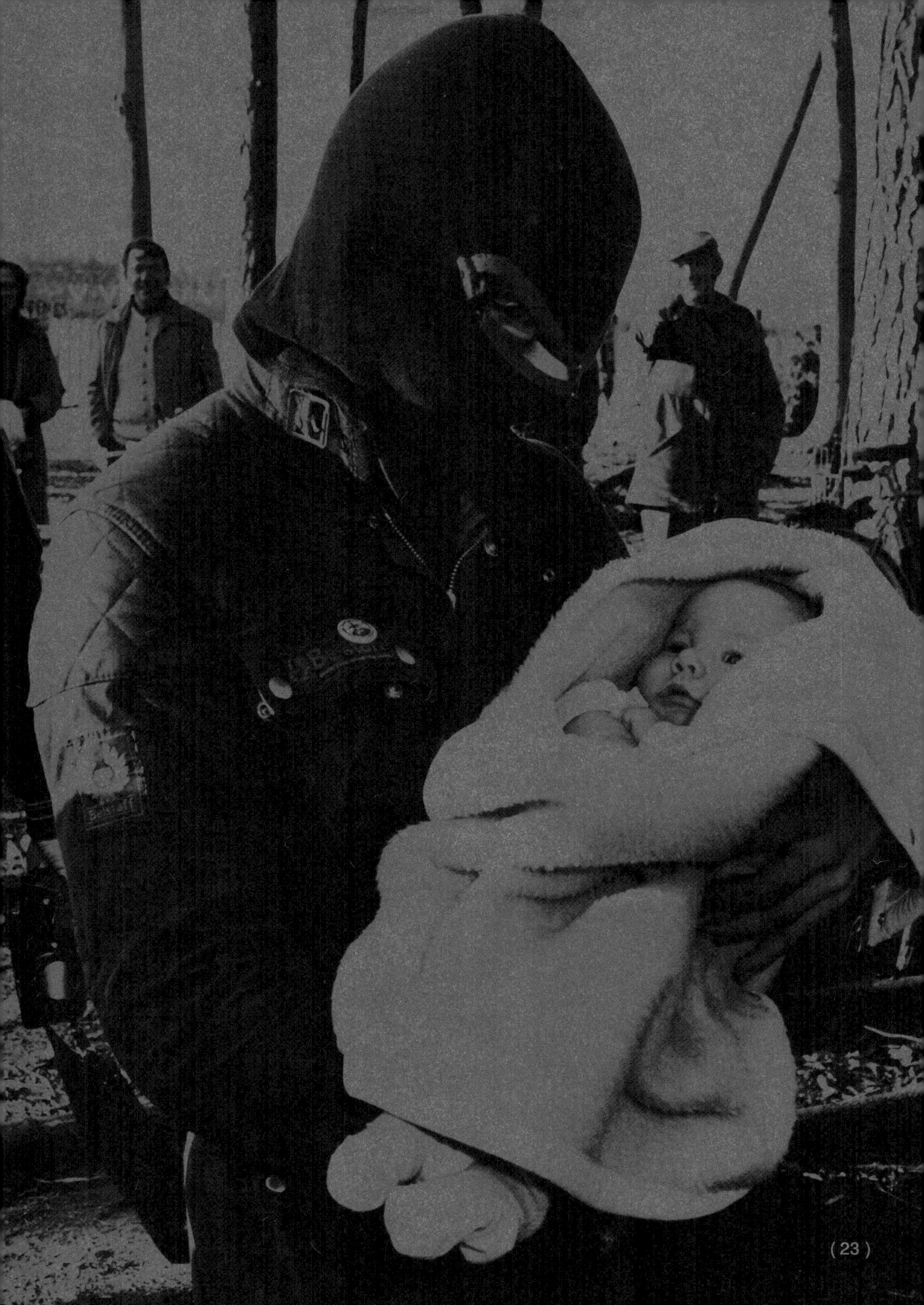

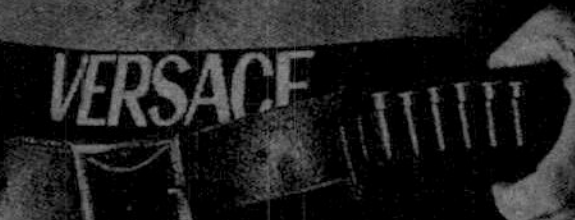

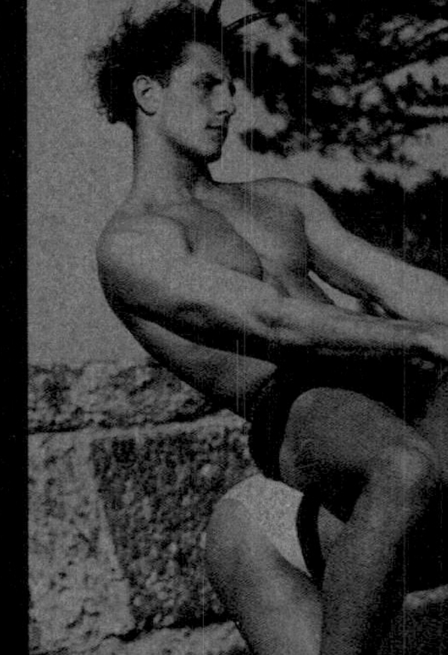

VERSACE
COUTURE

(24)

NEW YORK BEVERLY HILLS SAN FRANCISCO WASHINGTON HOUSTON ATLANTA SAN DIEGO
CHICAGO DALLAS LAS VEGAS BAL HARBOUR HONOLULU MEXICO CITY VANCOUVER TORONTO

„Aus dem Alltag von vier Hausfrauen". Rut Maggi, 36 Jahre, Eptingen/Schweiz: „Zu der Serie hat mich ein Ehemann angeregt. Er hat nämlich gesagt: „Ihr habt es ja schön, was macht ihr eigentlich den ganzen Tag?" Meine Bilder sind also Beweise, eine Dokumentation über das Tun im Haushalt, das auch Arbeit ist, auch wenn da freier eingeteilt wird als in anderen Berufen." AF zeigt nur einen kleinen Ausschnitt der Arbeit.

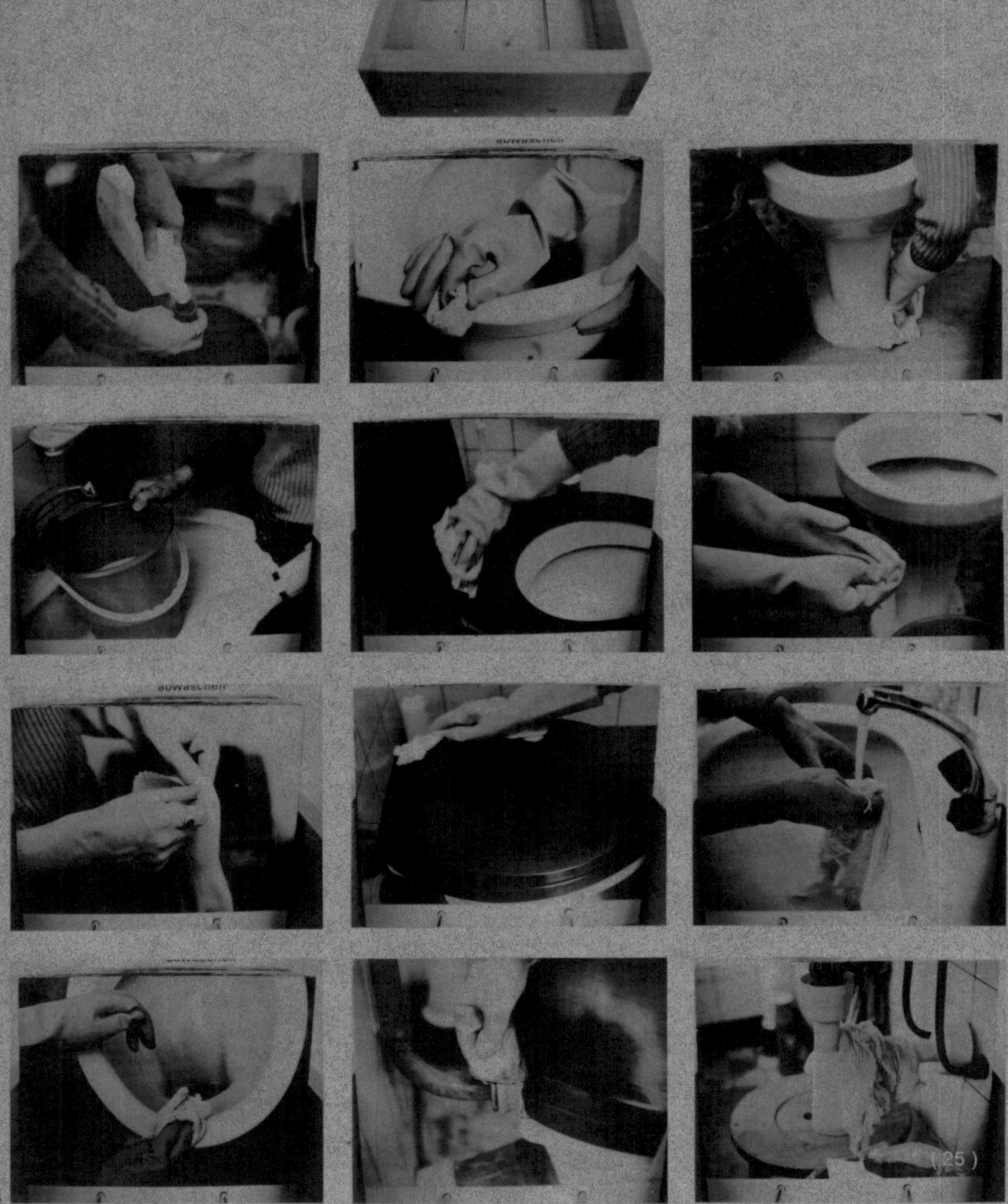

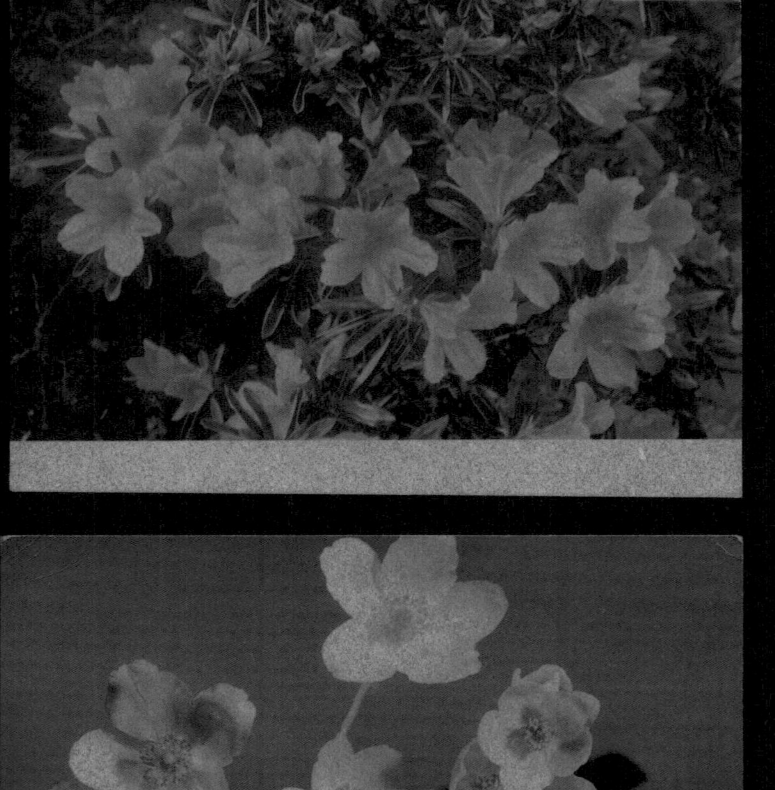
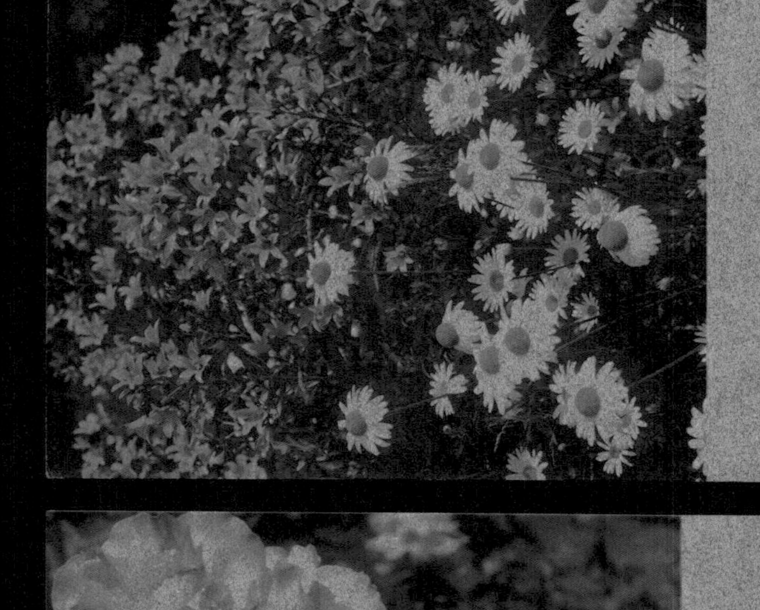
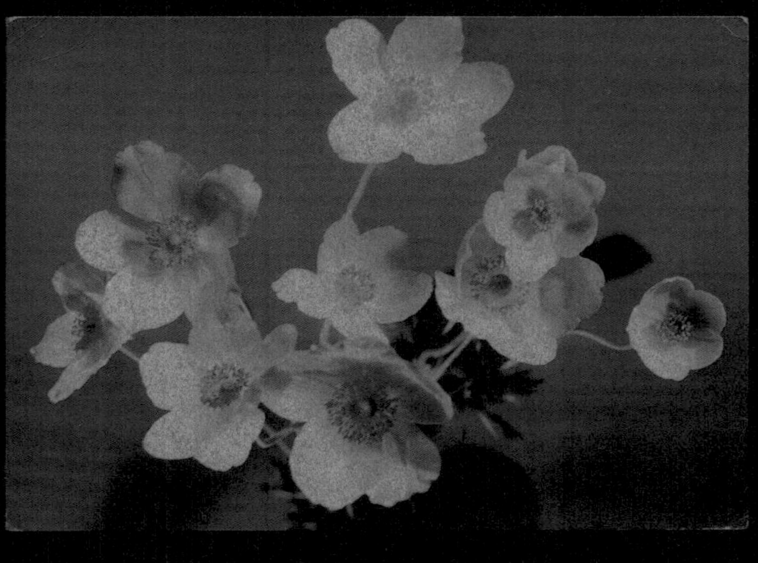
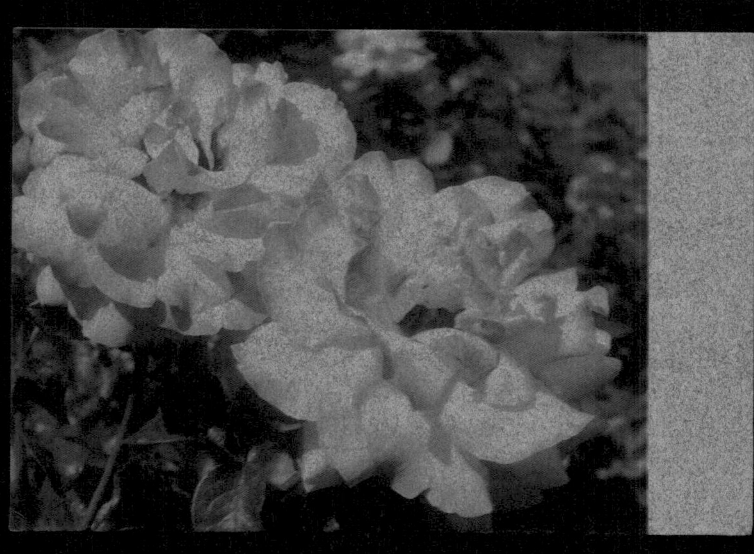
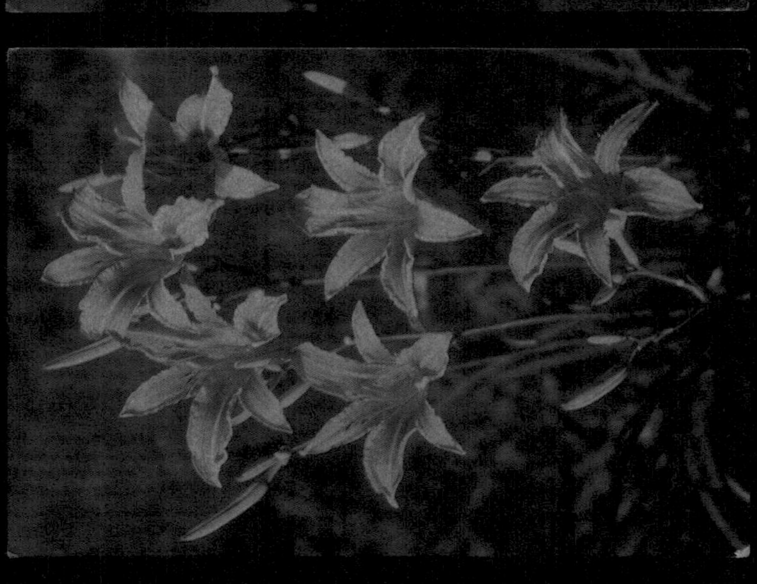
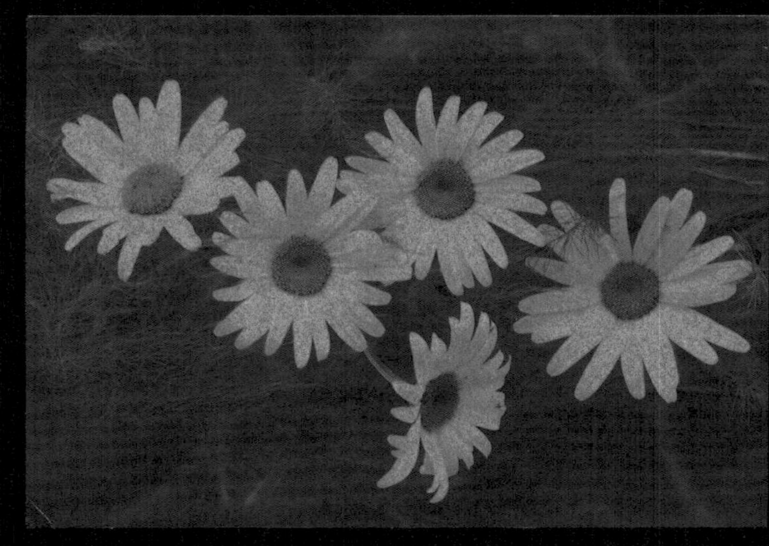
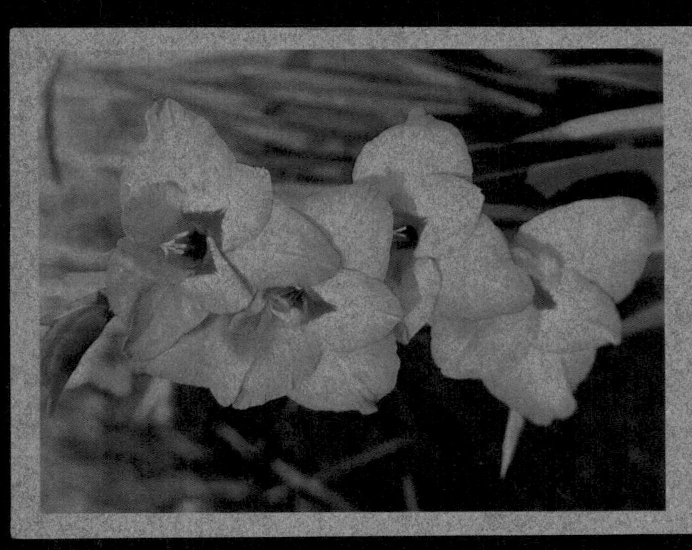
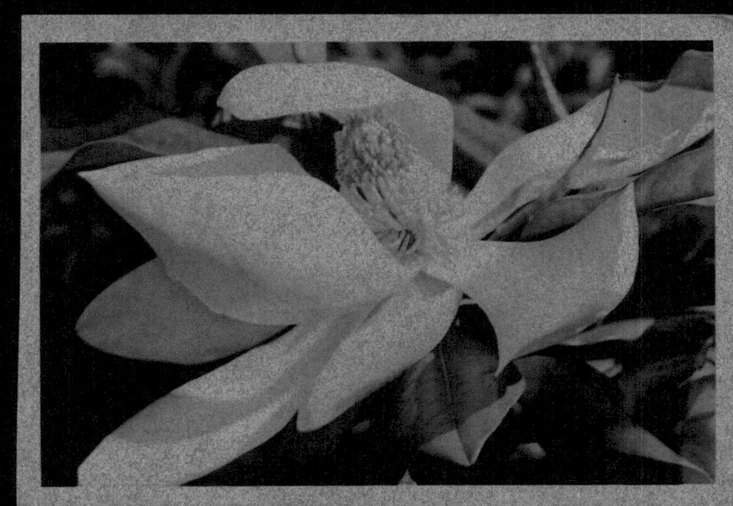

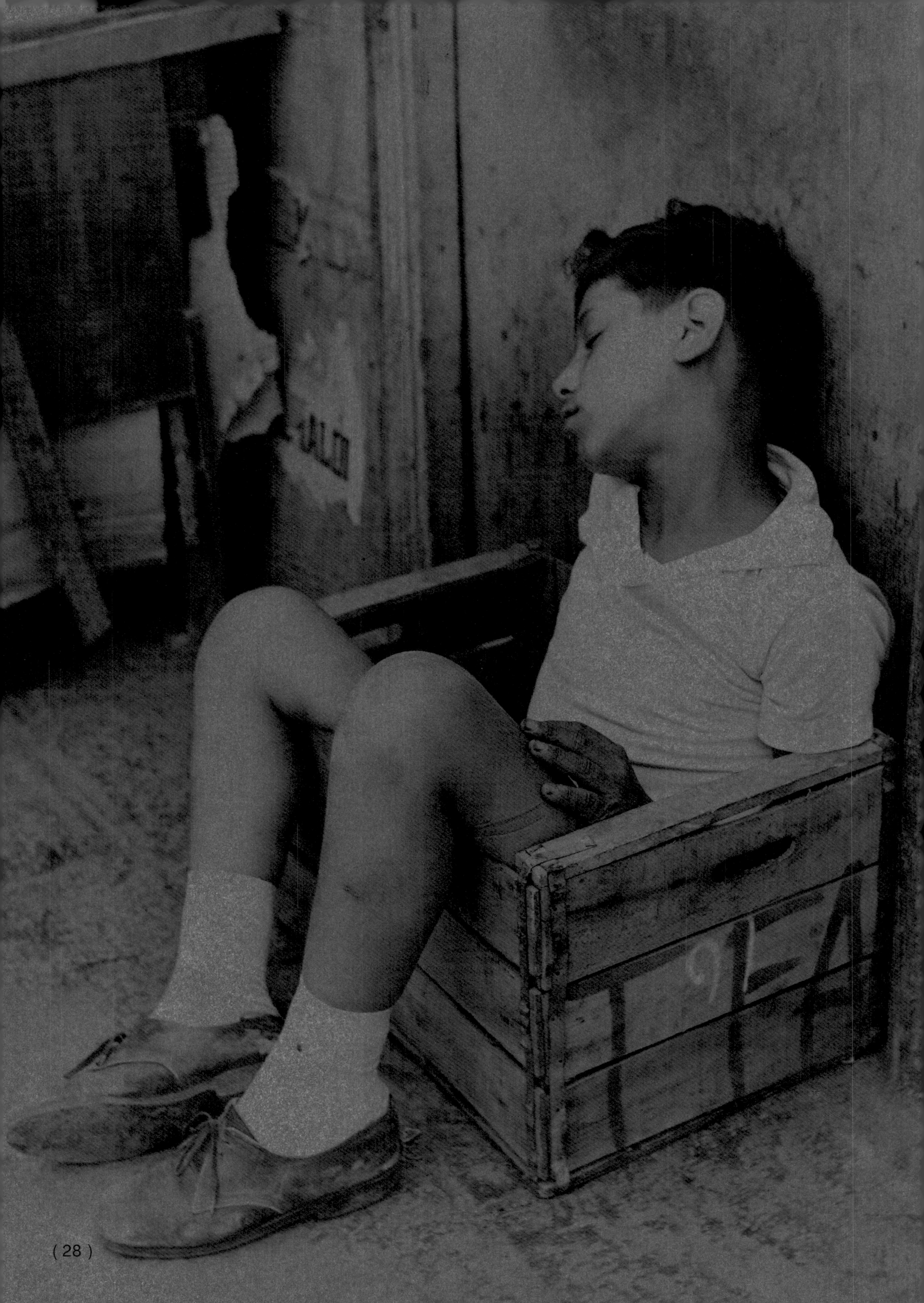

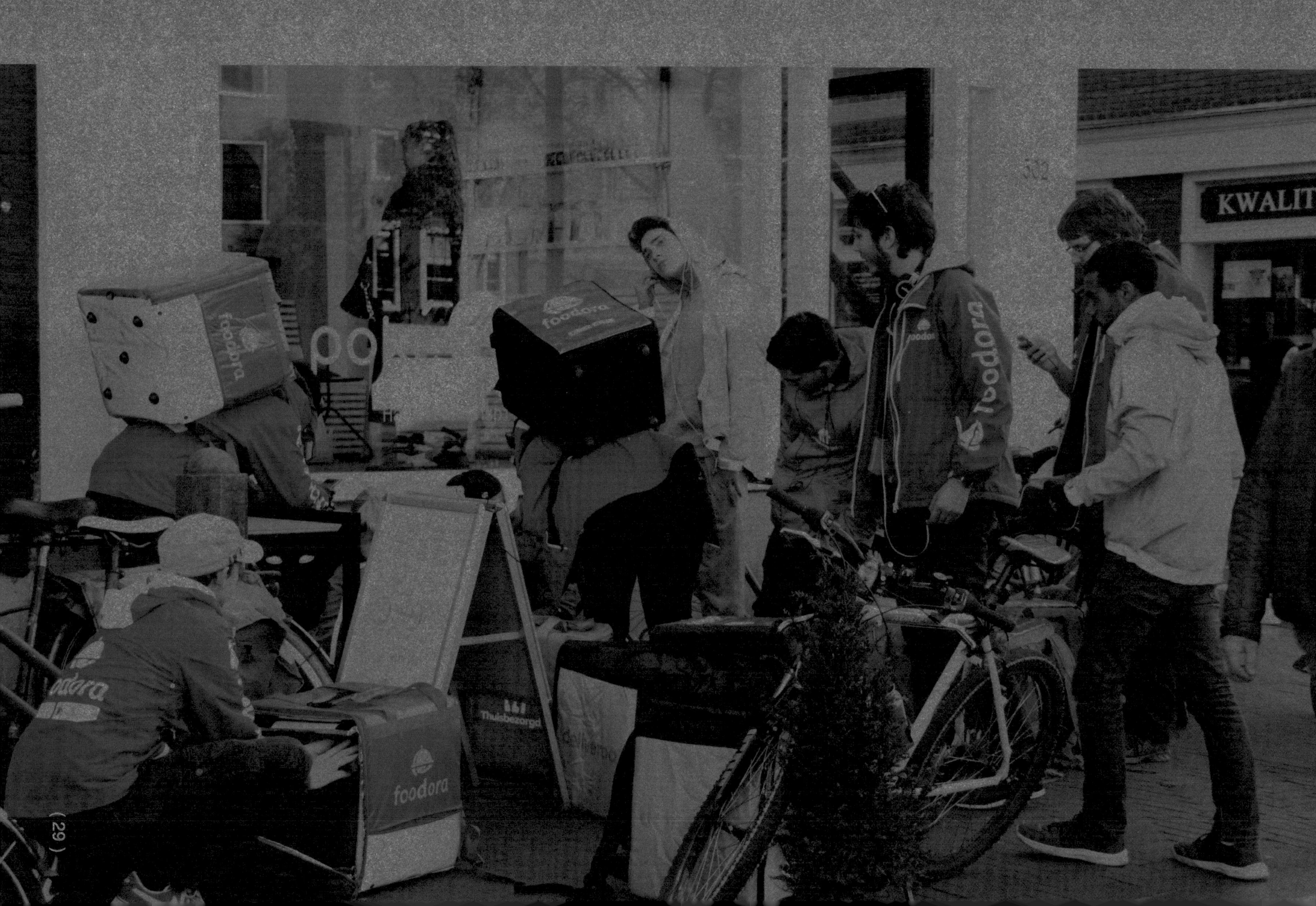

KWALIT
foodora
foodora
foodora
foodora
Thuisbezorg

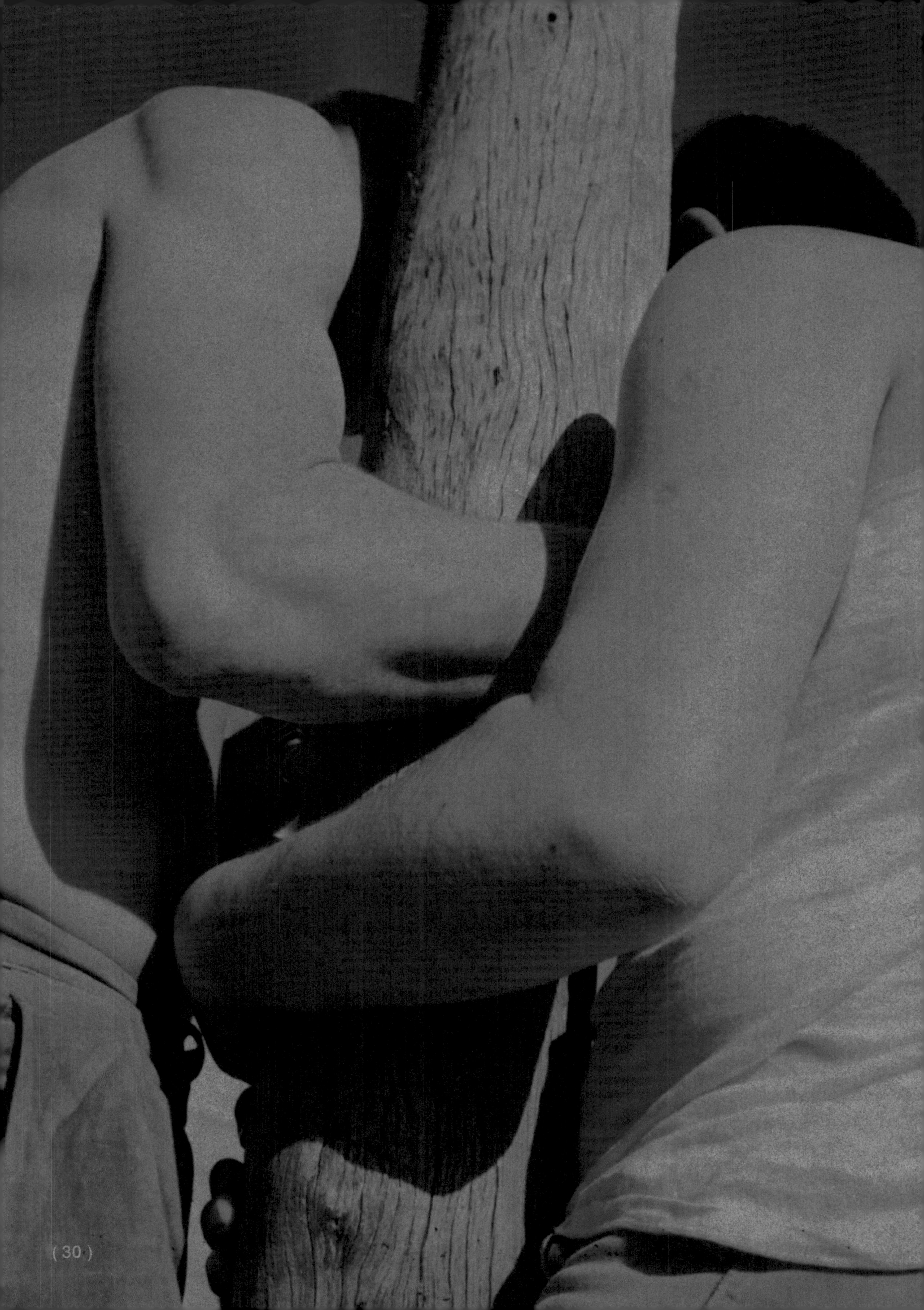

Condemned

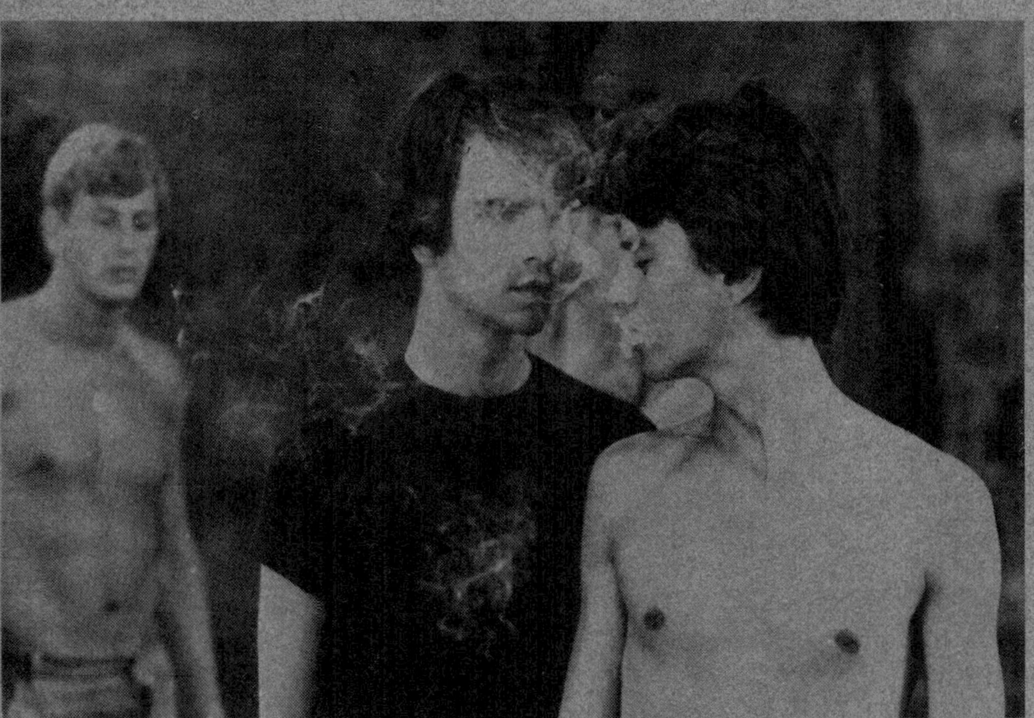

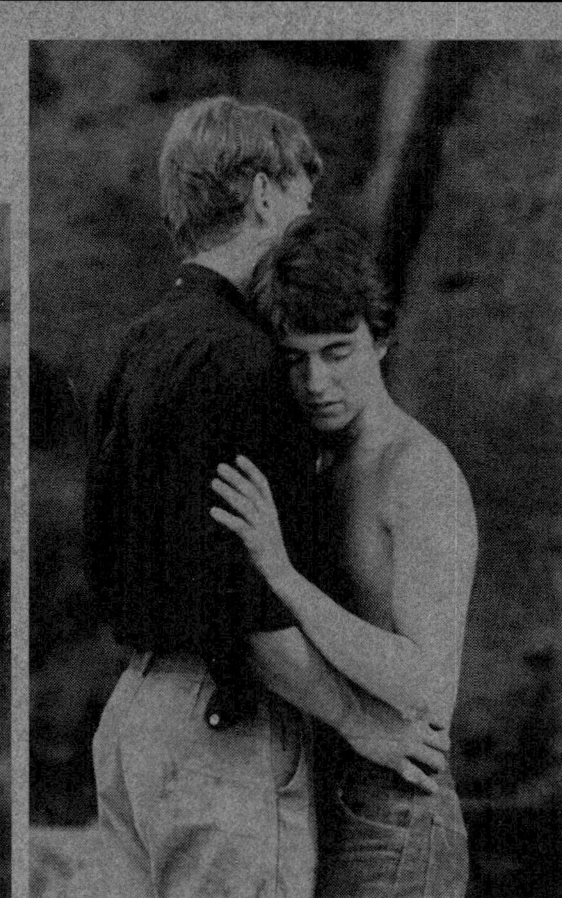

and Possessed

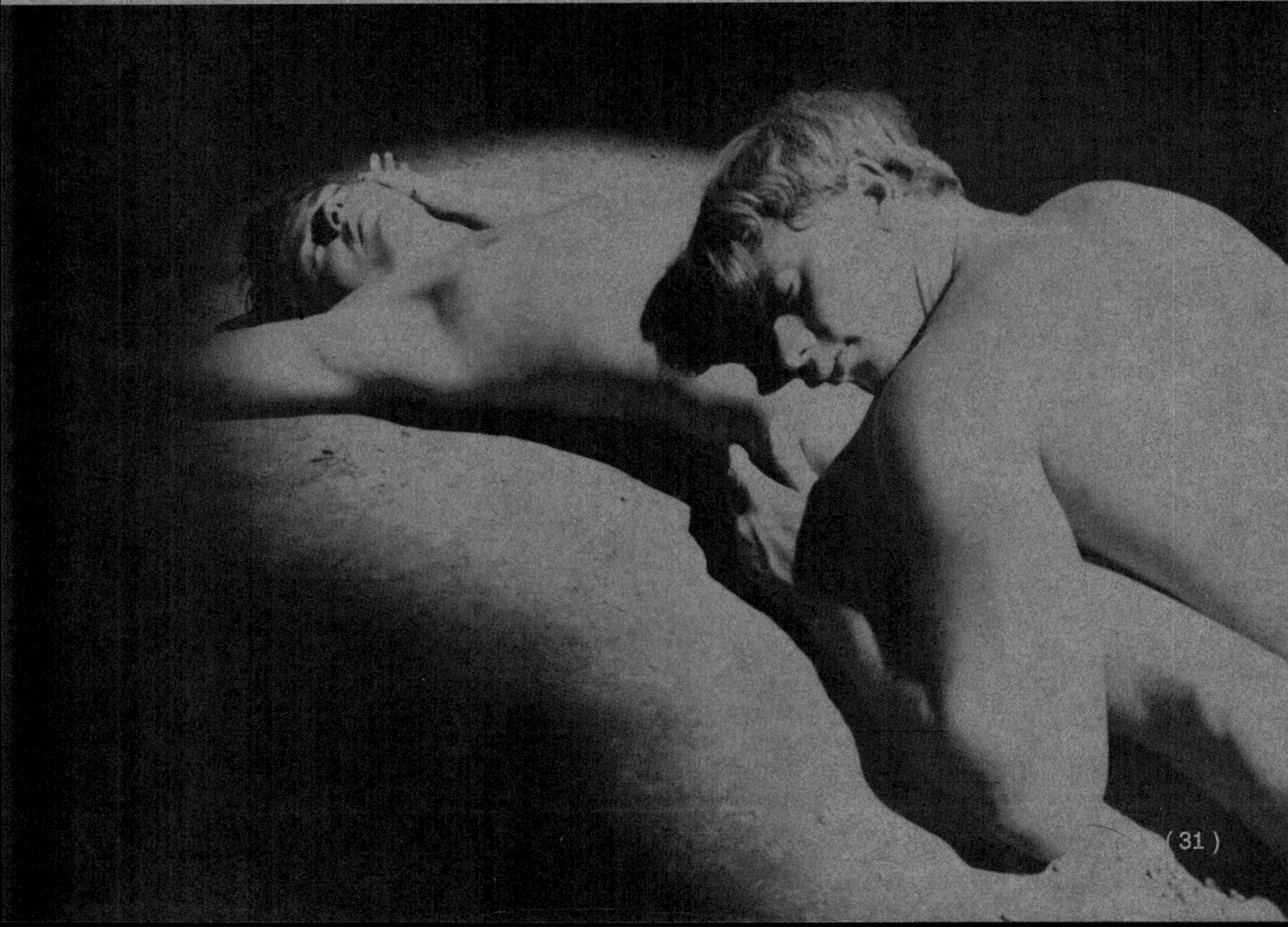

EUROPE MAGAZINE

REVUE HEBDOMADAIRE · 15ᵉ année · N° 685 · SEMAINE DU 24 AU 30 JUILLET 1958. BELGIQUE : 10 F.

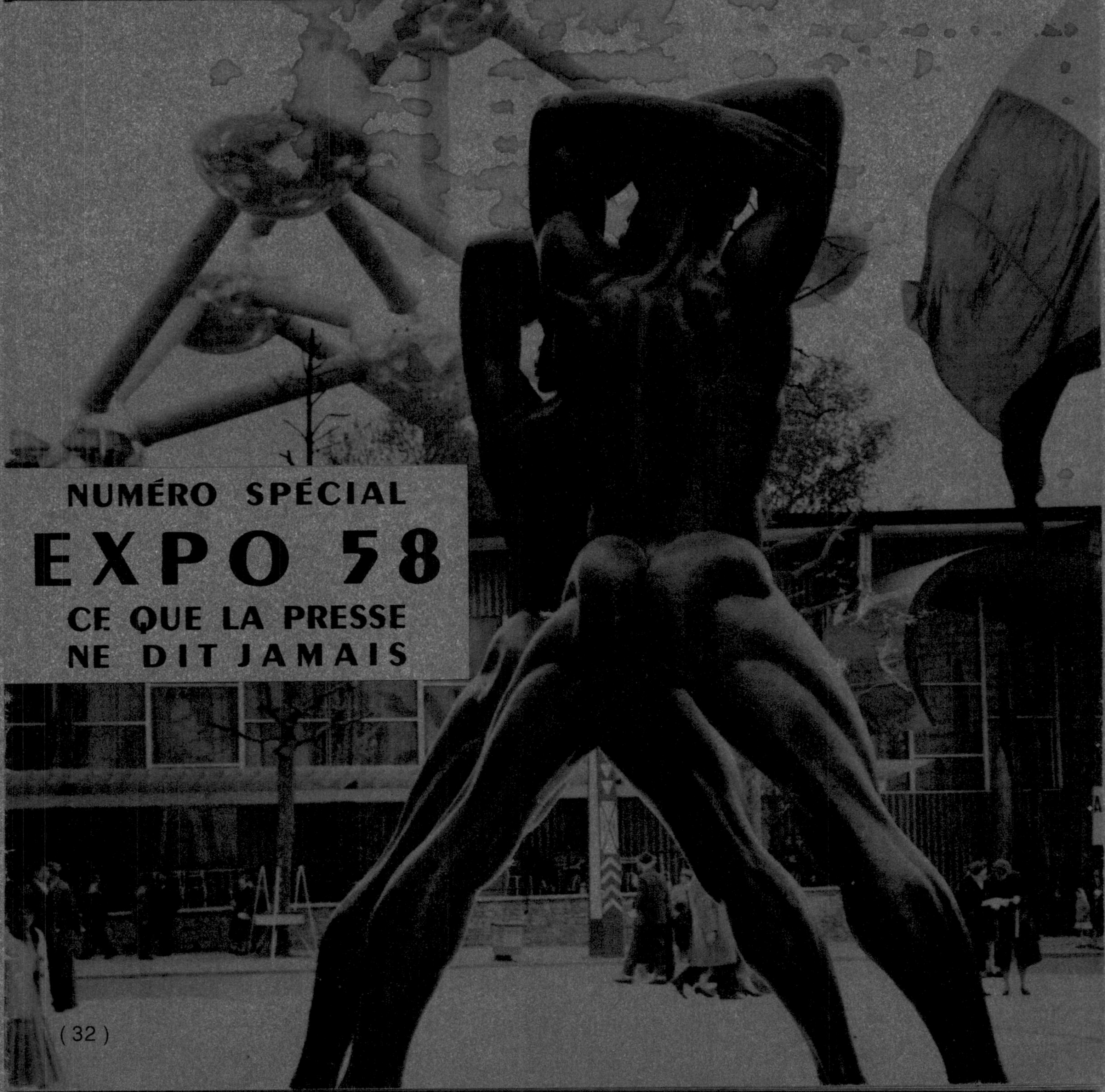

NUMÉRO SPÉCIAL

EXPO 58

CE QUE LA PRESSE NE DIT JAMAIS

(32)

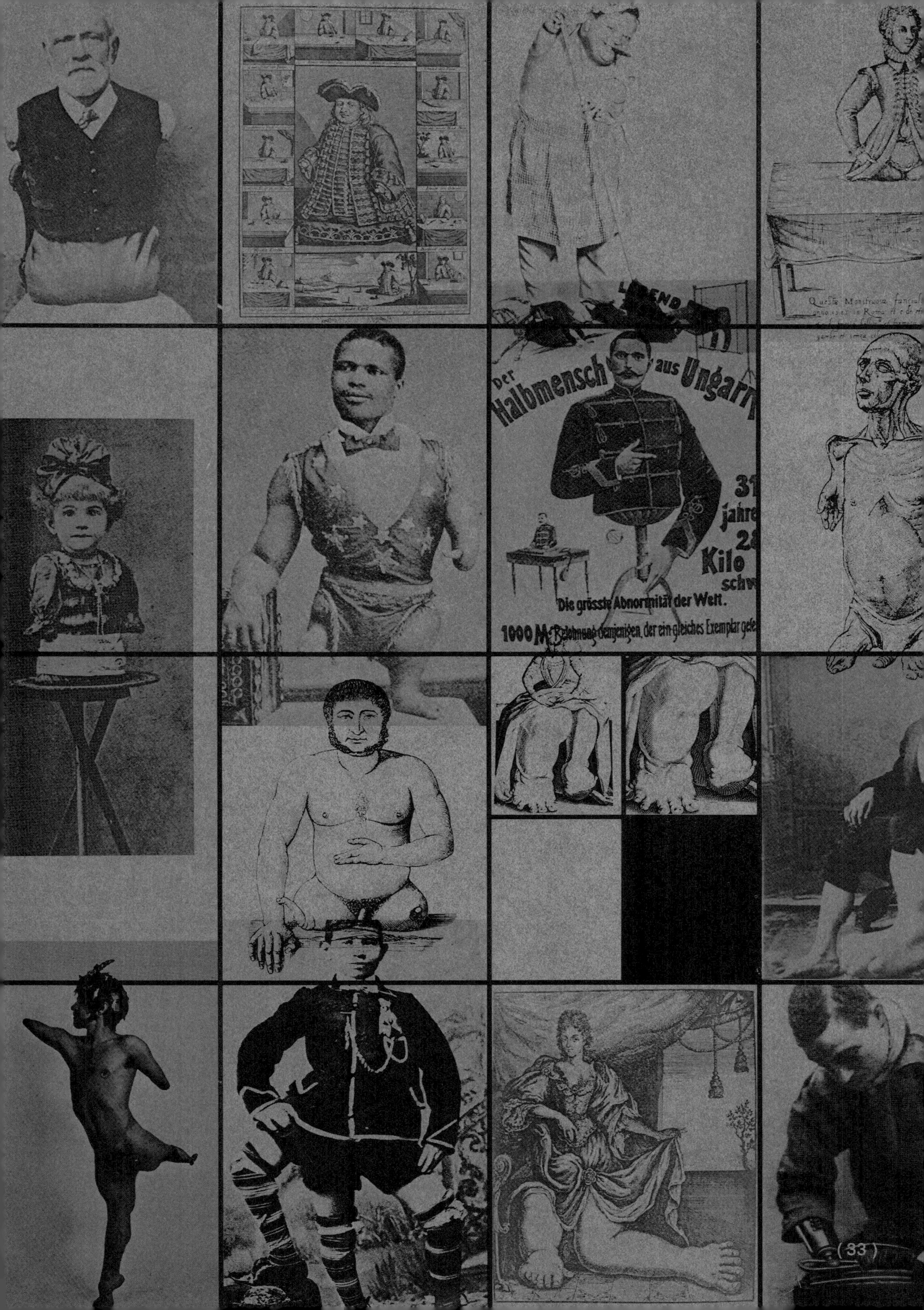

Der Halbmensch aus Ungarn
31 jahre 28 Kilo schw
Die grösste Abnormität der Welt.
1000 M. Belohnung demjenigen, der ein gleiches Exemplar gele

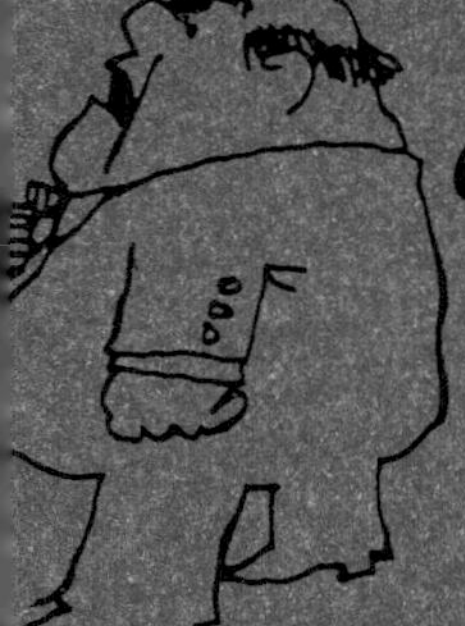

Injuries at work

all your fault'

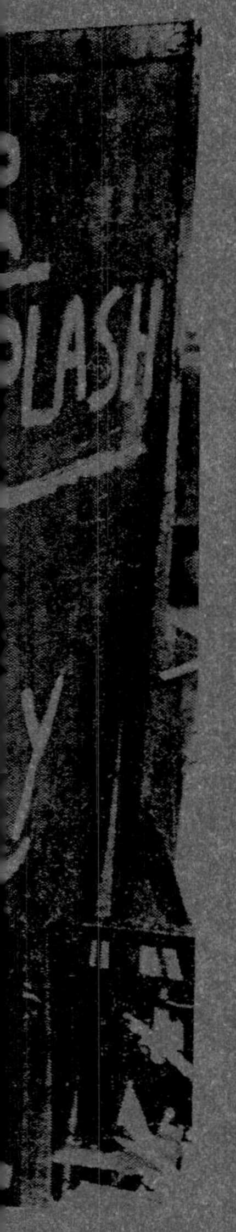

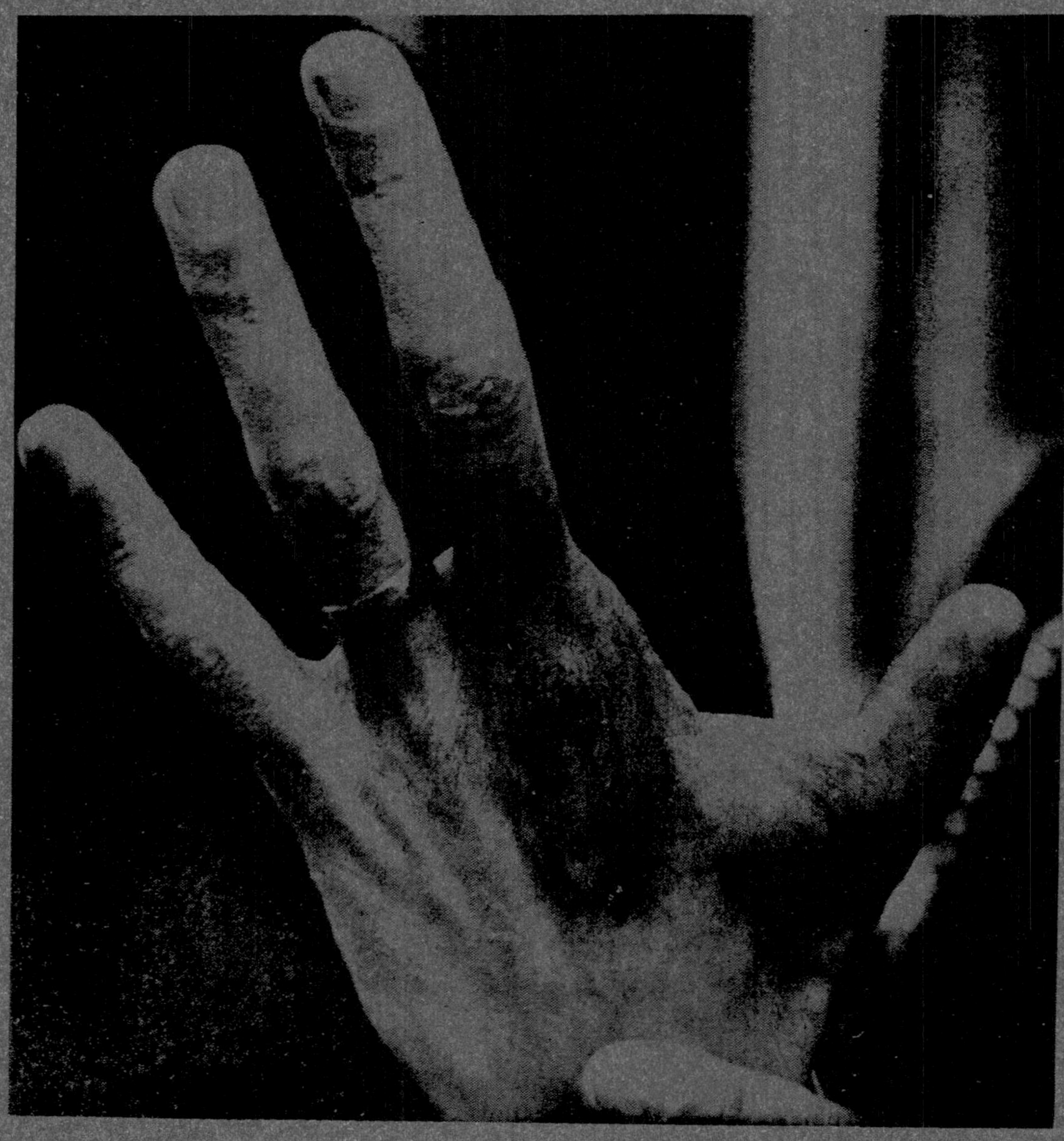

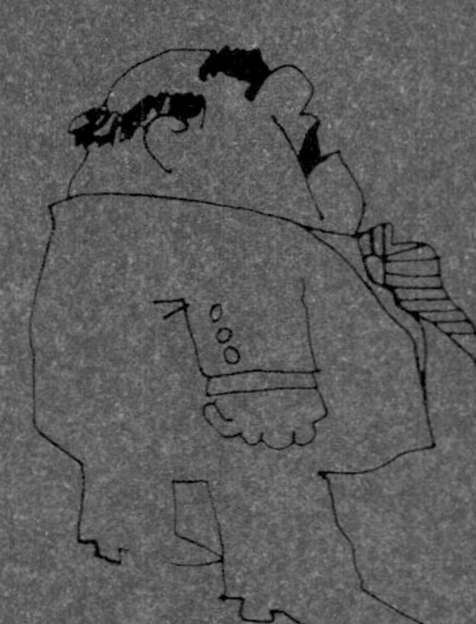

ITS HER
FAULT,
SHE PUT
HER
FINGERS
TOO
CLOSE

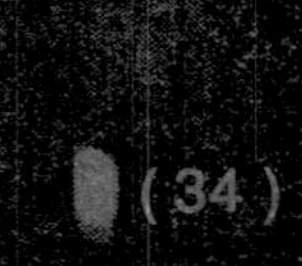

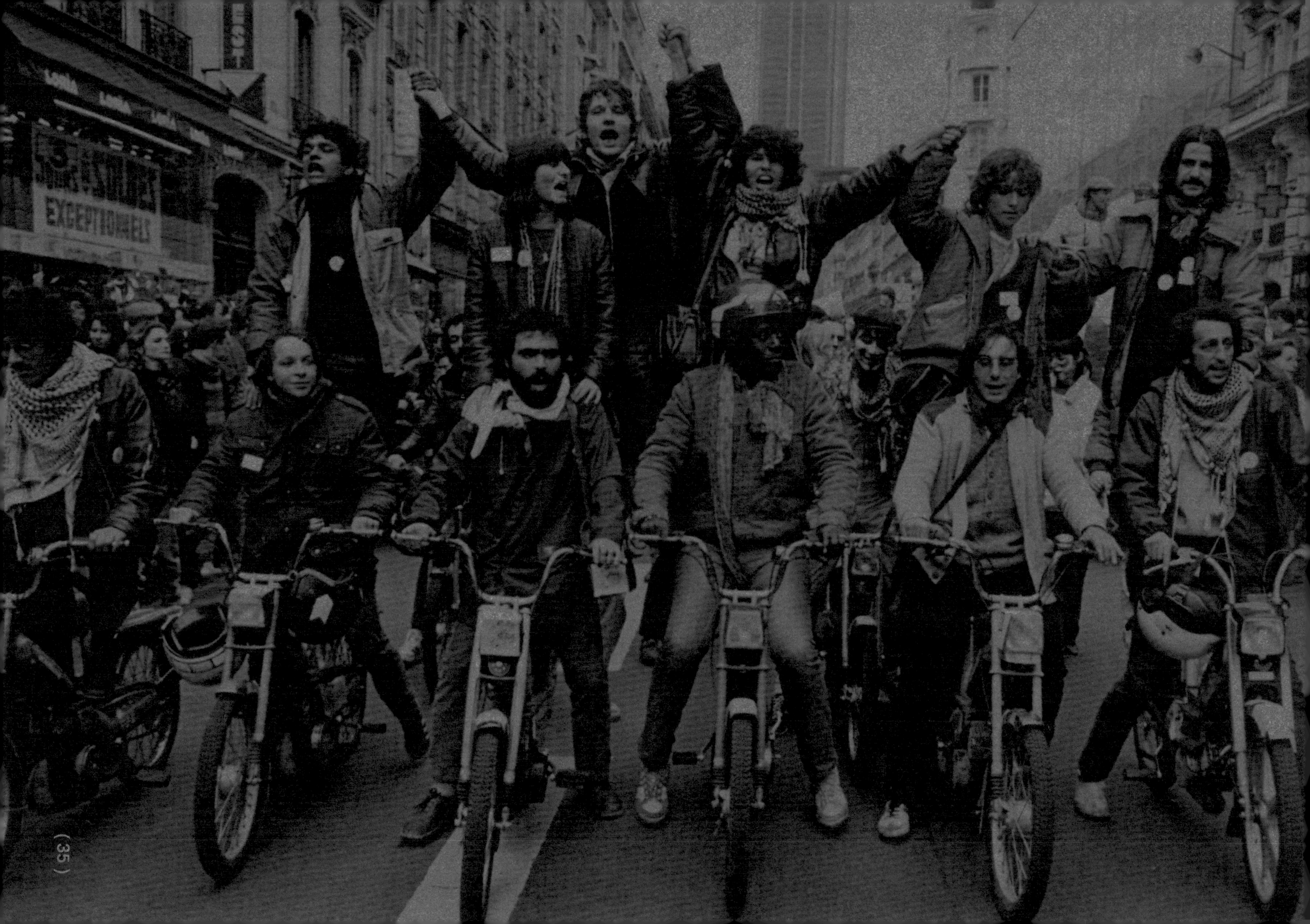

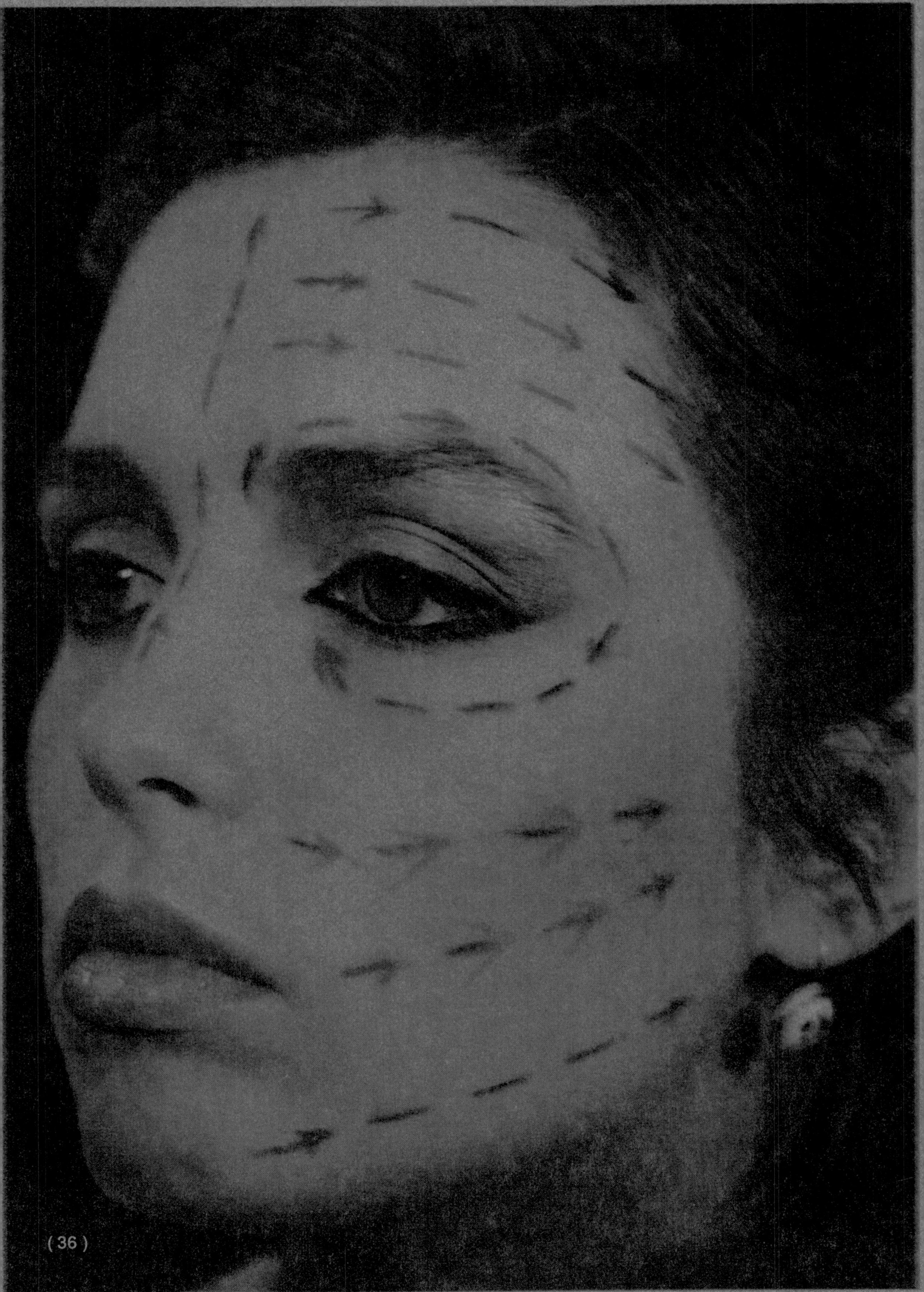

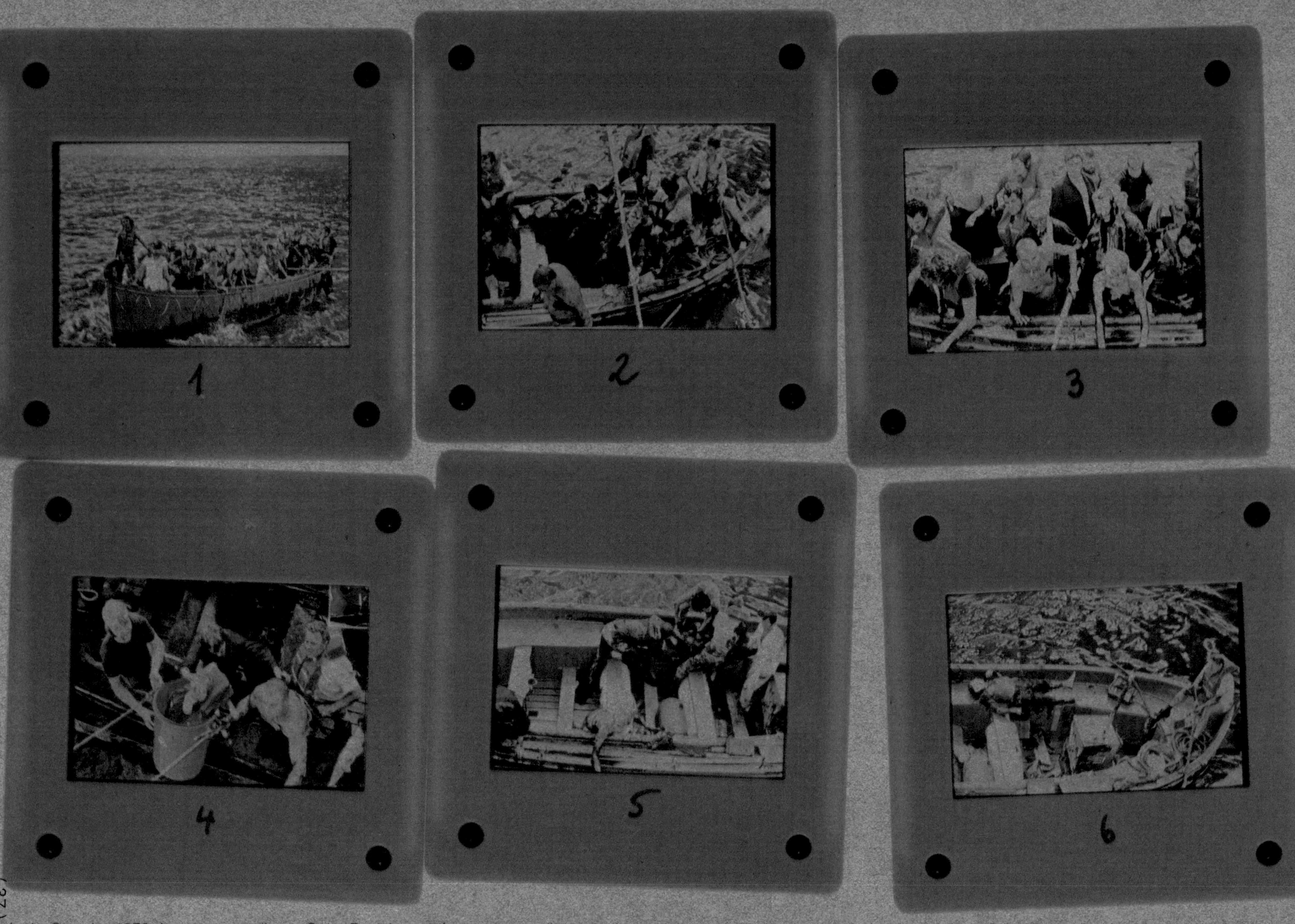

 Isole Canarie, 1970. La superpetroliera «Golar Patricia» naufraga a causa di una esplosione. I superstiti si imbarcano sul transatlantico «Cabo San Vicente». Una sola vittima.

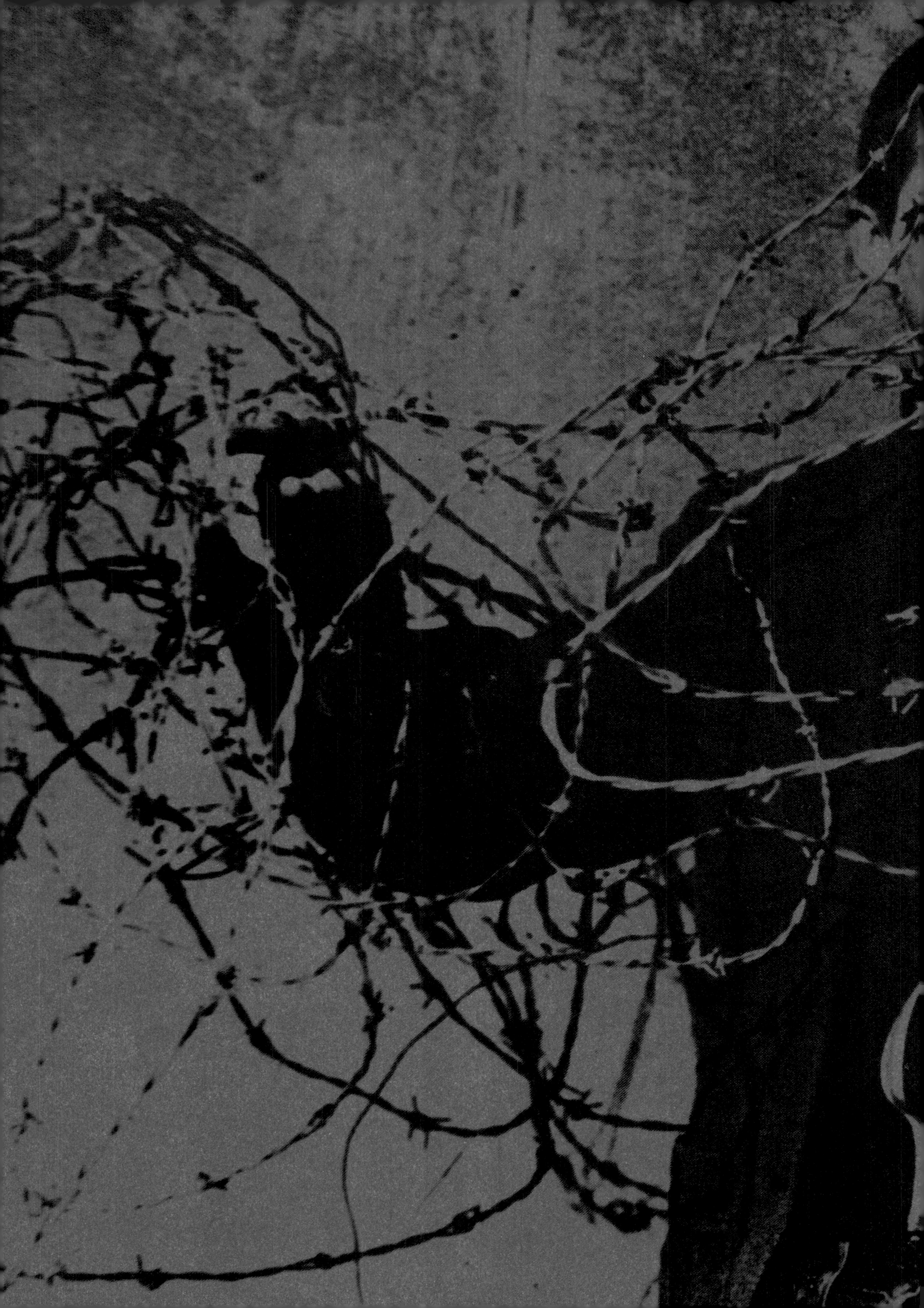

WERKER 2 / A GESTURAL HISTORY
OF THE YOUNG WORKER

SMYCHKA OF WORK AND DESIRE

Werker Collective compiled this publication in 2019, during an art residency in the Urals—the Soviet industrial heartland—where the strong, athletic bodies of workers, with severe and determined faces, firm and coordinated gestures, were once celebrated in painting, sculpture, and photography. The Soviet visual glorification of the worker rested upon the Marxist dialectical imperative to overcome alienation between different elements of social structure, namely the gap between physical and intellectual labour. In early Soviet political vocabulary, the word *smychka* indicated this drive towards collaboration and union in society. Soviet visual culture came up with different representations of *smychka.* During the industrialization of the 1920s and early 1930s, artists adopted a workers' ethos of collectivity through organising brigades that developed their artistic work on construction sites and factory floors. Soviet painting of the 1960s romanticised the idea of *smychka* by visually blurring the boundaries between physical and intellectual labour. The worker was portrayed as a thinker.

Gestures are the primary manifestations of bodies interacting with each other in social space, as they precede words in expressing desire, pain, excitement, fear, relaxation and anxiety. Gestural expression is especially relevant for marginalised and outcast bodies. Bodies whose capacity to speak is restricted by the environment in which they live, develop a vocabulary beyond the spoken word. Moving hips, a winking eye, a firm handshake, or a soft touch of shoulders, form the visual lexicon of resistance against the (hetero)normative assimilation of queered bodies and their desires. Gestures live short lives, they are hard to document, they tend to disappear. Gestures are always circumstantial and open to interpretation. So is the attempt of Werker Collective to (re)construct histories of the oppressed, the silenced, and the outcast. In this respect, publishing a visual history of gesture is a gesture in itself. Playful and painful, horny and reserved, tender and aggressive, liberating and oppressive, clandestine and up-front. *A Gestural History of the Young Worker* is a montage of anti-normative looks, moves, poses, smiles, and tears that stresses the dialectical character of the gesture of work which is often exploitative, enslaving, and abusive, yet which also contains the potential for becoming emancipatory.

Montage is a combination of two gestures; cutting and assembling. To cut off documents from their original context is an action that opens a symbolic space for seeking justice to a past that was repressed. Disconnected and reassembled—according to the method of montage—these reworked documents do not only reveal hidden histories, they also shed light on possible futures. A futurity that is lurking in this selection of documents is not a blueprint of a new society. It reveals the mere possibility of it, as an ephemeral hint towards solidarity between all bodies in pain, their shared desire for bodily mutuality, and their collective struggle. But also the possibility of work as a creative, fulfilling, and cumulative process.

Images and documents for this publication have been gathered collectively, from the margins of history. A variety of sources forms its corpus, such as propaganda and glossy magazines, museum and library archives, grassroots documentary photography, and paraphernalia found in flea markets. A photograph depicting a six-metre high statue of a naked man breaking chains—a monument to liberated labour, erected in the central square of Yekaterinburg in 1920—may still appear outrageous for its uncompromising physicality. Outrageous in different ways, but equally distressing, may be an image of two men cuddling, boys peeing on the street, or the frontal depiction of genitals from a male-to-male erotic phone line ad. However, it is not only full nudity and eroticism that can be perceived as unsettling. The Soviet photograph of a young Mansi reindeer herder, or a painting depicting workers on a factory floor looking at an easel, contrasted with impoverished, degraded and decomposed bodies of labour migrants, plantation workers, and food delivery couriers in flashy uniforms, appear naïve, artificial, and untrustworthy. Workers are no longer heroes; queers have never been depicted as such. Workers are queer. This is both a critical and a futuristic proposal. Throughout history, workers and queers have been pitted against each other. Right-wing regimes and politicians worldwide appeal to workers as a beacon of stability and tradition while depicting queers as a threat to traditional values. Opposing workers' interests with the interests of LGBTQ+ and feminist movements has been a remarkable characteristic of the international Left as well. Werker Collective, simultaneously inspired by the emancipatory politics of the labour movement and by the body liberationist politics of the radical queers and feminists, offers yet another kind of *smychka,* that is a utopian synthesis of work and desire.

Georgy Mamedov & Werker

СМЫЧКА ТРУДА И ЖЕЛАНИЯ

Данная публикация была подготовлена Коллектив Werker во время арт-резиденции на Урале, бывшем индустриальном центре Советского Союза, где когда-то в живописи, скульптуре и фотографии прославлялись сильные и спортивные тела рабочих с суровыми и решительными лицами, твердыми и слаженными жестами. Прославление человека труда в советском искусстве опиралось на марксистский императив преодоления отчуждения между различными элементами социальной структуры, в частности преодоления разрыва между физическим и умственным трудом. Для обозначения этого стремления использовалось слово «*смычка*». В советском искусстве разрабатывались разные образы смычки. Например, во время индустриализации 1920-х и начала 1930-х гг. художники, перенимая опыт рабочей коллективности, объединялись в художественные бригады для создания произведений искусства на строительных площадках и в заводских цехах; советская живопись 1960-х изображала рабочего как мыслителя.

Жест — первичное проявление тела в социальном пространстве. Жесты предшествуют словам в выражении желания, боли, волнения, страха, расслабленности и тревоги. Выражение при помощи жестов особенно актуально для маргинализированных и отверженных тел, чья возможность говорить всегда ограничена. Подмигивание, движение бедра, крепкое рукопожатие или мягкое касание плечами образуют жестовый словарь сопротивления (гетеро)нормативной ассимиляции ненормативных тел и их желаний. Жесты мимолетны и сопротивляются документированию. Таким образом, саму попытку (ре)конструкции истории угнетенных и изгоев, коей и является «Жестовая История Молодого Рабочего», можно рассматривать как жест. Этот жест одновременно художественный и политический, в нем находят проявление задор и боль, желание и сдержанность, нежность и агрессия. Организующий принцип данной публикации — коллаж антинормативных взглядов, движений рук, поз, улыбок и слез, раскрывающий диалектический характер жеста в процессе работы. Жест человека труда зачастую связан с (само)эксплуатацией, порабощением и унижением, но в то же время в нем всегда содержится потенциал освобождения.

Коллаж состоит из двух жестов: резки и сборки. Извлечение изображения или документа из его первоначального контекста открывает возможность для восстановления справедливости в отношении репрессированного прошлого. Однако вырезанные из контекста и повторно собранные изображения и документы не только восстанавливают историческую справедливость, но и проливают свет на возможное будущее. Образ будущего, проявляющейся на страницах этой публикации, не более чем указание на возможность мира, в котором присутствует солидарность между всеми угнетенными телами, объединившимися в борьбе за освобождение труда и превращение его в коллективный и творческий процесс.

Изображения и документы для этой публикации были извлечены из различных источников, включающих пропагандистские материалы и глянцевые журналы, музейные и библиотечные архивы, любительские фотографии и предметы с блошиных рынков. Шестиметровая статуя обнаженного мужчины, разрывающего цепи, — «памятник освобожденному труду», установленный на центральной площади Екатеринбурга в 1920 г., — как и сто лет назад, может показаться возмутительным бескомпромиссным изображением телесности. Такими же возмутительными могут показаться изображения двух обнимающихся мужчин, мальчиков, писающих на улице, или реклама «секса по телефону» для гомосексуалов. Однако не только полная нагота и эротизированные тела могут вызвать зрительскую тревогу. Советский фотопортрет молодого мансийского оленевода или картина, на которой рабочие в заводском цехе рассматривают собственные изображение на мольберте, могут показаться сегодня наивными и искусственными, особенно в сопоставлении с изображениями нищих и изможденных тел трудовых мигрантов, работников плантаций или курьеров по доставке еды в яркой униформе. Рабочие больше не герои, квиры же никогда героями не были. Рабочие — это квиры. И это заявление критичное и утопическое одновременно. На протяжении всей истории рабочих и квиров противопоставляют друг другу. Правые режимы и политики во всем мире обращаются к рабочим как к хранителям скреп стабильности и традиций, изображая квиров как угрозу этим скрепам. Однако противопоставление интересов рабочих интересам ЛГБТ и феминистского движений также характерно и для левой политики. Коллектив Werker, вдохновляемый одновременно освободительной борьбой международного рабочего движения и политической практикой радикальных квиров и феминисток, предлагает еще один образ смычки — утопический синтез труда и желания.

Георгий Мамедов и Werker

(1)

Манси—коренные жители Северного Урала.
Юный представитель династии охотников-
оленеводов Бахтияровых.

Свердловская Область Г. К. Краснов, В. Ф.
Дворянов. Средне-Уральское Книжное Изда-
тельство. Свердловск, 1978.

(2)

הכל תפוס!
על יד שולחן אחד יושבות שלוש בנות
ותוך כדי שיחה, אוכלות את המנות.
ועוד כיסא רביעי עומד לו שם ריקן,
אך לי נדמה היה, כי לא רועים בי כאן...

הינה שולחן אחר: יושבים שני בחורים
—תפוס—בשובבות אחד קולו הרים.
ישבתי לבדי, על־ יד שולחן אחד
וזרם הבאים—לתור מקום נדד

תופסים כבר שולחנות, אן לא בשכנותו
נותנים לר יחיד, לשבת במנוחה —

(1969)

״הגלבוע״, 1971 סידור: דפוס גולדברג, ירושלים פוטוליטו:
עדשה, רמת־ גן דפוס: אופסט ישראלי ליצוא, תל־ אביב.

(3)

Stufe: Ein Flaschenzug besteht aus vier Rollen;
zwei feste oben und zwei lose unten sind zu je einer
Flasche zusammengesetzt. An der oberen Schere
ist ein Seil befestigt, das von Flasche zu Flasche
verläuft. Bei einem Flaschenzug mit vier Rollen herrscht
Gleichgewicht, wenn die Zugkraft viermal kleiner ist
als das Gewicht der Last (einschl. untere Flasche).
Erklärung: Die Last hängt an vier Schnüren; an jeder
Schnur wirkt nur 1/4 der Last, so daß der Arbeiter
nur 1/4 der Kraft aufzuwenden hat. Hier wird Kraft
gespart, sie muß aber über den vierfachen Weg
wirken. Mögliche Folgerung: Einfache Maschinen
erleichtern zwar das Arbeiten, sie verkleinern aber
nicht die Arbeit.

Welche Aufgabe haben die festen Rollen in 74a, b, c?

*Werkunterricht und Technik. Handbuch der Kunst- und
Werkerziehung. Band 11/3. Willi Kaul. Berlin 1967.*

(4)

76. Ficus Elastica Roxb, Karet.

79. Het tappen van de rubber.

77. Castilloa elastica.

86. Assistenthuis op een rubberonderneming.

78. Latextransport door de tappers.

82. Stremmingskeet op een rubberonderneming.

81. Rubberfabriek

84. Interieur van een rubberfabriek.

De Wereld in Beeld. De Groote Indische Cultures.
Door Lr. L.J.M. Feber. Nijmegen 1931.

(5)

Die Weimarer Republik hatte auf die Forderung der
Arbeiterbewegung nach einem Einheitsschulwesen
mit gleichen Bildungs-möglichkeiten für alle mit
einem Chancengleichheitskonzept reagiert, das den
"Aufstieg der Tüchtigen" ermöglichen sollte. Wenn
auch die demokratischen und sozialistischen Kräfte
ihre Forderungen nicht annähernd durchsetzen
konnten, erreichten sie doch immerhin die Grund-
schule, eine vorsichtige soziale Öffnung der höheren
Bildung, den Ausbau von Mädchenbildung und Frauen-
studium sowie eine Verbesserung der Volksschulleh-
rerausbildung. Die Faschisten dagegen wollen weder
wissenschaftliche Bildung noch "Chancengleichheit
durch Bildung". Als Ersatz für individuellen Aufstieg
nach dem bürgerlichen Leistungsprinzip bieten sie
jedem "Volksgenossen", dem Kind wie dem Erwach-
senen, einen Platz in der Kolonne an, in der nach
autoritärem Führer-Prinzip organisierten "Arbeitsord-
nung des Volkes". Diese Erziehungspolitik führt zu
einer Bildungs-Begrenzung, einem drastischen
Rückfall hinter das in der Weimarer Republik bereits
Erreichte. Fachliches Wissen und Können werden
für die Faschisten erst zu einem Zeitpunkt wichtig,
als die Kriegsvorbereitung ein höheres Aus bildungs-
niveau erfordert, das durch Einführung der Berufs-
schulpflicht erreicht werden soll.

*Ein Bilder-Lese-Buch über Schule und Alltag Berliner
Arbeiterkinder. Von der Armenschule zur Gesamt-
schule. 1827 bis Heute.* Berlin 1981.

(6)

El caso de Cuba prueba como pocos que la educación,
tarea esencial en la vida de cada pueblo, depende,
en su naturaleza y desarrollo, de la organización
de la sociedad, determinada básicamente por las

estructuras económicas establecidas. Una escueta consideración del pasado y del presente de la nación cubana lo confirma cabalmente. Nuestra isla estuvo regida durante siglos por poderes extranjeros, metropolitanos, el de la España monárquica primero y el del imperialismo estadounidense después. La enseñanza y la cultura se mantuvieron marcadas, en todos sus niveles, por el interés de defender y prolongar la situación injusta y opresora inherente a la realidad colonial.

Por dos vías se mostró, primordialmente, la penuria de la acción cultural y educativa: por la orientación que la trascendió, dirigida a justificar y mantener la dominación extranjera, y por una vigilante limitación en su desarrollo, nacida del deseo de impedir que, con la multiplicación de la escuela y del libro, cobrase el pueblo conciencia de su larga servidumbre y se levantara contra ella.

La Educación en Revolución. Instituto Cubano del Libro. La Habana 1974.

(7)

Ces photographies ont été réalisées à Sidi Bou Saïd en 1945, lieu très fréquenté par les intellectuels et les cinéastes de l'époque. Ce photographe amateur et anonyme a pu faire ces images grâce à un cercle très protégé à cette époque et a magnifié tous ces garçons méditerranéens avec une grande liberté et sensualité. La crainte de la confiscation de ces images l'a contraint à en faire passer un certain nombre, complètement caché. Les négatifs ont été effectivement détruits à sa disparition. D'où le plaisir de cette découverte aujourd'hui dans cet ouvrage unique qui vous permettra de retrouver ces instants joyeux d'intimité.

Les amants de Sidi Bou Saïd, univers intime masculin d'un photographe amateur anonyme en 1945. Nicole Canet, Galerie Au Bonheur du Jour. Paris 2004.

(8)

Traditional Pastime

Playing Indians is so much a part of the American scene, especially among boys, that pictures of this highly imaginative activity certainly fall rightfully into the genre category. The serious concern of these two lads for authenticity, even just for fun, provided me with ready-made material for a series of dramatic photographs. My subjects, having made every item of costumes and props, insisted on directing each setup, and I was quite willing to cooperate. For this very realistic scene depicting the scalping of a fallen enemy, the setting was carefully chosen to avoid any signs of civilization. The large tree was included principally to improve the desirably open composition. A reflector used on the shadow side balances the

brilliant backlighting, which not only separates the figures from the background but also seems to darken the flesh tones appropriately. Altogether, this genuine-looking photograph convincingly records an exciting phase of the beloved diversion most of us can recall.

In Search of Young Beauty. A Venture into Photographic Art by Charles Du Bois Hodges. New York, London, 1964.

(9)

Tunis, le 18 mars 1904.

Mademoiselle, Ayant lu votre annonce dans les *Lectures pour tous* du mois de mars je vous propose d'échanger des cartes avec moi. Voici mes conditions. Contre dix timbres de votre pays, émission courante ou autres, je vous enverrai une carte de la Tunisie. Bien entendu les timbres doivent être le plus différent possible, si vous voulez même m'en envoyer de xxxxx, je vous enverrai un plus grand nombre de cartes. En attendant votre réponse pour savoir si vous acceptez mes conditions, recevez mes salutations.
Y. M. Orliac
Adresse: Y. M. Orliac. Intendance Militaire.
La kasbah, Tunis.

Cartes postales coloniales de la Tunisie ca. 1900. Courtoisie de Frédéric Mitterrand.

(10)

Фотография сделана на улице Гагарина в общежитии завода «Вектор».

МИЕ.

(11)

J'ai un coeur Monsieur!
Monsieur qui êtes assis face à moi.
Dans ce train dont je ne sais même pas la destination.
Ne me regardez pas ainsi.
Je n'ai jamais tué personne, je n'ai jamais volé non plus même si j'ai l'air d'un voyou. Je ne porte pas de costume, ni de cravate à pois seulement quelques trous, deux ou trois taches de cambouis si ce n'est du ciment, sur mes habits. C'est que moi monsieur, je ne suis pas un monsieur, je reste un homme.
J'ai deux mains pour travailler, m'habiller, me nourrir et serrer celle d'autrui.
Je n'ai ni chauffeur, ni serviteur, ni banquier. Mais j'ai un cœur monsieur. Le mépris et l'horreur dans vos yeux trahissent le vôtre. Crachez-moi dessus, je ne bougerais pas.
Avez-vous déjà rencontré un jour dans votre

vie, sur une route isolée cette vieille femme
amaigrie, édentée et ridée que l'on surnomme faim?

    Avez-vous déjà croisé sur un sentier perdu,
un vieillard courbaturé aux vêtements froissés,
qui marche les pieds nus et que l'on appelle froid?

    Moi, j'ai connu leur mère: Madame Misère
qui a été la maîtresse à mon école buissonnière.
Elle m'a enseigné à vivre. C'est pourquoi, monsieur,
crachez-moi dessus je ne bougerais pas.

    Moi j'ai un coeur monsieur et une famille sur
les bras.

Text: Maria Barbosa. *Sans Frontière, pour un hebdo
de l'immigration.* No 3. Mardi 29 Mai 1979 Paris.

    (12)

Ways of Denial—Al-Ahram Weekly

The Holocaust must be contextualised, and its
lessons learned, writes Azmi Bishara.

[…] The Zionist movement began, and had set its
sights on Palestine, long before the Holocaust.
Zionists only used the Holocaust to justify their
national project in hindsight, even if that justification
is what drove some Arabs to deny the existence of
the Holocaust. Yet, while there are people who
have felt that by minimising or even refuting the
Holocaust they undermine Jewish claims to a state
in Palestine, the majority of educated and informed
Arab opinion has never denied the Holocaust or the
existence of anti-Semitism in Europe. Rather, they
have argued—correctly— that since this horror
took place in Europe the Palestinians should not
have to pay the price. Although it vaguely existed
as a blend between the residue of a religious
culture and extremist nationalist ideas imported from
Europe even in early stages, anti-Semitism in the
sense of hostility towards the Jews only began to
spread significantly in the Arab world in the form
of cultural and intellectual output after 1967. Clearly,
the rise of this phenomenon coincided with the rise
of a metaphysical attitude that sought to explain
the overwhelming Arab defeat of that year in terms
of the confrontation with an absolute evil bent on
a global conspiracy of the nature of the "Protocols
of the Elders of Zion," which has been proven to be
an invention of the Russian secret service at the end
of the 19th century but which nevertheless found many
gullible ears in the Arab world in the wake of the 1967
defeat. Holocaust denial similarly emerged during
this period and in the same spirit of a fantastic
conspiracy theory that ascribed to an international
Jewish cabal the power to invent and dupe the entire
world into believing a stupendous set of lies. […]

Lidwien van de Ven, documenta 12. Kassel 2007.

    (13)

4.   Cf "…and will land them there." 1 Kin. (3 Kin.)
    V, 9.

5.   Cf. "And thou shalt carry it (the wood) up to
    Jerusalem." 2 Chr. 2, 16 (A. V.).

    Note :— In the time of Solomon the wood for
    the Temple was "carried" to Jerusalem. Today
    Arabs are busily engaged in depositing planks
    in the train which conveys the wood to the
    Holy City.

6.   "The carrier of the beam." T. B., B. K. In, M VI,
    p. 69.

7.   "… to carry burdens on their shoulders." 2 Chr.
    (2 Par.) II, 18.

8.   Cf. "Make thee an ark of timber planks."
    Gen. VI, 14.

    Note:—Timber planks on the beach of Jaffa,
    a reminder of the legend that—"it was there
    Noah built the ark." Lamartine, Travels in the
    East, p. 74 (From the French.)

    Cf. "And we bore him (Noah) in a vessel(*)
    composed of planks and nails," in the Koran.
    K., my, 13. The Moon, p. 511.

9.   "For the sea is his and he made it: and his
    hands formed the dry land." Jonah I, 3.
    Ps. xciv (95), 5.

10.   "By his magnificence the clouds run hither
    and thither." Deut. xxxm, 26.

11.   For he that wavereth is like—"a wave of the
    sea, which is moved and carried about by
    the wind." James I, 6.

Palestine Illustrated. 1 Jaffa, The Gate of Entrance.
Frank Scholten. Editions Jean Budry & Co. Paris.
Leiden, 1931.

    (14)

Routine search of a Gazan by security forces, 1984.
Gelatin silver print. Collection of the artist.

Joel Kantor. Born Canada, 1948, immigrated to
Israel 1976.

*Time Frame. A Century of Photography in the Land
of Israel.* Nissan N. Perez. The Israel Museum,
Jeruzalem 2000.

(15)

For Leroy, the riots — or uprising, as he prefers to call the events of several weekends that late summer in 1981 — were almost inevitable, given the dire relations between the community and the police and the economic policies of the Thatcherite government of the day.

"We are talking about a community established in this city since the days of the slave trade, here since the 1700s."

"With Margaret Thatcher, the vice was tightening on the working class, people were made to feel like second and third class citizens in their own country. We had between 70 and 80 percent unemployment amongst young men between 16 and 30 in the area."

"The riot was a symptom of there being something really wrong with our society. We smashed our own community up, we destroyed our own homes. There had to be something wrong. It was like a blistering, weeping spot right in the middle of your face which one day just explodes."

"The community had had a foot on its neck for years. I think the riots were basically historical chickens coming home to roost."

"I think we've got to acknowledge that at least three policemen had taken a bad kicking and they just tried to hang all three officers' wounds on me and made it seem like I was some sort of unbelievably violent, aggressive young man."

"When you meet me you see I'm completely otherwise, but that's the power of the media." After the riots, Toxteth became synonymous with violence, unemployment and, in the following years, drugs. But, argues Leroy: "Before the riots, we never really knew the area as Toxteth, it was the south end, or L8."

Leroy Cooper, the man whose arrest sparked the Toxteth Riots in 1981, tells Marc Waddington how it was a wake-up call to the establishment. *Liverpool Echo.* 4th of July. Liverpool 2011.

(16)

The existence of these two parallel mechanisms one of preventive censorship, the other to prohibit forbidden and clandestine transactions in printed matter or infractions of the rules governing booksellers — clearly indicates the keen awareness of the absolutist state and its rulers of the importance of the printed word. They, too, saw it as the principal vehicle of knowledge and thought, the medium of all political and religious discussion, the instrument for the expression of subversive criticism as well as intellectual obedience and acquiescence. Censorship existed to modify (or forbid) written material before it was published. The officers of the book police and the representatives of the publishing industry had the job of tracking down dangerous, prohibited, or clandestine works, and to this end they oversaw printers, booksellers, workers, and peddlers.

The system did not always work perfectly: From Richelieu to Colbert in the seventeenth century and from Pontchartrain to Maupeou in the eighteenth, the royal government was not fully in control of the situation. It was never able wholly to prevent the circulation of forbidden or condemned books, antimonarchist booklets, the innumerable pamphlets that floated around Paris and the provinces, writings, songs, satires — in fact, a whole body of printed criticism and controversy. But the political situation and the widening dissemination of "philosophical" works (a term eventually applied to all dangerous writing, all "bad books") distinguish the last decades of publishing under the Old Regime, and confer on them a character of their own. Never before had it been so clear what was at stake; never before had the internal contradictions of the censorship system, in its dealings with the publishing industry, become so evident. While booksellers pushed increasingly to expand their businesses, the inspectors of the book trade increased their efforts to keep it within the bounds of legality. The widening influence of the ideas of the Enlightenment in government circles made life easier for the bold and harder for the censors. Tugged as they were from repression to tolerance and back again, the censors and the book police never succeeded in keeping publishing and bookselling in chains.

Censorship and the Publishing Industry. Daniel Roche. Published in: Revolution in Print. The Press in France 1775–1800. Robert Darnton and Daniel Roche. University of California Press. Los Angeles 1989.

(17)

"Überreicht in Anerkennung der besonders guten Leistung im Reichsberufswettkampf der Deutschen Jugend vom Geschäftsführer der CONZ-Elektrizitätsges. M.b.h. Altona-Bahrenfeld. Juli 1936."

Olympia Der Arbeit. Arbeiterjugend im Reichsberufswettkampf. Artur Axman. Fotos: Georg L Hahn-Hahn. Berlin 1936.

(18)

Pour la Liberté et la Dignité des Jeunes Travailleurs

Mouvement Représentatif de
la Jeunesse Salariée,

Représentatif

par ses membres: de la dactylo au mineur
du vendeur à la cartonnière.

par ses dirigeants: employés, menuisiers,
imprimeurs, pris en pleine masse ouvrière.
par ses sections:

de la Belgique aux Indes
du Canada à Madagascar.

par ses journaux: tirant à 9.000.000
d'exemplaires par mois.

par ses services: de préparation au travail,
et de chômage, des loisirs et d'épargne,
des soldats et des malades.

par ses campagnes: pour l'apprentissage,
pour le salaire des jeunes
pour les loisirs éducatifs
pour la moralité au travail.

par ses démarches: auprès des patrons,
et des syndicats, des pouvoirs publics
et du B.I.T.
a entrepris une campagne mondiale pour

"La paix"

*Croisade Ouvrière. J.O.C. Jeunesse Ouvrière
Chrétienne,* Jeunesse Ouvrière Chrétienne Féminine.
Paris 1939

(19)

Some forty years later, AMG has in its files over
6,000 models, from athletes to cowboys, by way of
young GIs, leather boys straight out of a motorbike
gang, angel-faced hoodlums, street kids or simple
"boys next door." The aesthetic quality of his work may
sometimes be debatable, as it does have its kitsch
side, but given the evident sociological richness
of the material, even this can't detract from its value.
We have at our disposal here almost every type
of American boy, practically an anthropometric
archives on the subject. These photos have done
more than make their contribution to the various
physical culture magazines, they have offered a
dream, sharing the myth of California. And behind
them, their architect Bob Mizer has been able to
impose his vision and provide a unity, a subjective
reality, to his world.

*Athletic Model Guild. 160 Young Americans Photo-
graphed by Robert Mizer.* Los Angeles. Intermale.
Amsterdam 1987.

(20)

"Seit geraumer Zeit haben es einzelne Gruppen…
darauf angelegt, möglichst viele Polizeibeamte
abzubilden. Sie bezwecken damit ein frühzeitiges
Erkennen der … eingesetzten Polizeibeamten,
um so die polizeiliche Arbeit zu erschweren."
(aus: *Die Polizei*, Juli '78, Seite 212)
  Wir setzen hier ein Zeichen für Selbstzensur,
weil wir kein Interesse am Porträtieren von Polizei-

beamten haben. (Auf die Idee kamen wir durch den
Erlebnisbericht des Pressefotografen Günter Zint—
siehe vorangehende Seite—wo Polizeibeamten
aus seinen Negativen Polizisten-Gesichter heraus
gekratzt haben). Unsere Sorge ist die zunehmende
Überwachung des Staates mit Medien. Polizeibeamte
filmen mit "unseren" Geräten, sie nehmen uns auf.
Ihr Ziel ist es, uns "frühzeitig zu erkennen."
  (Wir haben auf durchsichtige Folie mit licht
abdeckendem Grafitstift oder Overhead- Projektor-
Stift gezeichnet. Während der Belichtung lag die Folie
auf dem Fotopapier. Die Bildschirm-Imitation haben
wir durch eine Maske aus schwarzem Karton erreicht).

Sünke + Michel, Mai 1979. *Arbeiterfotografie,* № 18,
Juni. Hamburg, 1979.

(21)

In the South the great planters form proportionately
a quite small class, but they have, singularly
enough, at their command some five million poor
whites; that is, there were actually more white
people to police the slaves than there were slaves.
Considering the economic rivalry of the black and
white worker, it would have seemed natural that
the poor white would have refused to police the
slave. But two considerations led him in the
opposite direction. First of all, it gave him work
and some authority as overseer, slave driver and
member of the patrol system. But above and
beyond this, it fed his vanity because it associated
him with the masters. To these Negroes he trans-
ferred all the dislike and hatred he had for the whole
slave system. The result was the system was held
stable and intact by the poor white.

Text: William E. B. DuBois, 1935. *A Matter of Colour.
Documentary of the Struggle for Racial Equality in
the USA.* Penguin Books. New York 1965.

(22)

Save Westminster's Services.
Rates up, Rents up, Services cut.

Cuts and privatisation in Westminster can be fought
off, and they must be. Lessons from around the
country show that joint action by workers and users,
even in Tory areas, can be successful. Public
services must be defended. But that is not enough:
there must be a campaign for the control of improved
and expanded services based on the needs of the
people of Westminster. Save Westminster's Services
has already begun that fight, but we need the support
of individuals, tenants' associations, women's groups,
parent-teacher associations and all others concerned
about public services. The tories' commitment to
selling off profitable public assets, nationalised
industries and public services, and cutting the rest,

threatens us both as workers and users. Cuts and privatisation by the government under Thatcher and by Westminster city council under porter are destroying our living standards.

North Paddington Community Darkroom. Exhibition panel. Save Westminster's Services, London ca. 1982.

(23)

Ja wir wollen eine politische, engagierte, zeitgemäße Fotografie.

Wer heute engagierte Fotos machen will, kann sich nicht an der Bilderflut der Massenmedien orientieren. Dort wird zu oft der visuelle Analphabetismus fort- geschrieben. 1973 haben wir die "Arbeiterfotografie" gegründet. Damals wurde die Geschichte der Arbeiter- fotografen von 1926 bis 1933 und der "Arbeiter- Illustrierten-Zeitung (AIZ)" gerade wiederentdeckt. Dabei haben wir mitgewirkt und diese Tradition nach 40 Jahren in unserem Lande wieder lebendig werden lassen. 1978 war es dann soweit. Aus den ersten Anfängen heraus hatten sich junge Gruppen von Arbeiterfotografen gebildet, die sich im November zum "Verband Arbeiterfotografie e. V." zusammen- schlossen. Die "Arbeiterfotografie" wurde zum Spiegel der Fotoarbeit in Bürgerinitiativen und in den neuen sozialen Bewegungen. Anfang der 80er Jahre rückten neue Fragen in den Vordergrund. Sind parteiliche Fotos schlechte Fotos? Und sind "gut" gestaltete Fotos politisch indifferent? Wie kann man für den Frieden fotografieren? Und wie fotografiert man eigentlich Arbeitslosigkeit? Kann man, soll man heute noch schöne Landschaften fotografieren? Ende 1983. 10 Jahre Arbeiterfotografie—10 Jahre Fotografie der Arbeitswelt. Unter diesem Motto haben wir Bilanz gezogen. Und wir konnten feststellen. Das gut gestaltete Bild, die ausdrucksstarke Serie sind wieder gefragt. Unsere Themen sind breiter, der fotografische Horizont weiter geworden, die Dokumentarfotografie bildet nur einen kleinen Ausschnitt. Seitdem führen wir mehr und mehr die Diskussion um bessere, wirksamere Fotos. Und da finden wir uns zusammen mit engagierten Foto- grafen und Fotojournalisten, die ihre überzeu- gendsten Bilder und Reportagen in der Presse oder in anderen Medien immer weniger veröffentlichen können, arbeiten wir mit allen zusammen, die Interesse an einer fortschrittlichen Fotografie haben. Wer heute mit der Fotografie etwas bewegen will, braucht die Arbeiterfotografie.

Arbeiterfotografie. Was den Stern Nicht Brachte. 12 Jahrgang Nummer 47. September-Oktober. Hamburg 1985.

(24)

Technicolor Dreams

[…] Sure, both the photos and articles deal [among other things] with lust. But lust is great. Why do Americans have such a problem with lust? It is nuts, because lust is part of loving another person: wouldn't you love to be adored? And isn't lust what being gay is about? Sooner or later, everyone loses control and has their lust anyway, so like, what's the big deal? It is only the repression of gay lust— lustophobia—that's an illness, and which causes us to hate ourselves. I want you to love your lust, because that's the only way to love yourself. The purpose of XY's photos—indeed, of all of XY—is to make young gay men feel happy and alive. And by that measure, I think we have been remarkably successful. Not only are our pictures funny. These pictures are also uniquely thrilling and passionate— so much so that they still make me gasp or laugh. I don't pretend that this issue shows all of young gay culture—for example, we haven't included any reader photos here. But this collection of photos is still more passionate than any magazine or book I've ever seen. I'm amazed by it. Such a range of emotions. What makes these pictures excite such fear, shame, thrill, and joy? All of it comes from something only gay boys can feel—a special passion, kept in a special secret place in only our souls. It is somewhere between validation and angst. Viewing the cover of XY4—which shows two menacing, but hot, jocks approaching in a deserted school corridor— our assistant editor Nathan Smorynski said the photo "sent him to the dark place." That "dark place" is our passion. You know what it is because gay boys live the feelings every day. Yet, though gay youth culture has become so loud lately, its actual feelings— the "dark place"— are never represented anywhere other than in XY. The real feelings are just way too scary, so anytime gay teens are shown, they are shown as decorative, nonsexual, nonpassionate smurfs—with no realness. It's as if someone altered all the mirrors in the world so whenever a gay boy looked in one, it showed no reflection. It is so terribly sad to repress our reflection, because the "dark place" is beautiful. Even the angst of secret lust is thrilling and reminds you that you are alive. When XY photos show a furtive glance in class, that approach of the scary yet hot jocks, a passionate kiss, a takeoff of an A+F ad, or just a shameless closeup [and why not?], we reflect people's deepest hopes, desires, fears, and [yes] dreams. […]

Text: Peter Ian Cummings. *XY Magazine,* Fall / November. № 34. San Fransico 2001.

(25)

Lieber Leser.

Das junge Forum, die Kulturabteilung der Gewerk-
schaftsjugend auf dem grünen Hügel in Reckling-
hausen, gab mit dem Kulturinfo 2 grünes Licht für
ihre Kulturarbeit. Eine Arbeitstagung von kultur-
schaffenden Kollegen war dem vorausgegangen
und formulierte die Kulturarbeit als Bestandteil der
Gewerkschaftsarbeit, die die Arbeit in Betrieb und
Gesellschaft unterstützt und Artikulationsmittel,
Mittel zur Selbstentfaltung und Entfaltung von Selbst-
bewußtsein, Agitationsmittel und Solidarisierungs-
mittel ist. Drei Jahre sind verstrichen. Ist diese
gedankliche Arbeit praktisch geworden, Gewerkschaftsarbeit der Kollegen geworden? Wie benutzen
sie Literatur, Theater, Musik, Malerei, Film, Video,
Fotografie in ihrer Arbeit? Welche Hilfestellung gab
die Bewegung der Arbeiterfotografen? Das vorlie-
gende Heft zeigt leichte und tiefere Verknüpfungen.
Wir fotografieren für die Öffentlichkeitsarbeit der
Gewerkschaft, Fotogruppen bilden sich, die von
uns angeleitet werden. Kollegen beziehen die
Fotografie ein in die betriebliche Arbeit.

Arbeiterfotografie № 13/14 March. Hamburg 1978.

(26)

SECURITY GUARD G/W/M, 24, 5'11", 195 lb.,
Italian/Irish, top, black hair, brown eyes, moustache,
pipe and cigar smoker, seeks white or Latin bottoms,
18+ to 35. You must have moustache and slim to
average build. I am Greek A, French A/P. Fems
O.K. I work as a security guard, live alone, and am
financially secure. Send letter with photo, will get
mine. [TIMOTHY, BOX S28–5971]

COLGATE STUDENT JOCK I love J/0, feeling you
and French action. I am 18 +, sophomore, 6', 140 lb.,
blond hair, blue eyes and 7" of hard, horny tool to
pacify you. If you want fun, sex or a lasting relationship, write me. No fats, ferns or T.V. [LOUIS, BOX
S28–5942]

EROTIC ENEMAS G/W/M, 29, 5'8", 145 lb., seeks
G/W/M, 18+ to 40 for erotic enema sessions, not
interested in J/0 correspondence. N.Y.C. metro area
only. [RICHARD, BOX S28-5965]

SMELLY PITS, WET JOCK Uniformed man, 37, 6',
160 lb., knows how to use his nose and please
yours. If you have rank armpits and crotch, let's talk
about it and maybe smell it. J/0, W/S, jockstraps,
balls, whatever, as long as it is raunchy and smells
like man [CAL, BOX S28-60321]

LONELY IN QUEENS W/M, 21, looking for friend in
my area and also on Long Island. I seek caring friend
for 50/50 sharing, honest, sincere, affectionate
relation and fun times. I also want sincere, honest
pen pals. Let's write first and get acquainted and
see what happens. Discretion assured and required.
Will answer all. [PETER, BOX S28–6011]

Stallion, The Magazine of the Alternative Lifestyle.
August. New York 1984.

(27)

Азалея. Фото Б. Раскина.
Ветреница. Фото И. Дергилеаа.
Красоднев. Фото Б. Подгорного.
Гладиолус. Фото Я. Смолякова.
Ромашки И Колокольчики. Фото Б. Раскина. Розы.
Фото И. Кропивницкого.

Издание Министерства Связи Ссср 1970.

(28)

[…] Proprio allora scoprii, a venti metri dalla pastic-
ceria Caflish, una delle innumerevoli piaghe di questa
città butterata, una fistola, un vicolo. Mi avvicinai
e la prima cosa che vidi, al centro d'un rigagnolo,
fu ancora un alimento—o piuttosto qualcosa da
mangiare: una fetta di cocomero (ricordavo ancora
i cocomeri di Roma spaccati, che avevano l'aria di
gelati al lampone e pistacchio picchiettati di chicchi
di caffè) macchiata di fango che ronzava di mosche
come una carogna e sanguinava sotto gli ultimi raggi
del sole. Un ragazzo coperto di stracci si avvicinò
a questa carne putrida, la prese e si mise a mangiarla
con naturalezza. Allora mi sembrò di capire quello
che i commercianti di via Roma nascondevano dietro
le loro oreficerie alimentari: la verità del nutrimento.
    Presi a sinistra, poi a destra, poi ancora a
sinistra: tutti i vicoli erano uguali. Nessuno mi notava,
ogni tanto incrociavo uno sguardo vuoto. Gli uomini
non parlavano, le donne scambiavano qualche parola
a lunghi intervalli. Stavano a gruppi di cinque o sei,
strette le une alle altre e i loro stracci facevano delle
macchie brillanti sulle pareti cineree. Ero stato
colpito, fin dalla mattina, dal pallore dei Napoletani;
ora non me ne meravigliavo più; cuocevano
nell'ombra a vapore; la carne delle donne, soprat-
tutto, aveva l'aria d'un bollito sotto il grasso; il vicolo
aveva digerito le loro guance: reggevano ancora ma
si sarebbe potuto staccarne dei pezzi tirando con
le dita. Vidi con sollievo le grosse labbra baffute
d'una ragazza: quelle, almeno, avevano l'aria di
essere crude. Tutta quella gente sembrava ripiegata
su se stessa, non sognava nemmeno più: circondata
anch'essa dal suo nutrimento, cibi vivi, scaglie, torsoli,
carni oscene, frutti aperti e macchiati, gioiva con
indolenza sensuale della propria vita organica. Dei
bambini si arrampicavano sui mobili che mettevano
in mostra, accanto a interiora di pesce i loro sederi
nudi; oppure si issavano sui gradini che davano
accesso alle camere, col ventre a terra, battendo

le braccia come se nuotassero, strofinando contro
la pietra i loro piccoli sessi tremolanti. Mi sentivo
a mia volta digerito: cominciò con un desiderio
di rimettere, ma molto dolce e zuccherato e poi
scese in tutto il mio corpo come un ridicolo solletico.
Io guardavo quelle carni, quelle sanguinolente,
quelle pallide, le braccia nude di una vecchia cieca,
la pezza rossastra che restava incollata a un osso
bianco, e mi sembrava che ci fosse qualche cosa da
fare. Ma che cosa? Mangiare? Carezzare, vomitare?

Text: J.P. Sartre. Translation: E. Ramondino, 1936.
Vicoli. Fotografie di Mario Cattaneo. Electa,
Napoli 1992.

(29)

Days of Sitting on a Bench. Photography: Laslo
Strong. Design: Jurgis Lietunovas. Amsterdam 2017.

(30)

דייש בשדות מרחביה אלי ניצן, פולדו.
נדב מן
מעבדת "ביתמונה" למקורות א"י

קיבוץ מרחביה, חודש ניסן תשס"ד, אפריל 2004.

(31)

Directed by Albert-Andre Yheunereux, based on
Jean Genet's Poem The Man Condemned to Death.
With Marin Denis and Christian de Wulf as the
protagonists in this "supreme love rite before death."
Described as bringing to the screen "the superb and
scandalous character of a poet obsessed by contemporary reality, which form the substance of his work,"
the film was shot in black-and-white by Michael
Baudour and produced by Robert Malengreau.

Films and Filming. Condemned and Possesed. Marin
Denis and Christian de Wulf. May. London, 1978.

(32)

On croyait que la puissance de la publicité avait
effacé, raboté, anéanti même, les particularismes
locaux et les caractères nationaux de chaque
peuple. La fermière de Peteghem n'adopte-t-elle
pas le même modèle de robe-sac que Grace Kelly
de Monaco ? Le noir de Stanleyville n'a-t-il pas été
persuadé, tout comme l'écolier de Paris, des vertus
douteuses du Coca-Cola? D'énormes magazines
imposent à des millions de lecteurs de tous les
continents une Olympe peuplée de quelques
divinités interchangeables Ingrid Bergman, Charlie
Chaplin, le comte de Paris et sa famille, Sophia
Loren, Soraya, etc… A intervalles réguliers et selon

la liturgie d'un véritable culte, on vous entretient des
amours, projets, déceptions et déplacements de ces
dieux et de ces déesses dont l'aspect physique
même finit par conditionner celui d'innombrables
humains. Il y a quelques mois, tous les petits crétins
du monde portaient des blousons de simili-cuir à
la James Dean ou s'aplatissaient la crinière à la
Marlon Brando. «La bêtise est l'axe de l'univers et
de la vie», a dit Courteline.

*Numéro Spécial. Expo '58, Ce que la Presse ne dit
Jamais.* #685 — Europe Magazine. Bruxelles, 1958.

(33)

Da sinistra a destra e dall'alto in basso: Foto C.
Eisenmann, la piccola Myrtle Corbin, New York;
Thomas Goy, l'uomo-tronco; Matthias Buchinger,
1732; Sealo, l'uomo-pinguino, 1949; Catherina
Mazzina in una incisione del 1585; Cari Herrmann
Unthan, 1890; la piccola Marta; Nicodemus;
manifesto teatrale per l'ussaro dimezzato; incisione
medica del XIX secolo; quattro incisioni mediche del
XIX secolo; caso di elefantiasi in un'incisione di
Gaspard Bauhin, Francoforte 1614; Eugene Berrey;
foto Gilles Larrain (da originale a colori, da «Idols»,
Links 1973); Francesco A. Centini; incisione del
XVIII secolo; grande invalido recuperato al lavoro.

PhotoTeca. Mostri Fantasmi Streghe & Baccanti.
Anno 1. № 2. Milano 1980.

(34)

Some considerations when making health and
safety photographs:

Only snapshot when it is unavoidable.

Remember photographs on their own won't tell
a full story — so get captions and additional
background notes every time. Nothing
happens in isolation or lacks a past history
and future implications... The pictures of the
actual incident or location are only part of the
story.

Don't sit on the material when you've collected
it. Write up the notes, process the film and
prepare a file for presentation and discussion
with those involved.

System and order help to win battles. Classify
and store your negatives and notes so that
they can be found quickly. Give people copies
but always retain control of original negatives
and notes.

The Worker Photographer. London ca. 1980. Courtesy
of Terry Dennett. Jo Spence Memorial Archive.

(35)

Paris 1/12/84. Arrivée de Convergence '84. Zineb, une des animatrices.

Courtesy of Pierre Ciot—Photo Imasud. Marseille 1984.

(36)

Всем, кто заботится о правильном уходе за кожей лица, необходимо запомнить линии наименьшего растяжения кожи. Это линии, по которым следует выполнять такие косметические процедуры, как самомассаж, нанесение крема и крем-пудры, а также косметических эмульсий для удаления декоративной косметики.

Косметика без секретов. С. Сикорская, Е. Бельченко. Дом русской косметики. Москва 1992.

(37)

Verrà la morte e faremo belle foto

La catastrofe viene bene. La catastrofe interessa. La catastrofe fa vendere i giornali. Quindi, la catastrofe occupa le prime pagine di giornali e riviste, e più catastrofe è, meglio viene evidenziata. Per dire la verità, se valesse la regola secondo la quale il cane che morde il bambino è una cazzata, mentre il bambino che morde il cane è una notizia, e che notizia!, se valesse dunque questa norma, le catastrofi dovrebbero venir ridotte a una «breve» a pagina diciotto, mentre copertine e titolini dovrebbero venir dedicati a: «Quest'autunno solo la tracimazione di una roggia, ce la siamo cavata», oppure «La foto dell'anno! Bimbo cade nella buca e viene salvato».
       E non è che sul piano della riflessione, come si dice, la catastrofe insegni qualcosa. Se così fosse, saremmo veramente un branco di idioti, visto che le dighe continuano a cedere, le alluvioni a tempestare, gli aerei a cadere.
       Ma l'arte di schivare le catastrofi, di renderle incruente, oltre ad essere difficile e costosa, non è fotogenica. Mentre il massacro scuote le coscienze, commuove anche gli iscritti alla P2, vien bene in copertina. Da qui nasce il genere. Dal genere la storia delle immagini usate, il loro successo commerciale.

PhotoTeca: Catastrofi batoste maledetta sfiga & soluzioni finali. Anno II, №5. Milano 1981.

(38)

Art and Working Class, Urban Environments

Much community arts activity takes place in the urban areas of our society, especially the cities.

It is right to question the value of such activity in an environment often consisting of bad housing, few jobs and a general denial of the opportunities available to others. Sticking plasters can not cure the ills of society—imaginative approaches have to be adopted by those seeking a cure. Community arts can only contribute to a wider desire for change which utilises a variety of techniques and approaches. Their value often lies in creating an atmosphere in which other approaches to society's problems can be explored.

Eddie Johnson. Arts in Action: A Community Photographic Project on Merseyside. Arts & Action. Liverpool 1980.

(39)

The cinema has grown up in the twentieth century. Its essential qualities of quick movement, quick thinking and candour (the camera is quick to reveal a lie) are the natural expression of an age of combustion engines, American journalese and "functionalism". But as usual, public opinion lagged far behind scientific and social changes and the surface common sense of the modern world hides a still Victorian heart. Functionalism becomes / how delightfully unfurnished my dear"—the corollary of the antimacassar; journalese is elaborated from a shortcut to a circumlocution; while engines built for speed are causing traffic blocks in Piccadilly.
       The time lag is nowhere more evident than in the cinema; whose mechanisms creaks laboriously in crane shots, trolly shots and panoramas; which is so slow-witted that it repeated in words what is— (or should be) already apparent from the action, camera angle and lighting; which is just as candid as the censor (i.e. the sum of die-hard opinion) will allow breeding the inverted prudery "leg shows" and semi-nudity.
       The cinema is backward because films are almost of necessity, enormous financial ventures. It is difficult to persuade a man to buy what has not already been tested, and this fact accounts.

Still from film *Bread.* Film and Photo league. London ca. 1930. Courtesy of Terry Dennett. Jo Spence Memorial Archive.

(40)

Trübungen im Glas, Ungenauigkeiten des Schliffes, Unsauberkeit der Oberfläche—für den Laien meist unsichtbare Dinge—können die Linse unbrauchbar machen. Jahrzehntelange Erfahrung des Fach-arbeiters ist um so ausschlaggebender, je stärker die Erzeugung "mechanisiert" ist.

Arbeit! Dr. Paul Wolf. Volk und Reich Verlag G.M.B.H. Berlin. Bechhold Verlagsbuchhandlung Frankfurt-M. 1937.

(41)

Before Jo and I met we had both wondered what
was here before us of a radical nature in the arts
so the first task for the workshop was to study and
hopefully try to revive the best of the forgotten
strands of social radicalism in the arts that would
be useful for our own age.

We started by reading the literature of the
historic labour and trade union. For this purpose
we got research permits to the library of the London
School of Economics. These were then available
to independent researchers. We set aside one
evening and Saturday mornings every week and
systematically worked our way through the library
reading and photocopying periodicals. Eventually
we spent a total of 8 years reading our way through
this collection—something very few people have
ever done. Parallel with this we also started to track
down and interview old activists we found mentioned
in the literature—they then pointed us towards
others who were still alive. In this way we became
aware of the hidden history of social radicalism in
the film, theatre, cartoons and graphic art.

Photography Workshop. Terry Dennett. Jo Spence
Memorial Archive. London 2012.

(42)

Celebrate, Construct, Select, Connote, Encode.

*Schools Photography Project. Work in Progress
1978–81.* Cultural Studies Department. ILEA
Cockpit Arts Workshop. London.

(43)

Les Meilleures Années de Notre Vie

La beauté est dans les yeux de celui qui regarde.
Pourquoi un visage, les contours d'un corps, le dessin
particulier d'un détail physique provoque-t-il cette
réaction? La réponse vient de notre inconscient et
peut illuminer notre vie ou au contraire provoquer
frustration et intolérance.

J'éprouve ces sentiments aussi bien face à
un jeune homme que devant un paysage marin,
et j'aime me souvenir de ce que j'ai vu de beau au
cours de mon existence.

J'ai eu une éducation stricte, et suivi des
études de mathématiques jusqu'au stade d'ingénieur
dans la marine australienne.

Dans les années 60, ma vie a été transformée
par l'apparition du Rock and Roll, par les mouvements
de révolte de la jeunesse. J'ai tout abandonné pour
suivre mes jeunes amis vagabondant de concert
en concert, partageant tout avec eux.

J'ai accumulé des milliers de documents sur
cette époque libératrice. Encore maintenant j'aime
photographier des jeunes qui ont cet esprit de révolte,
qui mènent leur vie hors des sentiers battus.

Il a fallu faire beaucoup de sacrifices matériels
pour subsister en tant que photographe, accepter
bien des petits boulots sans intérêt pour acheter des
pellicules, mais je ne regrette pas car la vie d'artiste
est la plus excitante qui soit.

Jeunes Hommes 3. Nos Plus Belles Années.
Ron Reid. Location and date unknown.

(44)

Lotta Continua. Bologna ca. 1970. Per cortesia dell'
Archivio Storico della Nuova Sinistra "Marco Pezzi".

(45)

Крупнейшей фигурой в бельгийском искусстве
XIX и начала XX века был Константин Менье
(1831–1905). Скульптор и живописец, он целиком
посвятил свое творчество людям труда. Его
работы, представленные на выставке бельги-
йского искусства, пользовались у нас большим
успехом. Искусство Менье близко и понятно
советскому зрителю. Последовательный реалист,
человек большой души и огромного таланта,
Менье в своих работах создал героический
образ пролетариата.

Одной из лучших его работ является скульптура, созданная мастером в последний год
жизни, — «Грузчик». Фигура молодого рабочего,
стоящего в свободной, непринужденной позе,
полна величавой силы и красоты. Той же
симпатией к простому народу, уверенностью
в его силах, глубоким состраданием к его
горестям отличаются и другие скульптурные
и живописные работы Менье.

В XX веке в Бельгии возник ряд художе-
ственных школ, придерживающихся различных
творческих методов, иногда далеких от
реализма. Но работы художников Бельгии всегда
посвящены человеку, его повседневной жизни,
его чувствам и переживаниям. Их отличает
живая симпатия к простым людям, умение
показать красоту жизни.

Работница, Общественно-политический и
литературно—художественный журнал. № 12.
Изд-во «Правда». Декабрь 1956.

(46)

The Mighty Micro was written and presented by the
late Dr Christopher Evans, computer scientist and
psychologists, from whose book it was adapted; this
series, expensively produced, extensively previewed,
and broadcast at peak-viewing time, was designed
to increase public understanding of the psychological,

social, political, and economic implications of the microprocessor revolution. The vision that emerges from its engagingly enthusiastic but essentially breathless narrative is of society rapidly metamorphosed by technological advance, into an affluent, leisured utopia.

Schooling and Culture. Issue 8. Published by the Cultural Studies Department ILEA Cockpit Arts Workshop. London 1980.

(47)

"כך הולכים".
קרן קיימת ומצלמת
תמוכות מהקופסה הכחולה 1903–2003.

בתחנת הכוח ההיסטורית רדינג א, של חברת החשמל ואפריל
2003.

(48)

"Zij noemen ons Ljoeberieten"

Enkele maanden geleden, in het voorjaar van dit jaar, is de kleine stad Ljoebertsy dicht bij Moskou eensklaps enorm populair in heel het land geworden. Deze populariteit is echter van zeer bijzondere aard. Men beweerde dat hier een jongerenorganisatie ontstaan was die oorlog verklaarde aan uur, "rockers", "panks" e.d. In ons land zijn er veel zogenaamde informele jongerenorganisaties, zoals liefhebbers van klassieke en pop-muziek, groepen voor het onderhoud van oude culturele en historische monumenten e.a. En nu geruchten over deze ljoeberieten, die op zich de rol van… "ordebewakers" zouden hebben overgenomen en die zelf zouden beslissen welke informele groepen en verenigingen goed en welke slecht zijn. Onze correspondent heeft een bezoek aan deze stad gebracht, waar hij met talrijke bewoners kon spreken. Zijn eerste conclusie: absoluut normale mensen. Minder intelligent, meer intelligent, goed opgevoed, slecht opgevoed, maar voor de rest: jongeren zoals overal, en geen bijzondere wens om "andersdenkenden" te vervolgen. Het enige specifieke kenmerk is misschien het feit dat zeer vele "ljoeberieten" deel uitmaken van verschillende sportverenigingen en bijzonder gek zijn op zware sporten. Maar het liefst laten wij ze zelf aan het woord komen.

Sovjet–Unie, maandelijks geïllustreerd tijdschrift in 21 talen. Nr. 9 (451). Moskou 1987.

(49)

Trentatré terzine per Tress: la Divina Commedia è ammalata da più di mezzo secolo di «doréite»: una malattia che ne ha seppellita l'illustrazione.

La resurrezione potrebbe essere fotografica.
Foto: Duane Michals.

Dante scrive non sopra la carta, che al principio del Trecento non si fabbrica, ma su pelle di pecora. Non per essere stampato ma ricopiato a mano su codici membranacei. Eppure, con la mirabile intuizione del genio paranoide, programma la «Commedia» per la pubblicazione a dispense settimanali in edicola. La più avveduta ricerca commerciale, oggi, non potrebbe essere migliore: tre cantiche, di trentatré canti ciascuna, 99 in totale. Più un canto introduttivo, che porta il totale a 100, immaginato per il primo fascicolo, doppio e promozionale, con in omaggio la prima copertina per rilegare l'Inferno. In due anni, tenuto conto delle sospensioni d'agosto, l'edizione si completa con il Purgatorio e il Paradiso. I canti hanno un numero pressoché eguale di terzine, alcune sembrerebbero scritte apposta per eventuali tagli dovendo pareggiare, per causa di mutevoli note, le trentadue pagine di ogni fascicolo.

In ciascuno dei quali si trova un episodio centrale, immaginato poeticamente per esserlo poi graficamente nella copertina. Dante a questo proposito non vuole lasciare a nessuno quello che si chiama l'imbarazzo della scelta: sceglie lui che conosce bene tutta la storia. Ma non invade il campo dell'editore e del redattore, lasciando ad essi di decidere il mezzo di fabbricazione delle immagini: xilografico, calcografico, litografico e fotografico. […]

PhotoTeca: Garibaldi lingualunga, rotte & rutti interessanti. Anno III, №8. Milano 1982.

(50)

See No. 43

(51)

Socialist emulation is a powerful factor for developing the creative initiative of the masses and fostering a spirit of socialist collectivism. Its purpose is not only to attain a higher level of labour productivity but also to show everybody how the best work performances are being achieved, to make advanced work methods available to all.

An Influential Force in Soviet Society. Profizdat Publishers, All-Union Central Council of Trade Unions. Moscow 1982.

(52)

[…] This is how I came to know a small group of gay men who met regularly in a sauna and then adjourned to the flat of one of the group. Innuendo and ambiguity were thick in the air despite the Rumanian Riesling. I suspect that frankness was not encouraged by my

presence since I was assumed to have the micro-
phones and cameras of the KGB trailing behind me.
The atmosphere resembled that of a stag party —
misogynist and hedonistic. It struck me as being their
way of not facing up to the real motive behind their
meeting; it was also a convincing explanation for
curious parents and wives. No-one was ever explicit
about his sexuality in this group, and I joined the
closet. During a Sunday afternoon walk one of the
group came out to me. I reciprocated and we became
friends. A couple of months later, when I was in the
woods with Pavel, I met Misha. This was three
weeks before I was due to leave. My relationship
with Misha is the basis of this cautionary tale of
paranoia and ejaculatio praecox. To avoid anxiety
I had chosen to be a sensible and chaste voyeur.
But now I lost my head with Misha. He was like
a fantasy come true, but in the most unlikely and
dangerous of places. I couldn't resist, despite the
signs that he was not interested in my mind or my
body. The first sign was a stolen cassette. When
he discovered that I had access to the "dollar shop",
he asked for a pair of fancy shoes. It was clear that
he expected something in return for any favours that
he might grant. Jeans were the next request. With
the bargaining came protestations of affection. "It's
better with you… why do you have to go away?"
A mutually exploitative relationship was built up on
the basis of desire and mistrust. The jeans were
provided before the event. The event needed a venue;
there was only my room which I was reluctant to use
because I was afraid that it was bugged. Alcohol,
lust and the corrupt feeling that I should get something
for my cast-offs blunted my judgement, and I invited
Misha back to my room. Afterwards he disappeared —
with 150 roubles. Paranoia and anxiety then began
in earnest. It started with the man who smiled at
Misha on the stairs ("No, I've never seen him before.")
I burnt my diary in the lavatory pan, drowning the
smell with eau de cologne. For the next five days
before my departure I saw agents everywhere and
expected to be arrested at any moment. […]

Paranoia in the USSR. Square Peg No. 3.
London 1983.

(53)

The Point of the Portrait. North Paddington Community
Darkroom. Exhibition panel. Croydon ca. 1988.
Courtesy of Philip Wolmuth.

(54)

[…] Erfreulicherweise zeigen die Bilder der Fotografen selbst eine Beschäftigung mit dem Leben
von heute. Mit einer Reduzierung dieser Fotos auf
Technik und anspruchsvolles Hobby allein wird
man diesen Fotografen nicht gerecht. Man sieht und
merkt deutlich ihre Betroffenheit über gesellschaft-
liche Zustände und ihr Engagement wird in einer
Reihe von Bildern deutlich, z. B. bei den Bildserien
und der einzigen Fotomontage, die sich auch unter
den ausgezeichneten Fotos findet. Wenn der Verant-
wortliche für diesen Bereich Amateurfotografie,
Dr. R. H. Ley feststellt: "Nur wenige Einsender
reichten achtlos geknipste Bilder ein, kaum einer
nutzte das Bild zur Agitation oder zu einer negativen
oder gar verfälschten Interpretation seiner Umwelt," —
so stellt diese Äußerung eher eine Charakterisierung der Schwierigkeiten des Photo-Industrie-
verbandes im Dialog mit der Jugend dar, als
eine Charakterisierung der Beiträge der Jugend-
lichen selbst.

Text: Norbert Ortmanns, Arbeiterfotografie Aachen.
Arbeiterfotografie. № 32. Dezember. Hamburg 1982.

(55)

An attempt to move the work on: setting up the
"studio" sessions

Our first concerted attempt to break the circuit had
been to ask the group to contribute to an exhibition
on youth style. We had pointed out to the group that
their photographs nearly always moved in the area
of representing peoples "style" and life-style. We
told them that our exhibition was relatively weak and
unspecific in the area of black people's style, yet
we could sense that amongst young black people
there was a whole spectrum of identities and
attitudes being expressed through style; that it was
a complicated scene. The group could easily build
upon what they were already doing to produce some
worked up exhibition panels. From our point of view
this would also be the point when we could colla-
borate with the students to provide forms and
conventions with which they could begin to articu-
late the meaning of the symbols and celebratory
motifs which were already established in their work.
They voted with their feet. No one turned up at the
session immediately following this discussion.

Youth, Culture and Photography. Andrew Dewdney
and Martin Lister. Macmillan Education. London 1988.

(56)

Мода приходит в цех. «Шейте сами — это красиво,
удобно, модно, практично» — эти слова были
девизом конкурса, впервые организованного
на заводе женсоветом металлургического
производства.

Газета «За тяжелое машиностроение» № 4 (9768)
за 6 января, 1984.

(57)

Сталевары вплотную приближены к зрителю
и занимают почти все пространство холста.
Художник любуется открытыми красивыми
лицами рабочих, лепит их широкими мазками,
кое-где сознательно преувеличивает пропорции
фигур. Чем больше вглядываешься в эту
небольшую группу из пяти человек, тесно сгру-
дившихся у этюдника, тем больше проникаешься
значительностью идеи, заложенной в полотне.
Да, вот такие могучие, физически красивые
парни, надежные в своих чувствах, являющиеся
мастерами своего дела, и есть подлинные герои
искусства. Это такие люди, как они, высоко
несут знамя советского рабочего человека,
трудом которого созданы все материальные
богатства нашего социалистического государства.

Искусство и Рабочий Класс. Е. В. Николаева.
Ленинград «Художник РСФСР» 1983.

(58)

"I think people were interested, but while the staff
seemed full of confidence, I think everyone else was
a bit "I don't think we're gonna get that far, it's just
not going to be taken seriously." Then we went further
and further into it, it became more interesting to do
and we realised we were surprising ourselves and that
we could make something really positive out of it.

    The production team was quite a small group
by the time we got nearer the end and we were really
getting a chance to say how we wanted the exhibition
to be done. I definitely started to take it more seriously
and people like David and Maio and Amy and I started
getting really involved with it. Not in the way of saying
"This is my work"—I couldn't have pulled off something
like that on my own. We all needed each other and
I felt quite proud.

    Young people had been able to say what they
wanted to, express the situation they were in. Actually
communicate with people. It was a way of putting
across to them how we felt about the situation we
were in and that we weren't going to just sit there and
take the kind of things that people were saying to us."

*What Can a Woman do With a Camera? Photography
for Women.* Jo Spence & Joan Solomon. Scarlett
Press. London 1995.

(59)

Population increases ceaselessly. It is only fifty-nine
years since the Revolution of 1911, but the face of
China has completely changed. In another thirty-one
years, that is, in the year 2001, or the beginning of
the twenty-first century, China will have undergone
an even greater change. She will have become more
densely populated than coastal India. And this is not
as it should be. In old imperialist times, each local
tyrant of the oppressive aristocracy was empowered
to keep as many wives and concubines as he could
afford and sire as many offspring by them as he
could afford. Since the wealth of feudal China was
improperly distributed, these oppressive landlords
and their bureaucratic lackeys were each able to
keep many women in a state of quadruple authori-
tarian domination (political authority, religious
authority, clan authority, and the authority of the
oppressing husband), and they each were able to
support many offspring by each woman. So it is that
China's present-day overpopulation crisis grows out
of two criminal pre-revolutionary injustices: feudal
improprieties in the distribution of the wealth, and the
subjection of Chinese women to the immoral institution
of patriarchal polygamy. Therefore, action to sharply
rein in the increase of population is not only materi-
ally necessary; it is as heroic and revolutionary a
program as a Peasants' Revolutionary Committee
seizing property from the landlord and redistributing
it democratically among the People.

Text: Dean Latimer. "*This Township Achieved Zero
Population Growth in the Second Year of the Great
Nonprocreative Revolution*" (December 12, 1971).
Mao's little Black Book—*or Please Don't Squeeze
the Chairman* published in *National Lampoon, The
Gentleman's Bathroom Companion.* New York 1975.

(60)

К Нашим Иллюстрациям

Рассматривая громадное количество работ,
присланных на конкурс (309 работ 1-й категории и
1170 работ 2-й категории), поражаешься настой-
чивости и любовью к фотографии, с какими
добивается фото-любитель усовершенствования
своей техники. Все же среди работ есть и доказа-
тельства того, что некоторые товарищи или еще
не окончательно осознали сущность фотографи-
ческого изображения (например, раскраска
фотографий красками), или не побороли еще труд-
ностей техники; кроме того, некоторые не учитывали
того впечатления, какое произведет на зрителя
размер изображения (напр., чрезвычайно малый
размер отпечатка). Среди авторов 1-й категории
встречаются еще, к сожалению, фотографы (из
числа профессионалов), не могущие отрешиться
от ретуши, варварски искажающей человеческое
лицо. Но тем не менее, суммируя общее впечат-
ление от просмотра всех присланных на конкурс
работ, не трудно видеть несомненный рост техники
массового фотолюбительства. Если среди работ
не нашлось выдающихся (чем и объясняется
отсутствие первой премии), то многие из них, и
особенно—отмеченные жюри, несомненно, заслу-
живают того, чтобы на них остановить внимание.

Советское фото, вып. 08, 1928 г.

(61)

Dear Heather,

At last I have a spare weekend, so that I can once
again communicate with you through the medium of
your marvellous magazine Smooth which continues
to be out of this world for all us rubber addicts.
    I have the flat to myself this weekend and
much as I enjoy entertaining and having fun with all
my rubber loving friends it does get a bit exhausting
both sexually and mentally and I'm looking forward
to a long weekend of peace and quiet (in rubber
of course).
    It is Friday evening and as always I am wearing
a tight fit latex rubber suit and hood (open face), long
black latex mackintosh, hooded and tightly belted,
over a rubber gas mask, long rubber gloves and
high heeled black rubber riding boots in glossy black
finish—divine!
    A few comments on recent issues of Smooth—
how sad that it is now only published regularly, I do
sincerely hope that you will be able to resume
monthly publication very soon—as it is I can hardly
wait for the next issue to appear. Mrs.L.B. from the
Midlands looked very alluring in her various rubber
outfits. The large photo on the centre page, with
rubber gloved hands on her wide open thighs, and
particularly the zip of her rubber panties leads the
beholder to seductive thoughts of tweaking open that
zip, inserting rubber gloved fingers to gently mastur-
bate her clitty, while she takes one's throbbing penis
into the smooth rubber gloves and stroke one to a
full magnificent erection. Meanwhile one's own rubber
gloved fingers ever busy, she finally urges one's
pulsing organ right up into her warm vagina. One's
slow firm thrusts become quicker and quicker. As
one's sex urges are further stimulated by the sound
of the swish and ripple of rubber against rubber,
the smell of hot latex and sex until the final climax
takes place.[…]

        Yours always,
        Rubberwise

*Smooth. For Those Appreciative of the Sensual
Properties of Rubber.* №60. Swiss Publications Ltd.
London (date unknown).

(62)

Barvou mládí je královská zeleň. Barva naděje. Barva
odvahy. Není náhodou, že je to základní barva i tito
spanilé, slavně země, která jaro co jaro žene do listů
a do květů, plná sil a šťáv a neklidu a touhy. Ano,
mládí je v této zemi doma. Má tu svá místa prvních
přísah a prvních velkých snů, má tu svá zátiší i
domovské přístavy, kde si lze promluvit se stromy,
s oblaky i s dávnou minulostí… Mládí tohoto času
je stokrát veselé a stokrát mládí tohoto času je
stokrát samo—á stokrát se sbíhá do houfů, kde

zní zpěv a silák verš a zvony navzdor bouřkám.
Mládí je láska. Mládí je První čin. Mládí je chuť slízat
všechna pohoří, co jich má svět, i nořit se až k
samým hlubinám tajemné planety. Mládí je dotýkání
hvězd. Mládí je troufalost. A taky vědomí, že být pro
radost je někdy příliš, příliš málo. Ze někam patříme.
Že jsme i pro druhé. A že tu někde čeká dobré dílo.
Neboť ne přicházíme na svět první, ani poslední.
V každé pídi země, v každém cípu lesa, v každém
růžovém keři, v každém jezu na řekách, v každém
nově zastřešeném stavení je kus poselství, které tu
zůstalo po dědcích i po otcích. Poselství s desítkami
čistých, nepopsaných stran. Mládí je nádherná úzkost
před prvním vlastním krokem po zemi— ale i
hladová pýcha vyšlapovat si po ní jako král. Mládí
je závrať. Mládí je hrom a blesk. Mládí je nenávratný
čas, v němž se ráno s dívčím ostychem či s chla-
peckou drzostí skloníš nad plynoucí řeku, abys v
ní večer uhlídal svou vlastní dospělou tvář. Mládí je
touha po kráse. Mládí je samo tvoření. Mládí je velká
lidská moc. A jeho barvou je proto královská zeleň.
Barva naděje. Barva Odvahy.

Má Mládí. Jakou Barvu. Mladá Fronta.
Československo, 1980.

(63)

Монумент «Освобожденному труду» скульптора
Степана Эрьзя был установлен на постаменте
памятника императору Александру II Освободи-
телю в 1920 и простоял на центральной площади
Екатеринбурга-Свердловска до 1926. Скульптура
получила негативную оценку в народе и
приобрела прозвище «Ванька голый».

МИЕ.

(64)

"The street where I find a room will be what
I photograph"

[…] There were two bars in the rue André Antoine.
"François Villon" was presided over by Joseph. He
had a very distinguished manner, as though of old
aristocratic stock, in striking contrast to his clientele.
He became Roswitha's fatherly friend. One photograph shows him in "François Villon" with his wife
and her dog. The patron of "Chez Sylvain" was
Sylvain. We see him in one picture with his wife
and their two children behind the counter. The whole
family worked in the bar, which was the transvestites'
chosen haunt. Here they all convened, haggled,
gossiped, drank Pernod, displayed jealousy and
desire. Roswitha Hecke's first important contact was
Michel, whose female persona was called Barbara.
It was his charisma that made him stand out. He was
the first one she took pictures of.

She returned to "Chez Sylvain" with the prints; the
photographs were passed round and everyone was
thrilled. Then Belinda, Huguette and Alice also
wanted to be portrayed and suggested settings and
poses. Word got about. Soon so-called "normal"
residents of the district began turning up, too. Finally,
even the seemingly grumpy and bitter concierge
asked to be photographed, along with her best
friend and a couple of black mecs in their Sunday
best. Gradually a small cosmos began to grow,
centred on the cobblestone street with its live-in
personnel, at one end bordered by a flight of stone
steps, at the other spilling out along a gentle curve
onto the Place Pigalle. "The street where I find a
room will be what I photograph," Roswitha Hecke
had pledged. She kept her promise, and her photographs tell us of the openness with which she
approached all these people, of her frequently
intimate participation in the game of the sexes, which
involves pleasure as well as taboos and is marked
more by contradiction than by a lack of danger. [...]

Text: Joachim Sartorius. *Pigalle.* Rosita Hecke.
Verlag der Buchhandlung Walther König, Köln 2007.

(65)

See № 19.

(66)

— Привет, Андрюша, — сказал он. — Устал? —
Как… Откуда вы узнали…
— А! — Пафнутьев беззаботно махнул
рукой. — Ты же сам попросил меня найти Свету…
Подняли на ноги все… Ее отец вспомнил про эту
деревеньку… А здесь уже мне показали на
тебя… Вон, говорят, на речке купается… Свету
нашел?
— В сарае спит.
— А что ж ты с ребятами так круто?
— Они всю ночь насиловали ее… А перед этим
силой напоили… И при мне еще собирались…
Вертолет, говорят, тебе покажем…
— Вертолет? — Пафнутьев, казалось,
удивился. — Тогда ладно, тогда все правильно.
Как же тебе удалось справиться с ними?
— У меня был пистолет.
— Где взял? — Не помню…
— Ты что, сначала их перестрелял, а потом сжег?
— Нет… Они еще живы были… Я по яйцам
стрелял.
— Надо же! — ужаснулся Пафнутьев.
— Больно ведь!
— Я же не по своим. — А, тогда ладно, тогда
ничего… Послушай, — Пафнутьев положил руку
на тощеватое плечо Андрея, — ты в самом деле
должен был в меня стрелять?
— Да. Тогда, говорят, и Светку не тронем, и мать
жива будет…

— А винтовка где? — В сарае. — А патроны? —
Патрон был только один.
— Почему был? Его уже нет?
— Использовал. — Удачно? — Не знаю… Кажется,
да. — Если имеешь в виду Заварзина, то удачно.
Не сомневайся. А почему в меня не стрелял?
— Я бы тогда совсем завяз.
— Тоже верно… Значит, девчонкой пожертвовал?
— Я не жертвовал. Я ее спрятал в другой
квартире. Они как-то узнали… Обманом
выманили и увезли. Я не знал. Я не стал бы
ею жертвовать… Даже ради вас… — Мог бы
и выстрелить?
— А куда деваться… Светкой я бы не стал
рисковать.
— Спасибо за откровенность.

Банда. Опасный Человек. Виктор Пронин. Вис.
Санкт — Петербург, 1995.

(67)

De cel was een klein vertrek met een vloeroppervlak
van ongeveer zestien vierkante meter en een hoog
plafond. De wanden waren kaal, hard en glad met
aan één zijde, of in oudere gestichten aan twee
zijden een dubbele deur van zwaar massief eikehout
met een kijkgaatje en in enkele gevallen een voedsel-
luik. Hoog in de muur of in het dak zat meestal een
klein venster van gepansterd glas waardoor schaars
licht naar binnen scheen. Ergens in de muur was
achter een ijzeren rooster een verwarmingstoestel
geplaatst en in een aantal gestichten was het
versterkte vertrek voorzien van vastgeklonken
meubilair: een stoel, een krib en een (heimelijk)
gemak. Over het algemeen waren de cellen echter
leeg op een enkele matras of een hoop zeegras na.

*Krankzinnigen Gesticht. Psychiatrische Inrichtingen
in Nederland 1880–1910.* Joost Vijselaar. Fibula-Van
Dishoeck. Haarlem 1982.

(68)

The defused light inside the photographer's parents'
home in Carroll Gardens, Brooklyn, illuminated a
young man's flesh differently than it did outside in
broad daylight. On the street the sunlight was harsh.
It blared like a delivery truck's horn, sparked like
a welding iron, crackled like a transistor radio on full
volume. It matched the temper and bravado of the
boys in their cars and on the basketball courts;
at every moment proving its power to the neighborhood. But inside the photographer's home, upstairs,
where the young men removed their clothes, lit a
cigarette, and sat naked in a void between the pale
wall and the photographer's camera, the sun's quiet
illumination gave everything an honest focus,
a sensual solitude. It poured through curtains of
lace, airborne dust, and fresh smoke as it would

through stained glass, providing the young men a silent retreat directed by a master of light and composition, and the photographer himself a focus for the many incongruities in his own life between inside and out. In that space, the photographer created some of his most exquisite works of art.

Surprisingly contemporary in his approach to both the male physique and photographic technique, the photographer behind the studio Les Demi Dieux was little known among collectors until after his death. Danny Fitzgerald (1921–2000) was born in Brooklyn, New York, to first-generation Italian-Irish parents and developed a love for art and film from an early age. Though he would travel the world with his camera and his partner Richard Bennett at his side, the working-class Italian-American neighborhood of Carroll Gardens, Brooklyn, remained his home and the backdrop to much of his photography.

Brooklyn Boys. Danny Fitzgerald and Les Demi Dieux. Edited by Robert Loncar and James Kempster. Berlin 2013.

(69)

Designer labels were ripped out, or razored off, in an ever-increasing desire to get ahead. Britain's major cities became known for rapidly-changing casual styles, their ebb and flow partially dependent on the relative success of the local football clubs and whether or not they had qualified for European competition. Liverpool's unrivalled record in this respect (stretching back to the mid-60s and forward to Heysel, after which, until 1991, they were indefinitely banned) gave Merseyside fans the best opportunity to bring back spoils of their European conquests-scarves, jewellery, casual tops, trainers, shoes or just personal memories of bitter battles and unforgettable away victories on "foreign" soil.

[...] At Heysel itself, what the Italian counterparts of Liverpool fans were wearing really mattered. The "Juve" fans' expensive styles were a stinging reminder of the economic decline of a once-great port economy and, though there were plenty of "traditional" football fans at Heysel, what some of the Italian "Ultras" were sporting wasn't lost on fashion-conscious Liverpool boys. In this tale of two cities, the motto was, as always, "if you can't beat them, look as if you can."

Football with Attitude. Steve Redhead. Wordsmith, Progress Centre. Manchester 1991.

(70)

—Mykull Tronn: "the world" is an innovative spectacle of fabulousness and it is "it".
—Gym: I love clubs so much, last night I was at the world, I had such a good time that coughed up a curtain rod.
—Larry Tee: "the world" puts a tingle in my hipbone.
—La Homma: it's the hottest place on earth—lord, god is it hot, and i love those boys in their underpants.
—James St. James: "the world" is fierce, "the world" is fun, "the world" is best when one on one. I have a thing for big black men, I love to stand in the middle of the dance floor and say, "take me, i'm yours."
—Michael Musto: "The World" keeps growing like a fungus. I hope nobody kills it. It is the world, it is the children, it is a place to make a better day, so let's start giving attitude amen, if the world fails, love will save the day.
—Reinaldo Herrer: "The World" is the place where the top meets the bottom.
—Brian Desantis: if I didn't work here, i would be here anyway.
—Lincoln: "The World" is fabulous… I'll never stop loving it.
—Stana: it's like my second home.
—Darrel: sometimes it's heaven, sometimes it's hell, it all depends on you.
—Heather Sommerfield: "The World" is the place your mother warned you about.
—Really Denise: "The World"—how did I get here, anyway?

The World. Captured by Stephan Lupino. Graphics-Photo-Art Verlag und Vertrieb. Munich 1988.

(71)

Vorläufer der Freikörperkultur

[...] Zitat: "Das Proletariat muß zu seiner eigenen Sittlichkeit kommen," das ist ein Marx-Zitat, hätte der Schreiber sagen sollen, "wenn es mit der verlogenen Moral von gestern ein Stück von den herrschenden sexuellen Zuständen überwinden will." "Nacktheit erzieht zu sexueller Unbefangenheit und Aufrichtigkeit." "Nacktkultur ist ein Stück notwendiger Sexualerziehung." "Ob das Nackte als sittlich gilt oder nicht oder unter welchen Umständen es moralisch Anstoß erregt oder nicht, hängt von der Gesellschaft und Klasse ab, die es betrachtet."

"Die Arbeiterklasse wird mit ihrer neuen Moral dem Schamgefühl im Proletariat eine neue Richtung geben."

"Sie wird es als sittlich betrachten, den Körper gesund zu erhalten und nach seiner Schönheit zu streben." Das ist eigentlich alles ganz scharf und links formuliert.

"Unsittlich wird ihr dagegen alles erscheinen, was dem Bürgertum sittlich erscheint." Ein schöner Satz! "Ist dem Bürgertum der nackte Körper des

badenden Menschen unsittlich," das gilt für damals,
"die Abbildung eines nackten Menschen aus
sexuellen Motiven unter dem Deckmantel der Kunst
dagegen sittlich, so findet das Proletariat umgekehrt
jede Leistung einer pornografischen Kunst
anständig, den nackten. Menschen in der Natur
dagegen moralisch." Darüber kann man natürlich
gewaltig streiten. [...]

Arbeiterfotografie. № 69. 3. Quartal. Hamburg 1991.

(72)

Einige GFK-Fotografen beschlossen, mit der Z-Side
Kontakt aufzunehmen. Zunächst mal um zu über-
prüfen, was von dem Bild der Massenmedien eigentlich stimmte. Die Z-Side schien aus einer hetero-
genen Gruppe junger Leute zu bestehen. Man kann
sie nicht ohne weiteres als aggressiv, rassistisch
oder faschistisch abstempeln. Allerdings fällt das
aggressive Verhalten im Gruppenverband ins Auge.
Aus Gesprächen wurde deutlich, daß diese Aggres-
sion eine Ventilfunktion für verschiedene Probleme
hat. Das GFK beschloß daraufhin, ein Fotoprojekt
über die Z-Side durchzuführen mit dem Ziel, ein
nuancierteres Bild von der Z-Side zu zeichnen als
dies die Massenmedien taten.

Arbeiterfotografie. № 34. Juni–August.
Hamburg 1983.

(73)

1980—Олимпиада в Москве. Высылка из
столицы, принудительное психиатрическое
лечение и тюремное заключение гомосексуалов
перед приездом иностранцев.

1981/82—После провала операции «Олимпи-
йские игры-80» милиция начинает облавы
на гомосексуалов. По с. 121 посажено более
2000 человек.

1986—Подпольная «Голубая Лаборатория
Ленинграда»—диссидентская организация,
основанная в 1984 Александром Заремба,—
разгромлена сотрудниками местного КГБ.

1987—По центральному ТВ и в кинотеатрах
показан фильм «Группа Риска», где освещается
проблема СПИДа и секс-меньшинств в СССР.

1989—Начинается выпуск первой в СССР гей-
газеты «Тема» (ред. Роман Калинин). В 1990
зарегистрирована Моссоветом как частное
издание; выходила до 1993.

1990—Москва. Роман Калинин и Евгения
Дебрянская учреждают Либертарианскую
партию защиты сексуальных меньшинств.

1990/91—Появление первой ЛГБТ-периодики:
газеты «Риск» и «Арго» (ред. Влад Ортанов),
«IMO» (ред. Дмитрий Лычев), «Gay, славяне!»
(ред. Ольга Жук).

1991—Мила Уголькова и Любовь Зиновьева
создают Московское Объединение лесбийской
литературы и искусства.

1991—Москва-Ленинград. «Фонд Чайковского»
и «Ассоциация сексуальных меньшинств» при
поддержке IGLHRC провели первый междуна-
родный гей-лесби кинофестиваль и конференцию
в ходе фестиваля на Советской площади. У
Большого Театра были проведены первые гей-ма-
нифестации против уголовного преследования.

1991—В журнале «Литературное Обозрение»
напечатана статья Семена Карлинского об истории
гомосексуальности в русской культуре. Парал-
лельно в газете «Тема» появляется текст Ольги
Жук о лесбийской субкультуре в советской тюрьме.

1991—Министерство юстиции России отказы-
вает в регистрации ЛГ-организации «Союз
Освобождения».

1991—В Ленинграде зарегистрирована первая
гей- организация «Крылья» под руководством
Александра Кухарского и Ольги Краузе.

1991—На концерте «Рок против террора» группа
АукцЫон выступила с заявлением и петицией
в защиту сексуальных меньшинств и за отмену
121 ст. УК РСФСР.

1992—Первая в России конференция, посвя-
щенная правам ЛГБТ. Опубликована брошюра
Маши Гессен о положении геев и лесбиянок
в России.

1993—В Томске зарегистрирована Ассоциация
сексуальных меньшинств «Астарта».

1993—27 мая 1993 указом Б. Ельцина отменена
ст. 121.1 УК РСФСР. Закон имеет обратную силу,
однако официальной реабилитации его жертв
не последовало.

1993—В Омске проходит Фестиваль геев Сибири.

1993—На основе 27 региональных организаций
учреждена общенациональная ЛГБ-ассоциация
«Треугольник». Московские власти отказывают
ей в регистрации с формулировкой: «противоречит
общественным нормам нравственности».
«Треугольник» проводит конференцию, освеща-
ющую участие гей-активистов в борьбе со
СПИДом, правовые вопросы ЛГБТ, роль СМИ
и проблемы лесбийского движения.

1993 — Налет московского ОМОНа на гей-бар
«Андеграунд», где накануне лидеры «Треуголь-
ника» провели пресс-конференцию о бойкоте
выборов в ГосДуму.

1994 — Начинает работу Информационный
центр геев и лесбиянок.

Квирфест 2013. 20 Лет Отмены Ст. 121 Ук
РСФСР.

(74)

Gestatten, wir sind die Jugend.

Um ein möglichst breites Bild von den Einsendungen
zum Fotowettbewerb zu geben, haben wir nur je ein
Foto pro Teilnehmer ausgesucht, auch wenn die
Fotos dadurch ab und zu aus dem Zusammenhang
einer Serie gerissen werden mußten. Trotzdem kann
aufgrund des Platzmangels nur ein Teil der Einsender vorgestellt werden.

Arbeiterfotografie. № 27. September. Hamburg 1981.

(75)

"We dress for our own pleasure and get off on each
other. It's our own small world; within it we under-
stand and are understood—and we do what we
want. When we put on our clothes, we feel free."
      "If other people want to share in our joy and
freedom, they're welcome to. There's strength and
self-confidence in the way I dress. Suddenly I don't
feel ugly anymore!"

Idols. Gilles Larrain. Studio Gilles Larrain, Inc.
New York 1973.

ВЫХОДНЫЕ ДАННЫЕ

WERKER 2 / ЖЕСТОВАЯ ИСТОРИЯ МОЛОДОГО РАБОЧЕГО была представлена в 2019 году в рамках 5-й Уральской индустриальной биеннале современного искусства в Екатеринбурге, Россия.

Издание подготовлено КОЛЛЕКТИВ WERKER в сотрудничестве с Георгием Мамедовым.

Дизайн и верстка: WERKER

Перевод на русский: Максим Кульбида, Георгий Мамедов и команда 5-й Уральской индустриальной биеннале современного искусства.

На момент публикации WERKER 2 / ЖЕСТОВАЯ ИСТОРИЯ МОЛОДОГО РАБОЧЕГО была представлена на: 5-ой Уральской индустриальной биеннале современного искусства, Екатеринбург, 2019; *In the Presence of Absence — Proposals for the Museum Collection*, Stedelijk Museum, Амстердам, 2020; *¡Ratas! ¡Ratas! ¡Ratas! La Gramática Poética del Hack*, CaixaForum, Барселона, 2022; *The Work of Love, The Queer of Labour*, Pratt Institute, Нью-Йорк, 2022; Public Research Residency, Looiersgracht 60, Амстердам, 2023.

WERKER выражает благодарность за предоставленное разрешение на воспроизведение материалов, защищенных авторским правом, в этой публикации. Были предприняты все усилия, чтобы определить правообладателей и получить их разрешение на использование материалов, защищенных авторским правом. WERKER приносит свои извинения за любые ошибки или упущения и будут признательны, если будет сообщено о каких-либо исправлениях, которые должны быть включены в последующие издания.

WERKER 2 / ЖЕСТОВАЯ ИСТОРИЯ МОЛОДОГО РАБОЧЕГО осуществлена при финансовой поддержке Фонда Мондриана, Посольства Нидерландов в Российской Федерации и Фонда Яапа Хартена в Нидерландах.

ОБ АВТОРАХ

ГЕОРГИЙ МАМЕДОВ — куратор, публицист и исследователь. Главные темы в его работе - история и практика радикального воображения и реинтерпретация и присвоение советского социалистического наследия для целей прогрессивной левой политики. Георгий со-автор "Манифеста квир-коммунизма" и нескольких книг: "Книга о счастье для молодых (и не очень) ЛГБТ (и нетолько) людей" (Бишкек, 2021); первый русскоязычный сборник феминисткой и квир-фантастики "Совсем Другие" (Бишкек, 2018); "Квир-коммунизм это этика" (Москва, 2016); "Понятия о советском в Центральной Азии" (Бишкек, 2016); "Бишкек утопический" (Бишкек 2015). Георгий также пишет о современной политике, культуре и искусстве для международных периодических изданий вроде Jacobin и OpenDemocracy, а также является старшим преподавателем факультета "Кино и медиаискусств" Американского университета в Центральной Азии в Бишкеке. В 2015 году Георгий стал кавалером французского ордена "Искусств и литературы". Живет и работает в Бишкеке, Кыргызстан.

ОБ АВТОРАХ

WERKER — экспериментальная издательская инициатива, соединяющая в себе рабочее движение, экофеминизм и ЛГБТИК+ в пользу имиджевой критики повседневной жизни, для анализа того, что делается видимым, а что остается скрытым или замалчивается в различных политических контекстах. Она была инициирована Марком Роигом Блезой и Рогиром Дельфосом в Амстердаме в 2009 году, когда были выпущены десять выпусков журнала WERKER MAGAZINE.

WERKER черпает вдохновение с Der Vereinigung der Arbeiter-Fotografen (Ассоциации рабочих фотографов), группы политизированных фотоклубов, возникших в 1920-х годах в Германии, следуя по стопам первых экспериментов социалистической фотографии в СССР, распространившихся на остальную Европу, США и Японию. Начиная с 2012 года, под названием КОЛЛЕКТИВ WERKER, они проводят мастерклассы по фотографии, дизайну и публикации со студентами, работниками культуры, самоорганизованными союзами домашних работниковмигрантов, мигрантов без документов, в поддержку активистов против выселения, феминистских групп, ЛГБТИК+ сообществ и люди с неврологическими или функциональными отклонениями, среди прочих. Посредством этих семинаров, КОЛЛЕКТИВ WERKER сплетает интернациональную и транснациональную сеть союзников, оживляя угнетенные истории и добиваясь солидарности рабочих через совместную художественную практику.

ПОСЛЕСЛОВИЕ

Данное издание выходит в печать в 2023 году с четырехлетним опозданием. В 2019 году издание подверглось цензуре со стороны руководства 5-й Уральской биеннале современного искусства. В результате этого цензурного запрета, екатеринбургская типография, в которой публикация должна была быть напеча-

тана, отказалась исполнять заказ. В 2022 году
вторая попытка выпустить издание была
отложена из-за недостаточного финансиро-
вания, необходимого для компенсации растущих
расходов на бумагу, печать и распространение,
вызванных последствиями пандемии COVID-19
и экономическими последствиями вторжения
России в Украину в том же году.

В 2019 году в Екатеринбурге была впервые
представлена инсталляция "Жестовая История
Молодого Рабочего, частью которой является
данная публикация. Тем временем политический
климат вокруг темы репрезентации негетеронор-
мативных тел обострился. С декабря 2022 года
новый закон в России запрещает любое изображение или поддержку ЛГБТК+ сообществ в
публичной сфере и искусстве. Данный закон в
еще большей степени ограничивает права ЛГБТ-
людей на репрезентацию по сравнению с законом
принятым в 2013 году о так называемой "гей-пропаганде", вводившим запрет на публичное обсуж-
дение гомосексуальности среди несовершенно-
летних. Новые ограничения распространяются
на все население Российской Федерации. Цель
данной публикации - способствовать созданию
образа квир-будущего, свободного от политической инструментализации и исключения квир-
жизней в глобальном масштабе.

Согласно так называемому закону о
"гей-пропаганде", принятому в России в 2013 году
"с целью защиты детей от информации, пропа-
гандирующей отказ от традиционных семейных
ценностей", инсталляция в Екатеринбурге была
представлена с возрастным ограничением "18+".
Однако, несмотря на соблюдение всех предпи-
санных законом мер, на последних этапах
продакшена организаторы Биеннале проинфор-
мировали нас, что считают неприемлемым демон-
страцию откровенной мужской наготы даже для
взрослой аудитории и предложили исключить из
инсталляции и русскоязычной версии публикации
шесть изображений. После длительного внутрен-
него обсуждения, мы приняли решение оставить
шесть изображений, вызвавших возмущение
организаторов, но покрыть их черными пленкой.
Для нас было важным показать проект, пусть
и в подвергшимся цензуре варианте, обращаю-
щейся к темам труда и квирности именно в
Екатеринбурге, — где незадолго до открытия
выставки, в августе 2019, Ресурсный центр для
ЛГБТ-сообществ вынужден был временно
прекратить свою деятельность

в связи с угрозами физической расправы
над сотрудниками. Мы посчитали наше решение
более адекватным жестом в текущей политической ситуации, чем полный отказ от участия в
выставке в связи с цензурой.

Ирония цензурных ограничений заключа-
ется в том, что сам этот жест исключения и
запрета вплетается в художественную ткань
произведения и наделяет его новыми и непред-
сказуемыми смыслами. С самого начала работы

над этим проектом мы отдавали себе отчет в
его политическом подтексте. Однако попытка е
го цензуры только усилила политическое напря-
жение, содержащееся в предложенном нами
синтезе классовой борьбы и борьбы против
гетеронормативного угнетения наших тел.
Цензура проекта функционерами Биеннале
вывела "Историю жеста молодого рабочего"
из поля художественной спекуляции в пространство политического противостояния, преобразуя,
таким образом, его изначальный политический
подтекст в действенную форму политического
высказывания. [...]

Коллектив Werker и Георгий Мамедов

*   Смычка труда и желания — организаторы
        выставки о квирной телесности рабочих в
        промышленном центре России рассуждают
        об искусстве, цензуре и политике" Автор:
        Георгий Мамедов, опубликовано на
        tribunemag.co.uk 16 ноября 2019.

COLOPHON

WERKER 2 / A GESTURAL HISTORY OF THE YOUNG WORKER by Werker Collective has been developed in 2019 during the Artist-in-Residence Program of the 5th Ural Industrial Biennial of Contemporary Art in Yekaterinburg, Russia.

Compiled and edited by Werker Collective with Georgy Mamedov.

Design and production by Werker.

Translation to Russian by Maksym Kulbida, Georgy Mamedov and the 5th Ural Industrial Biennial of Contemporary Art Team.

Special thanks to the entire team of the residency program of the 5th Ural Industrial Biennial of Contemporary Art. We would also like to thank Sara Benaglia, Pierre Gramond, Stephan Kuderna, Maksym Kulbida, Antoine de Mena, Gilad Reich, Babken Srtashian, Pieter Verweij, Rijksakademie van Beeldende Kunsten and the LGTB Resource Center of Yekaterinburg for their contributions.

At the time of publication, A GESTURAL HISTORY OF THE YOUNG WORKER has been presented at The 5th Ural Industrial Biennial of Contemporary Art in Yekaterinburg, 2019; *In the Presence of Absence, Proposals for the Museum Collection*, Stedelijk Museum Amsterdam, 2020; *¡Ratas! ¡Ratas! ¡Ratas! La Gramática Poética del Hack*, CaixaForum Barcelona, 2022; *The Work of Love, The Queer of Labour*, Pratt Institute, New York, 2022; and Public Research Residency, Looiersgracht 60, Amsterdam, 2023.

Werker gratefully acknowledges the permission granted to reproduce the copyright material in this publication. Every effort has been made to trace copyright holders and to obtain their permission for the use of copyright material. Werker apologises for any errors or omissions and would be grateful if notified of any corrections that should be incorporated in further editions.

WERKER 2 / A GESTURAL HISTORY OF THE YOUNG WORKER is made possible with the financial support of the Mondriaan Foundation, the Embassy of the Netherlands in Russia, and the Jaap Harten Fonds.

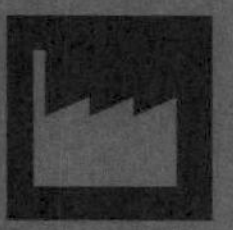

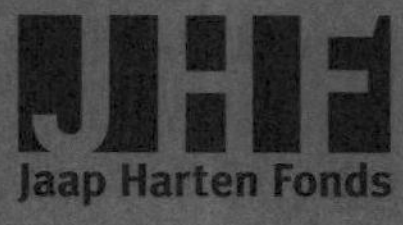

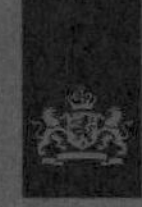

PUBLISHED BY

SPECTOR BOOKS, Harkortstraße 10, 04107 Leipzig
spectorbooks.com

&

WERKER, Geldersekade 74, 1012BL Amsterdam
werkercollective.net

© 2023, Spector Books, Leipzig
© 2023, Werker, Amsterdam

First edition: 2023

Printing by Die Keure, Brugge.

ISBN 978-3-95905-471-3

DISTRIBUTION

GERMANY, AUSTRIA:
GVA, Gemeinsame Verlagsauslieferung Göttingen GmbH&Co. KG, gva-verlage.de

USA, CANADA, CENTRAL AND SOUTH AMERICA, AFRICA:
Artbook / D.A.P., artbook.com

SWITZERLAND:
AVA Verlagsauslieferung AG, ava.ch

SOUTH KOREA:
The Book Society, thebooksociety.org

FRANCE, BELGIUM:
Interart Paris, interart.fr

JAPAN:
twelvebooks, twelve-books.com

UK:
Central Books Ltd, centralbooks.com

AUSTRALIA, NEW ZEALAND:
Perimeter Distribution, perimeterdistribution.com

ABOUT

GEORGY MAMEDOV is a curator and writer based in Bishkek, Kyrgyzstan. History and practice of radical imagination and progressive re-interpretation and appropriation of the soviet socialist legacies are the central themes of his artistic and research projects. Georgy is the co-author of *Queer-Communist Manifesto* and several books including *A Book on Happiness for Young (and not so) LGBT (and not only) People* (Bishkek, 2021), the pioneering Russian language collection of feminist and queer science fiction, *Utterly Other* (Bishkek, 2018); *Queer Communism is Ethics* (Moscow, 2016); *Concepts of the Soviet in Central Asia* (Bishkek, 2016) and *Bishkek Utopian* (Bishkek, 2015). Georgy also regularly writes on politics, culture and art for international media such as Jacobin and OpenDemocracy.

Georgy holds a position of Assistant Professor of film and media arts at the American University of Central Asia in Bishkek. In 2015, Georgy became a chevalier of the French Order of Arts and Letters.

ABOUT

WERKER is an experimental publishing initiative operating in the intersection of labour, ecofeminism and the LGBTQ+ movements in favour of an image critique of daily life, to analyse what is made visible and what remains hidden or silenced in different political contexts. It was initiated by Marc Roig Blesa and Rogier Delfos in Amsterdam in 2009 with the release of ten issues of a publication called WERKER MAGAZINE.

WERKER takes inspiration from Der Vereinigung der Arbeiter-Fotografen (the Association of Worker Photographers), a group of politicised photo-clubs that appeared in Germany in the 1920's, following in the steps of the first Socialist photography experiments in the USSR which extended into the rest of Europe, the United States, and Japan. Since 2012, under the name WERKER COLLECTIVE, it has been hosting photography, design and publishing workshops with students, cultural workers, self-organised unions of migrant domestic workers, undocumented migrants, in support of anti-eviction activists, feminist groups, LGBTQ+ communities and people with neurological or functional diversities, amongst others. Through these workshops, WERKER COLLECTIVE is weaving an intersectional and transnational network of allies, reactivating oppressed histories and inquiring worker's solidarity through collaborative artistic practice.

AFTERWORD

This publication was belatedly launched in 2023 after two unsuccessful attempts during the last four years. In 2019 the publication was subjected to censorship by the 5th Ural Biennial of Contemporary Art officials. Subsequently, the publication underwent a boycott by the printing house that was assigned to print the publication in Yekaterinburg. In 2022, a second attempt to launch the publication was postponed because of insufficient additional financing necessary to compensate for the rising costs of paper, printing and distribution caused by the aftermath of the COVID-19 pandemic and the economic consequences of the Russian invasion of Ukraine in that same year.

At the date of publishing, nearly four years have passed since the artwork *A Gestural History of the Young Worker* was first presented in Yekaterinburg. Meanwhile, the political climate around the topic of representation of non-heteronormative bodies has exacerbated. Since December 2022, a new law in Russia has illegalised any depiction or support of the LGBTQ+ community in the public realm and the arts, taking the so called "anti-gay propaganda" law from 2013 (which targeted people under 18 years of age) one step further, extending it to the entire population of the Russian Federation. Let this publication contribute to the task of imaging a queer future, as an antidote against the political instrumentalization and erasure of queer lives internationally.

"When *A Gestural History of the Young Worker* by Werker Collective was first presented in Yekaterinburg in 2019, the so-called "anti-gay propaganda" law (introduced in Russia in 2013 "for the purpose of protecting children from information advocating for a denial of traditional family values"), obliged the 5th Ural Biennial of Contemporary Art to display the work with an 18+ age warning. Despite these legal precautions, during the final stages of production the biennial organisers informed Werker that they found it inappropriate to depict male frontal nudity, even for adult audiences. They suggested removing six images from the installation. After debating this act of censorship, Werker decided to exhibit the project without altering its content. Instead, patches of black vinyl were added to cover the six images. In August 2019, prior to the opening of the biennial, the LGBTQ+ Resource Centre in Yekaterinburg had to close its doors because of death threats by far-right extremists. Therefore, the fact that a project which combines labour and queerness could be seen in Yekaterinburg, even in a censored rendering, seemed to be a more relevant and acute political gesture than the complete withdrawal from public display.

The irony of censorship in artistic practice is that these acts of restriction and prohibition become interwoven into the fabric of an artwork and inform its meaning in a new and unpredicted way. From the very beginning of the research Werker was aware of the project's political implications. However, this act of censorship seemed to sharpen their proposal for a synthesis of class struggle and the oppression of non-heteronormative bodies. This episode of censorship shifted *A Gestural History of the Young Worker* from the realm of imaginative speculation into the realm of actual political confrontation, thus placing the project into a localised and embodied political reality. […]" *

Werker & Georgy Mamedov

* Published in its original form on the 16th of November 2019: "*A Union of Work and Desire — The makers of an exhibition on working class queer bodies in the industrial heartland of Russia reflect on art, censorship and politics*" by Georgy Mamedov, in tribunemag.co.uk

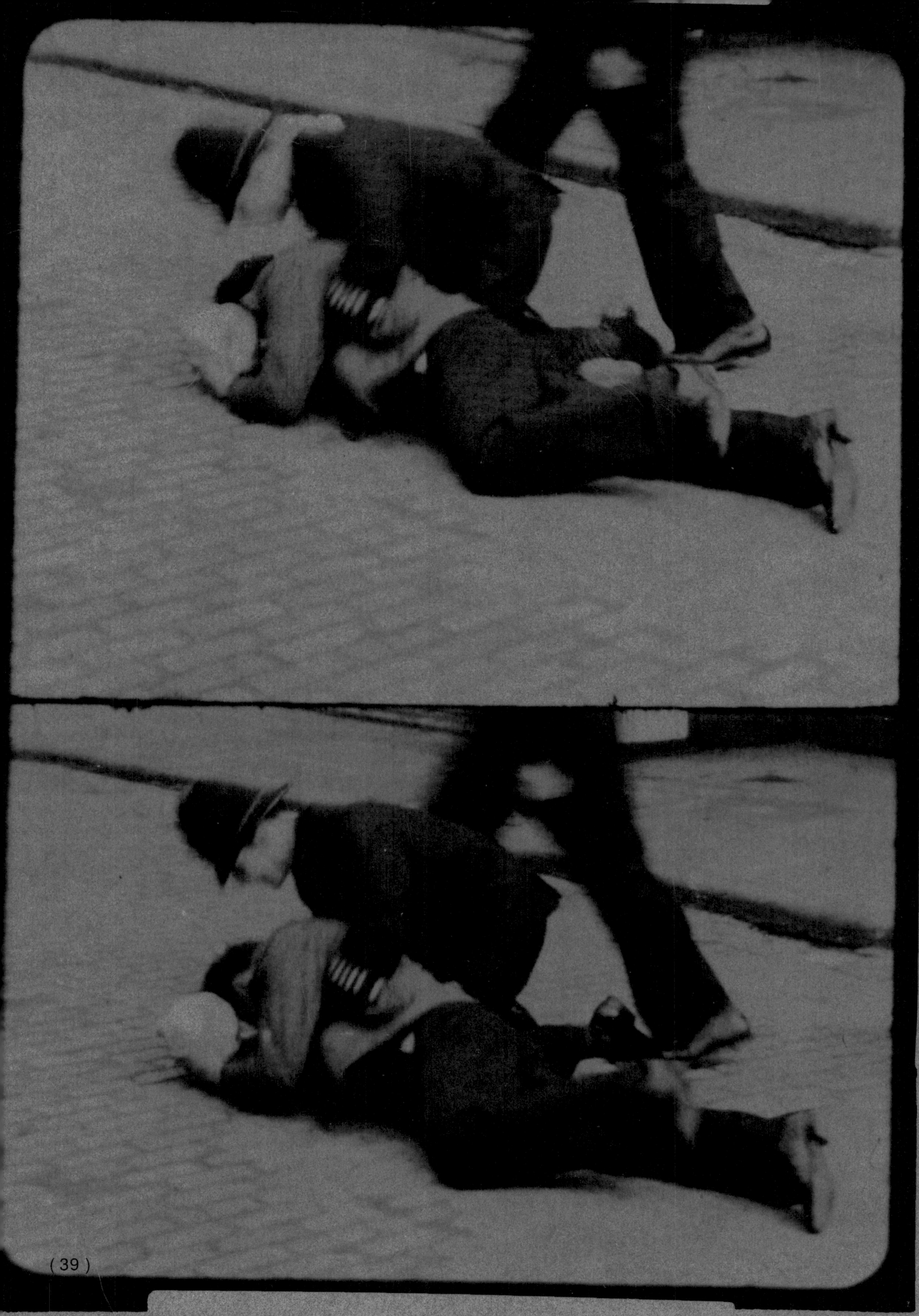

(39)

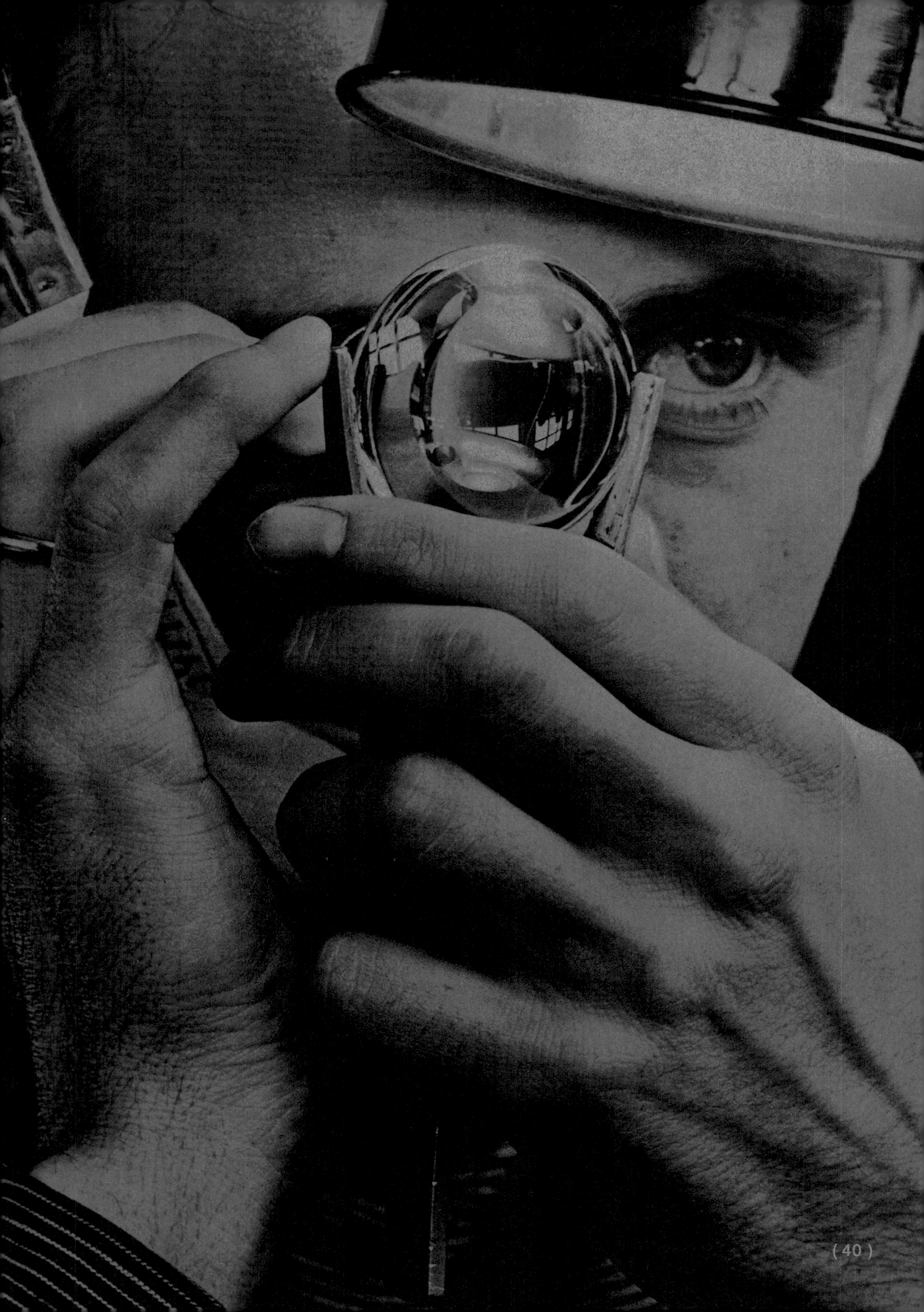

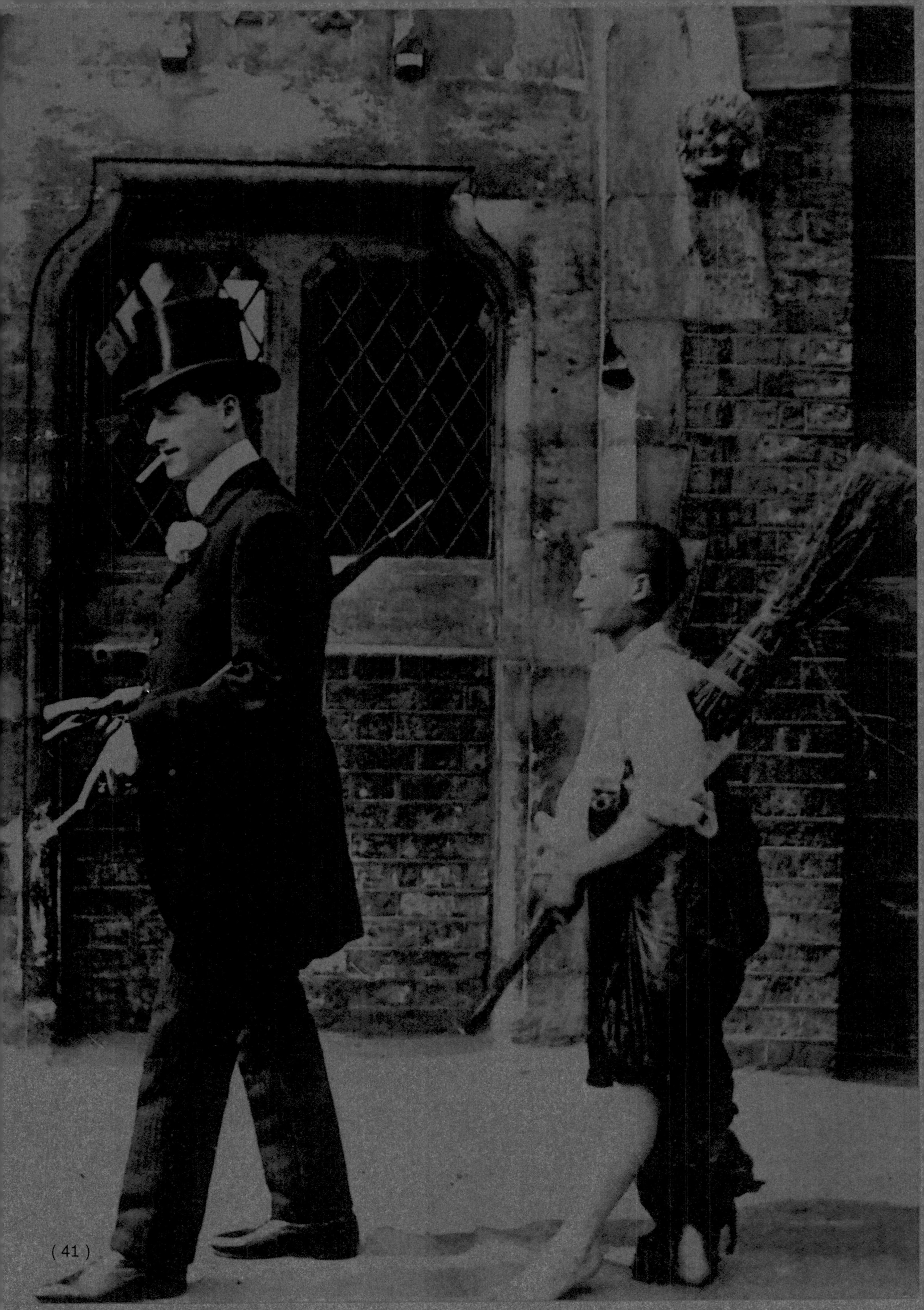

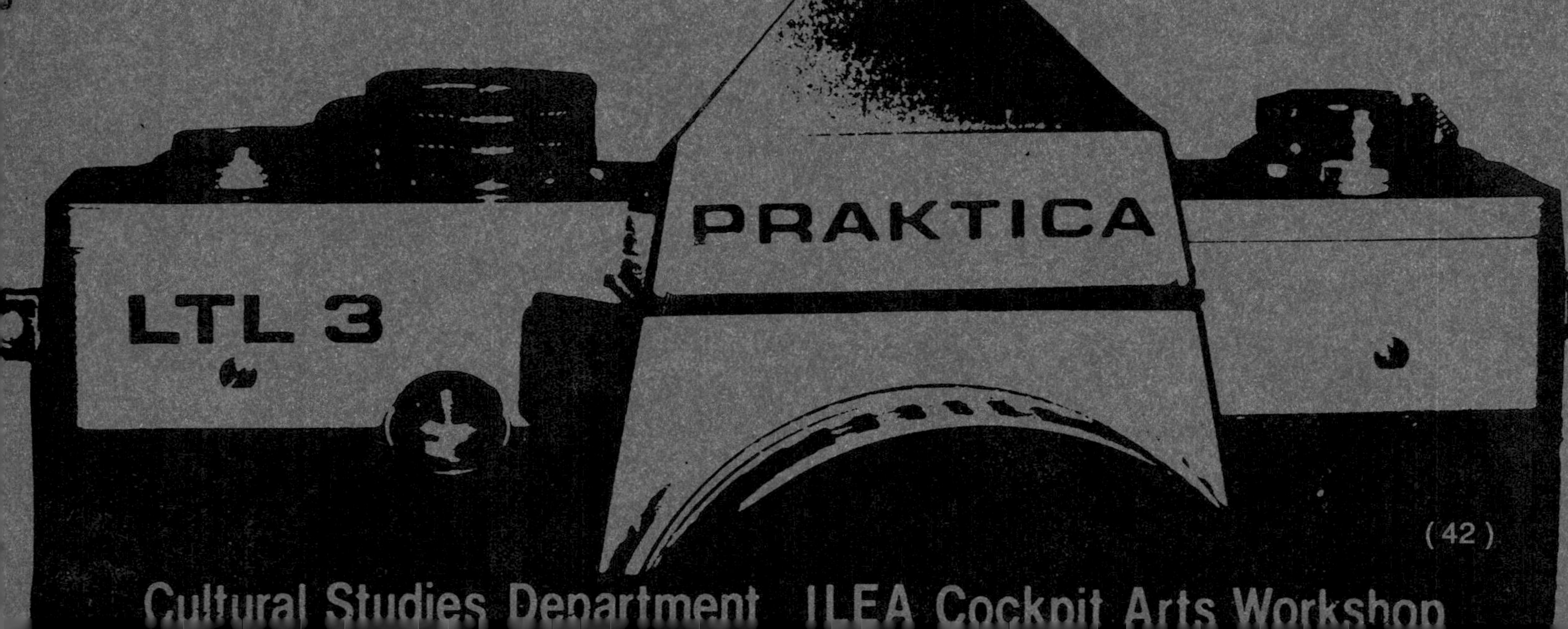
CELEBRATE
CONSTRUCT
SELECT
CONNOTE
ENCODE
PRAKTICA
LTL 3
(42)
Cultural Studies Department   ILEA Cockpit Arts Workshop

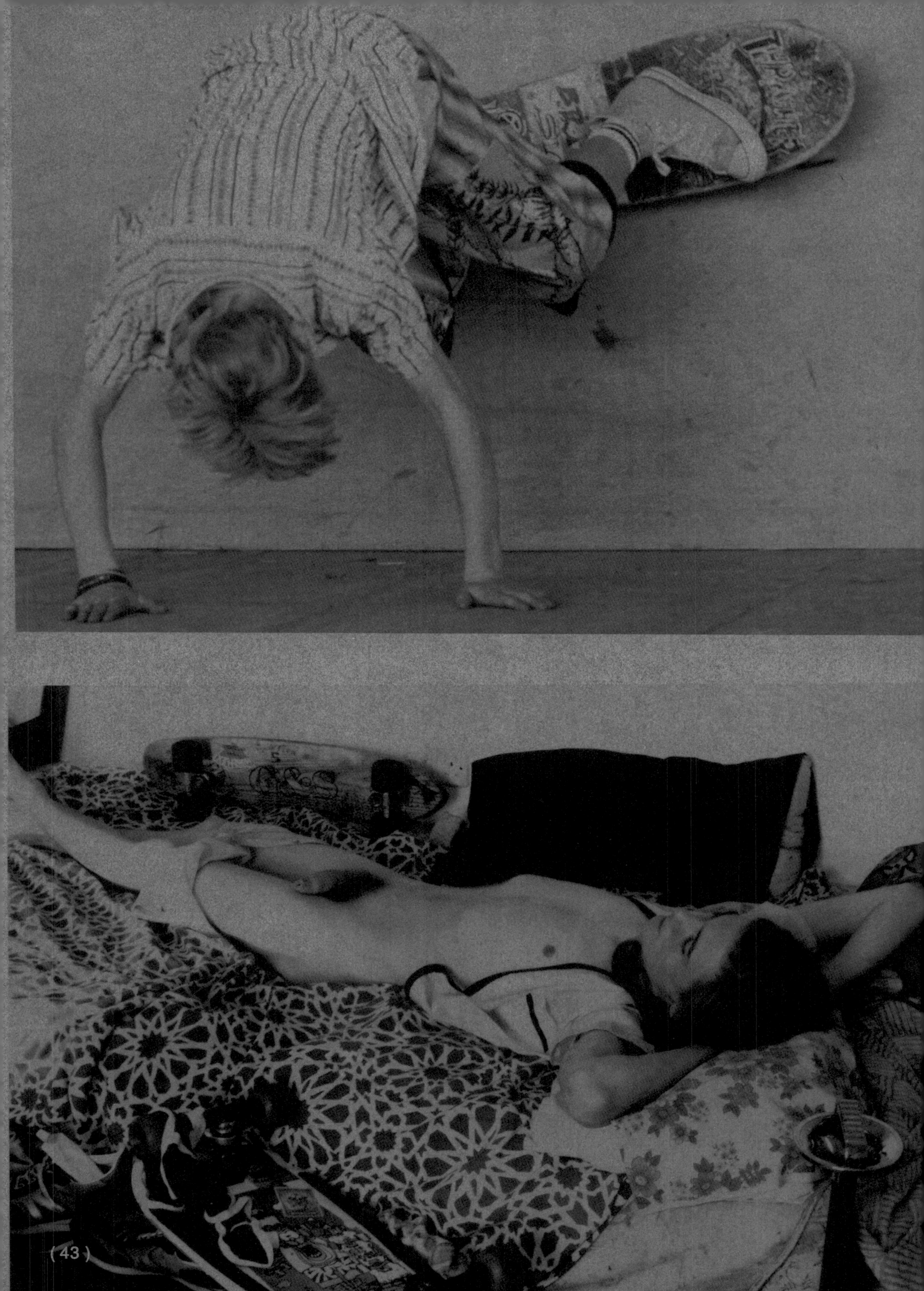

La Lotta Continua

Abbiamo scioperato perchè vogliamo:
- Turno unico (di mattina)
- Libri gratis
- Palestra più grande e bella

I professori ci trattano male ma loro non fanno niente e leggono il giornale. Dicono che parliamo male e ci bocciano così poi siamo tutti disoccupati in mezzo alla strada -

Oggi scioperiamo le scuole medie di pomeriggio. Nei prossimi giorni organizziamoci pure la mattina. E colleghiamoci con i compagni delle scuole elementare -

W lo sciopero. Gli studenti che lottano

2/Dicembre

КИ

...ьностью пользуются его
...ни «Сто видов Фудзи»,
...0-х годах XIX века. Одна
...серии воспроизведена
...е.

...низованная в основном
...авюрного кабинета Го-
...музея изобразительных
...А. С. Пушкина, а так-
...ет достаточно полное
...национальном япон-

* *

*

...игурой в бельгийском
...начала XX века был
...е (1831—1905). Скульп-
...он целиком посвятил
...юдям труда. Его рабо-
...ые на выставке бель-
...за, пользовались у нас

...е близко и понятно со-
...ю. Последовательный
...большой души и ог-
...Менье в своих работах
...ий образ пролетариата.

...их его работ является
...нная мастером в по-
...зни, — «Грузчик». Фи-
...бочего, стоящего в сво-
...жденной позе, полна
...красоты. Той же сим-
...у народу, уверенностью
...боким состраданием к
...наются и другие скульп-
...ные работы Менье.

...льгии возник ряд худо-
...л, придерживающихся
...еских методов, иногда
...зма. Но работы худож-
...егда посвящены чело-
...евной жизни, его чув-
...ниям. Их отличает жи-
...ростым людям, умение
...жизни.

* *

*

...зведений Пабло Пикас-
...в связи с 75-летием

...ло известно советским
...крупнейших худож-
...век огромного таланта,

(45)

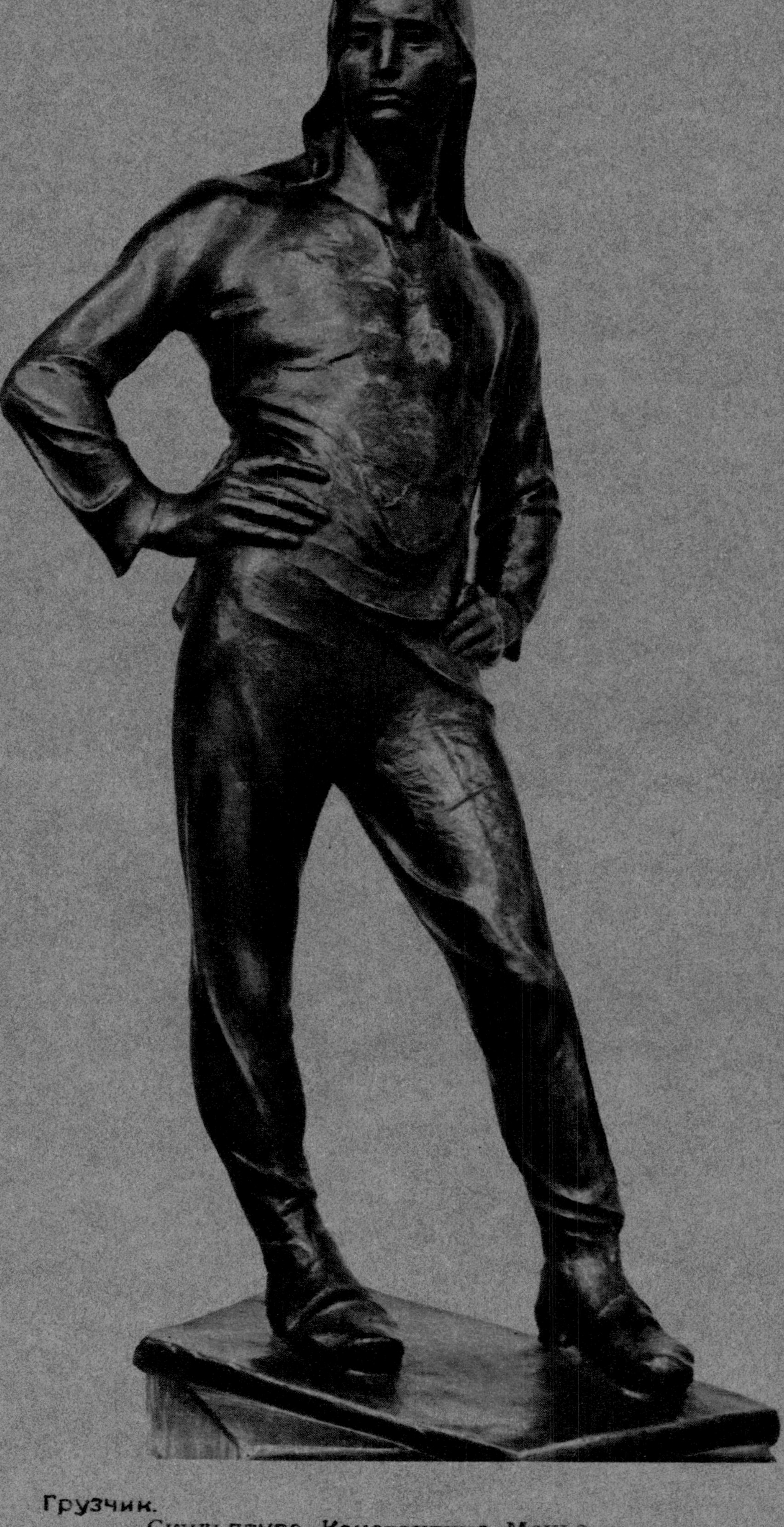

Грузчик.
Скульптура Константина Менье.

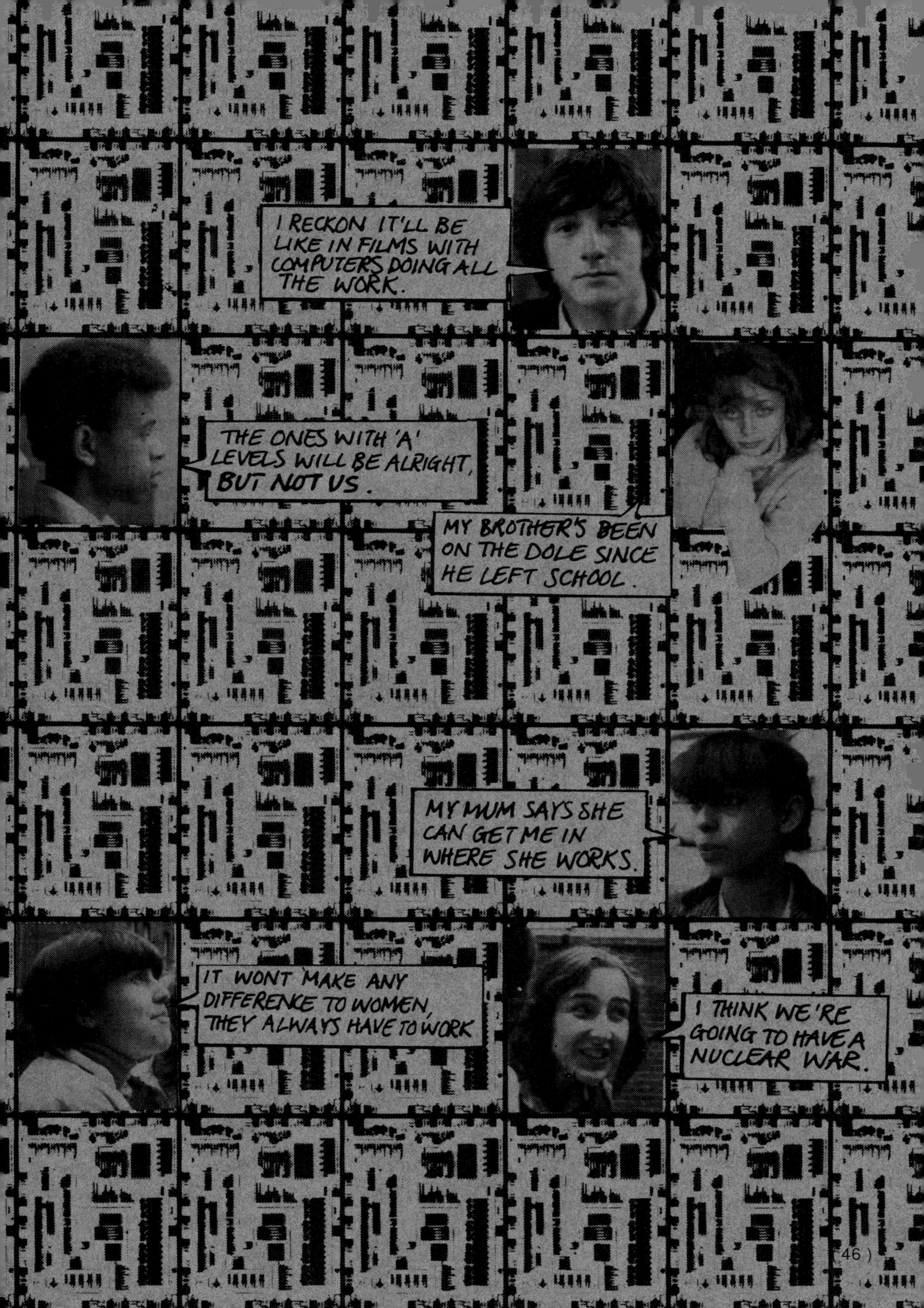

I RECKON IT'LL BE LIKE IN FILMS WITH COMPUTERS DOING ALL THE WORK.
THE ONES WITH 'A' LEVELS WILL BE ALRIGHT, BUT NOT US.
MY BROTHER'S BEEN ON THE DOLE SINCE HE LEFT SCHOOL.
MY MUM SAYS SHE CAN GET ME IN WHERE SHE WORKS.
IT WONT MAKE ANY DIFFERENCE TO WOMEN, THEY ALWAYS HAVE TO WORK
I THINK WE'RE GOING TO HAVE A NUCLEAR WAR.

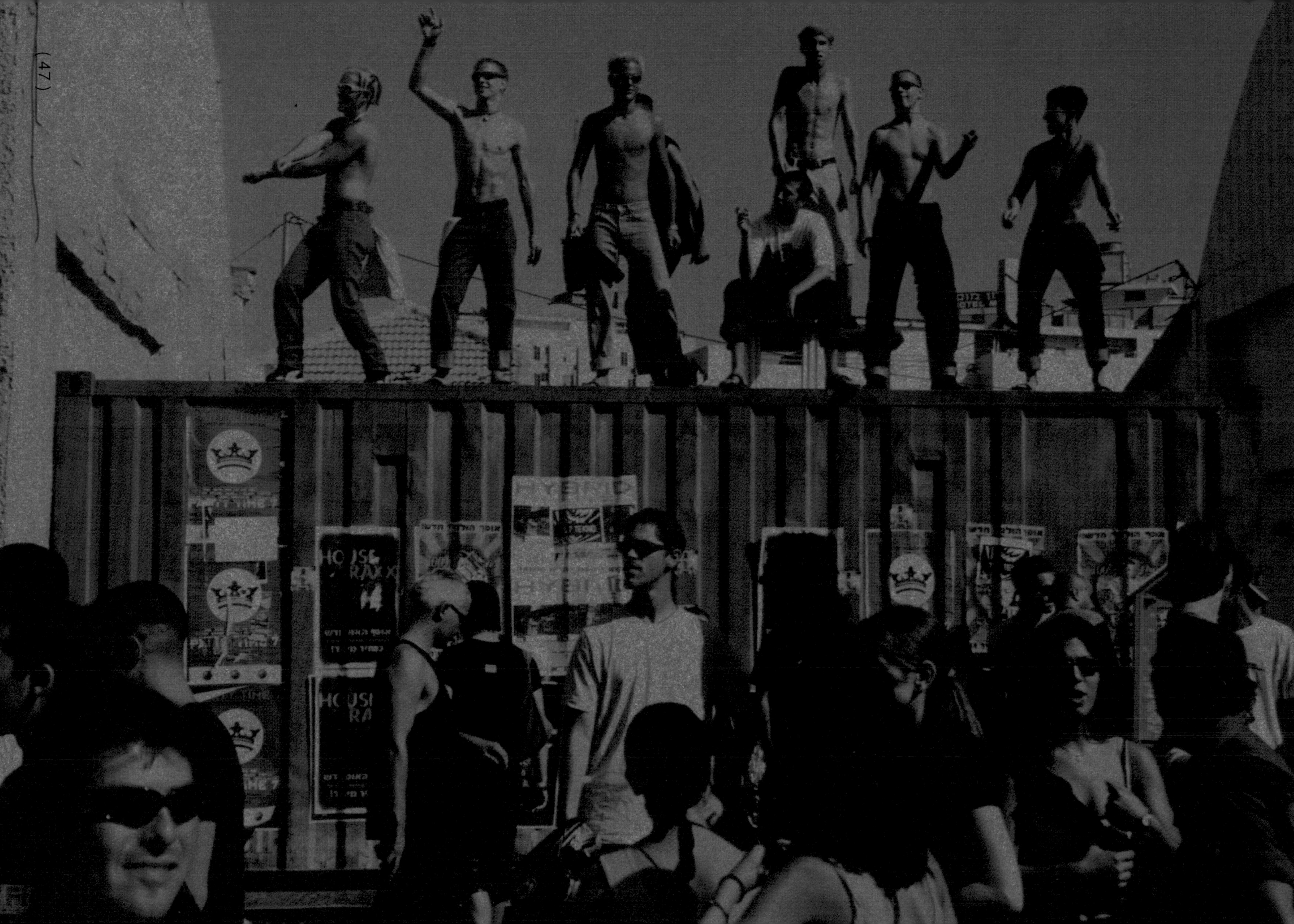

Весной этого года Люберцы, небольшой
промышленный город на границе с Москвой,
обрел популярность особого рода. Говорили,
будто в городе существует некое объединение
подростков, «объявивших войну» всякого рода
«металлистам», «рокерам», «панкам»,
которые мир своих увлечений
заимствовали на Западе.

Неформальные объединения молодежи
привлекают к себе внимание общества. Они
разные. Одни — любители самодеятельной песни,
другие вызвались охранять и реставрировать
памятники старины, третьи борются
с браконьерами и обсуждают вопросы
охраны рек и лесов.

САМЫЕ ОБЫЧНЫЕ ПАРНИ

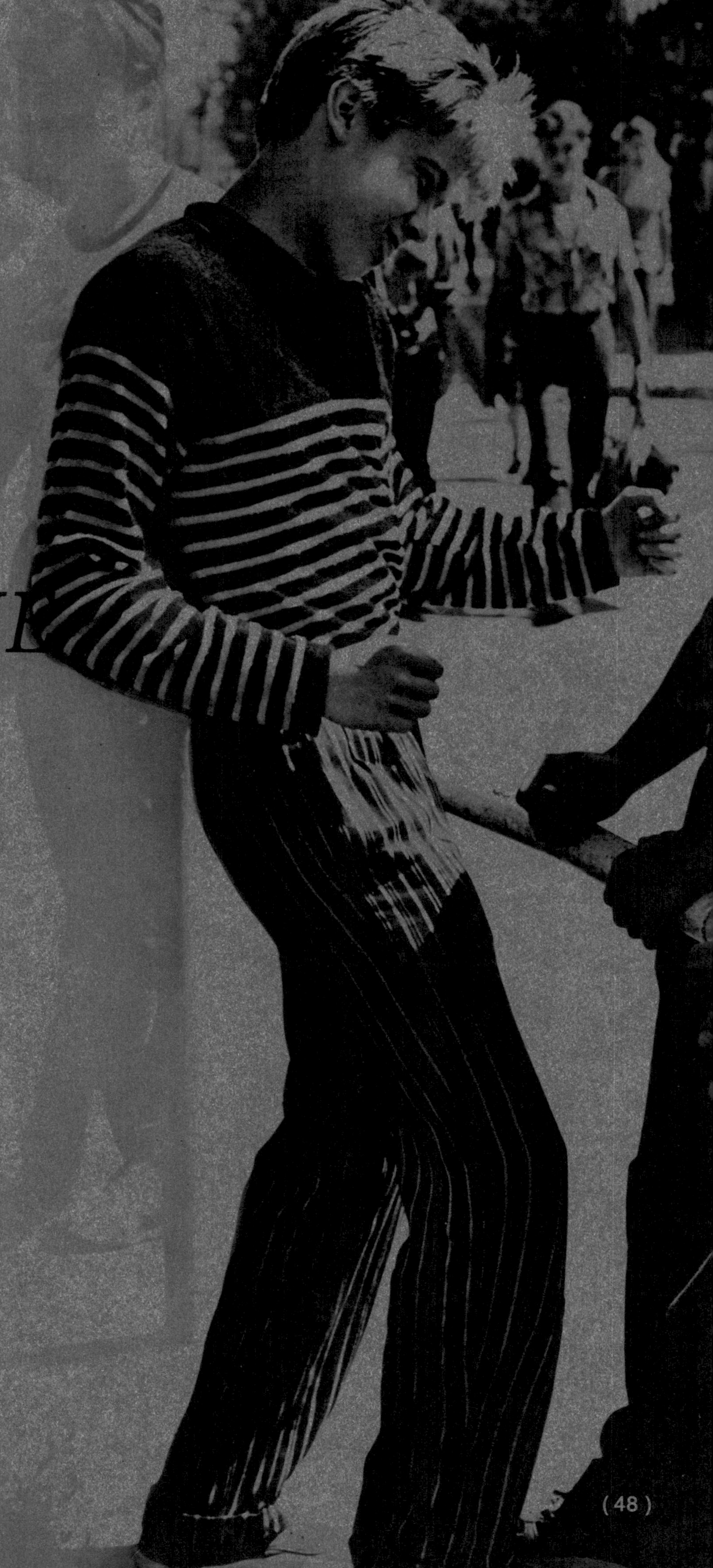

Проблемы у каждой группы свои, о них много
пишут в прессе в последнее время. Обсуждает их
и комсомол, крупнейшая общественно-политиче-
ская организация советской молодежи (кстати,
среди членов неформальных объединений немало
комсомольцев). Увлечения подростков далеко не
всегда готовы принять люди взрослые. Иной раз
это приводило даже к конфликтам, хотя, как
правило, «нарушители традиций» —
самые обыкновенные ребята.

И вдруг — слухи о люберецких. Якобы они
приняли на себя роль «блюстителей нравов».
Говорили так: подмосковные ребята, лишенные
прелестей культурной жизни столицы, взяли на
себя право решать, какая из неформальных групп
хороша, а какая плоха. «Плохим», мол,
предложено немедленно исправиться.
Большинству москвичей это стало известно из
слухов, которыми обросли разного рода
публикации. Пошли разговоры о «тысячных
драках» в московских парках, о жестоких
расправах над «панками» и «металлистами»,
о мобильной организации «темных сил» из
Люберец. В лексиконе появилось новое слово —
«любер», для обозначения подростков,
поклоняющихся силе, исповедующих, как писала
американская газета «Нью-Йорк Таймс»,
«жестокий культ бдительности».

Что же было в самом деле? В Люберцах мы
беседовали с жителями города. Вот первый
вывод: подростки и в Люберцах
опять же самые обыкновенные.
Кто-то воспитанный, а кто-то драчун;
кто-то образован, а кто-то не очень. Никаких целей
по искоренению «инакомыслия» у сверстников
они перед собой не ставили. Впрочем, судите сами.
Предлагаем вниманию читателей несколько
интервью, взятых в Люберцах.

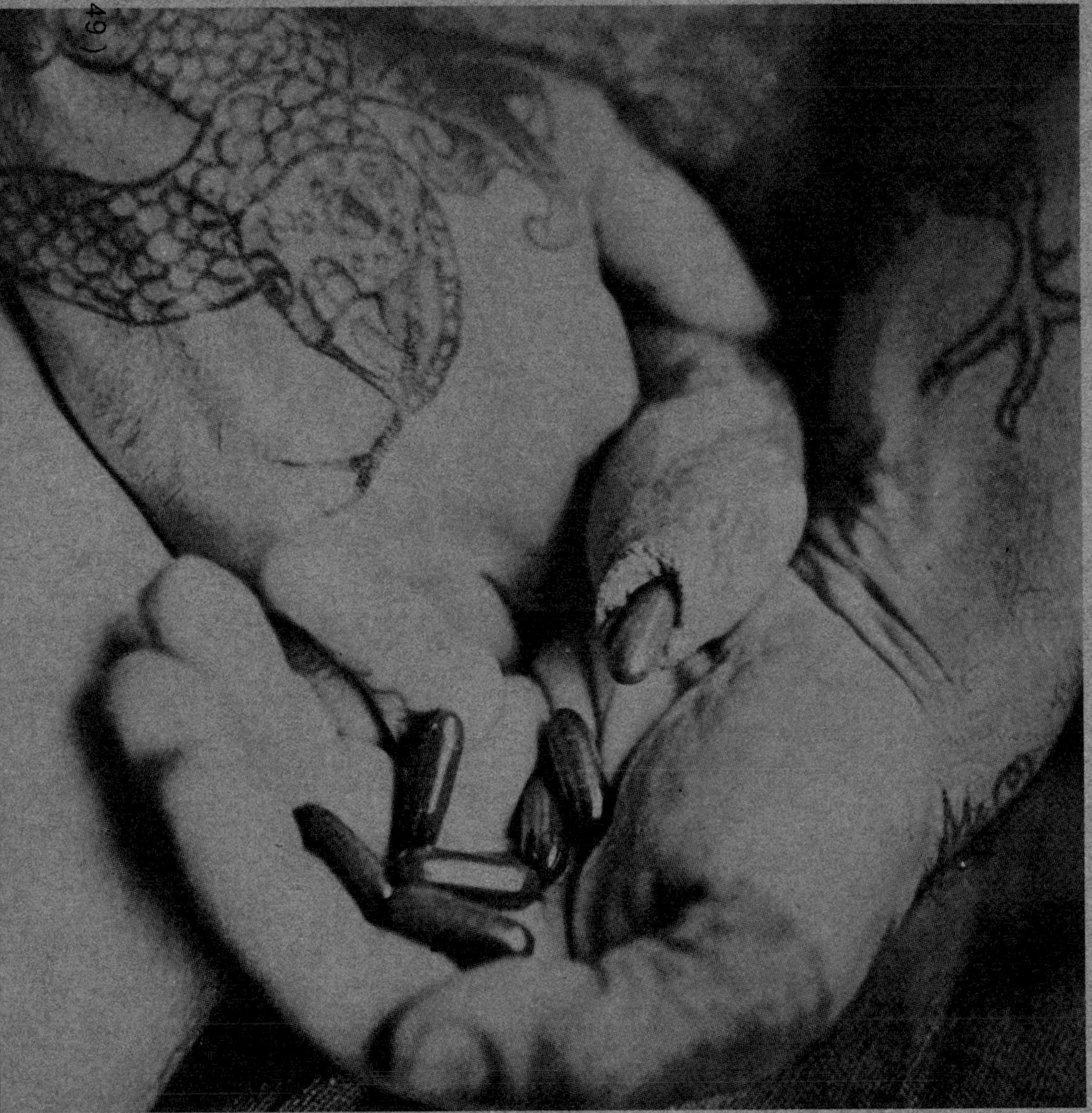

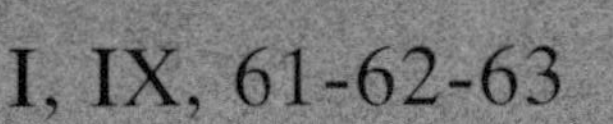

O voi, che avete gli intelletti sani,
Mirate la dottrina che s'asconde
Sotto il velame degli versi strani...

I, IX, 61-62-63

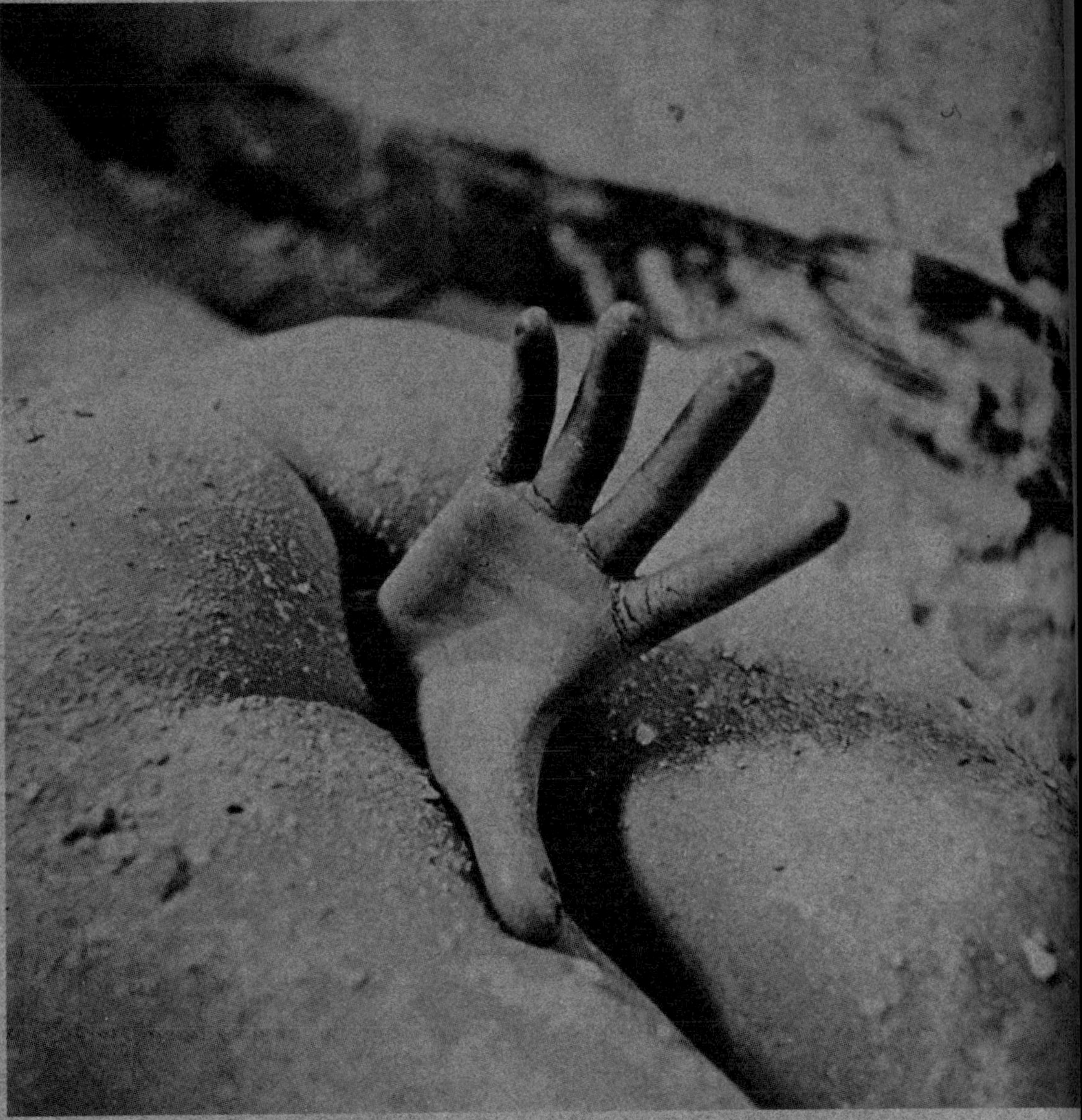

S'egli avesse potuto creder prima,
Rispose il Savio mio, anima lesa,
Ciò ch'ha veduto pur con la mia rima,
Non averebbe in te la man distesa...

I, XIII, 46-47-48-4

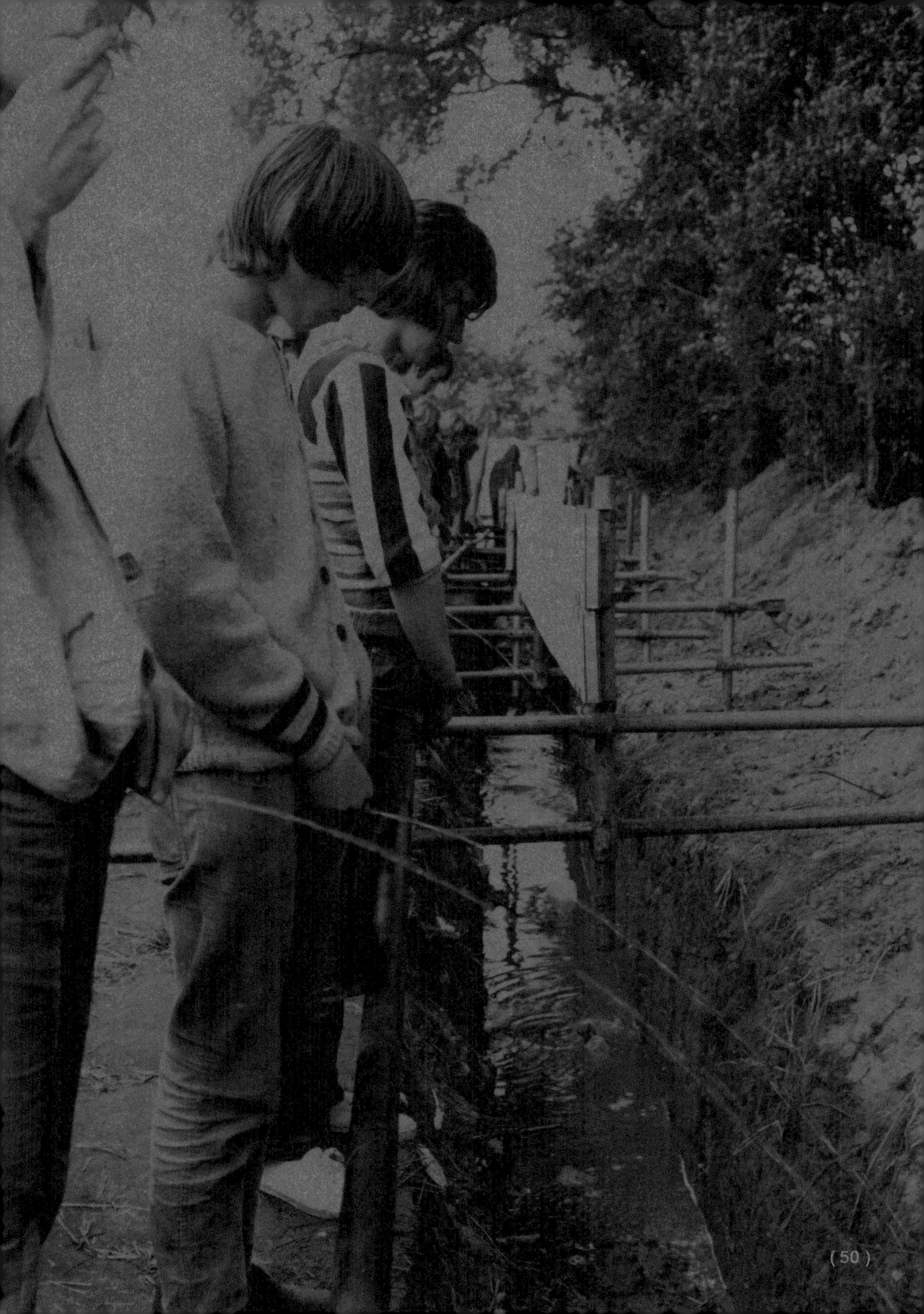

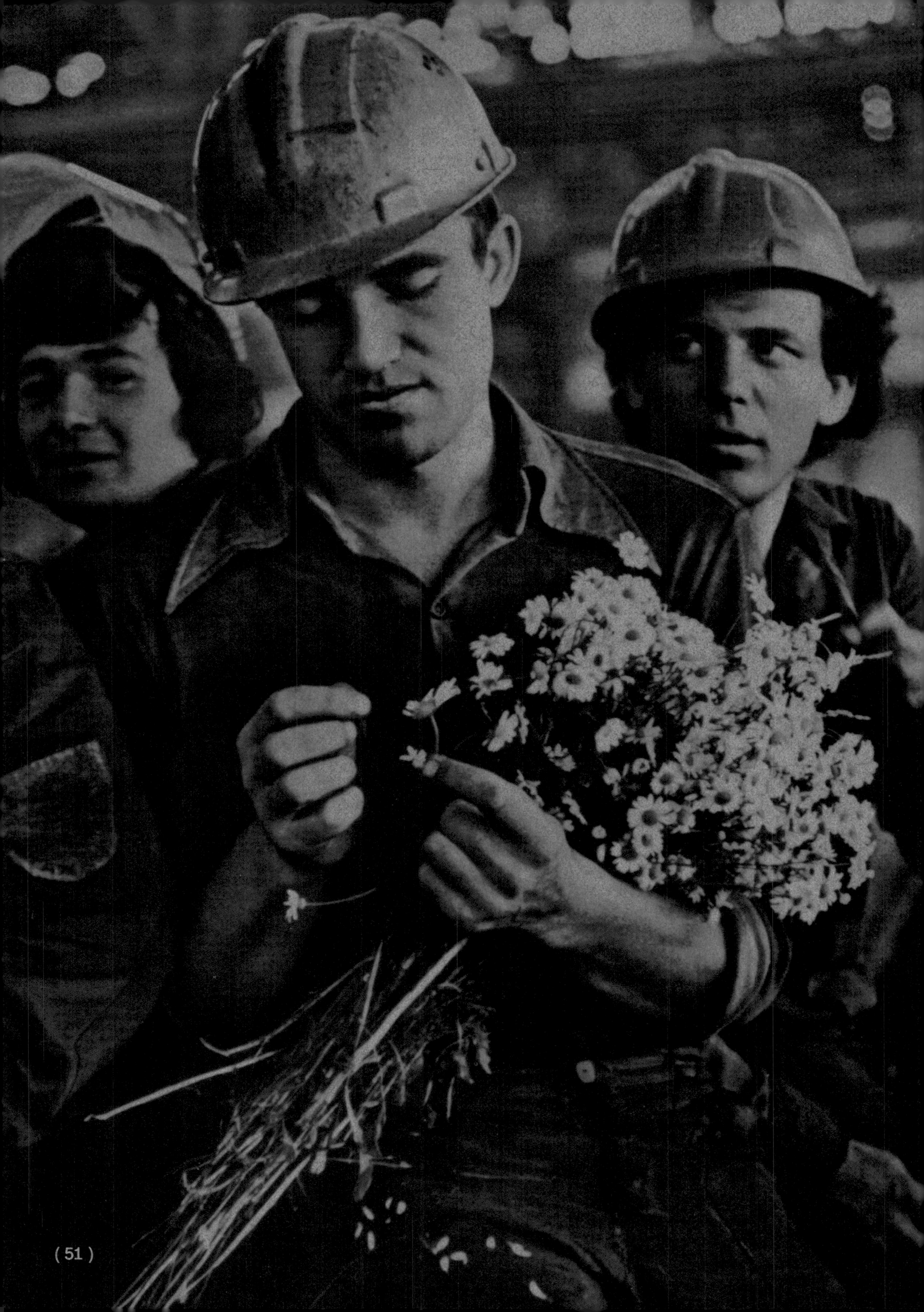

GAY DESIRES . . . .

Gay Icebreakers

is a collective of socialist gay men
working for radical change through the gay movement
providing support and solidarity to other gay people

with our helpline
meetings for people coming out
open discussion groups about the politics of being gay (2nd & 4th
Tues of each month in Gay's The Word at 7.30 pm)
the disco, with Gay CND and Nightworkers, on Fridays at the Bell
and doing other things when we can.
We would like to hear from you,
if you can help us or if we can help you.

01-274 9590 Mon to Fri 7.30 – 10.30 pm

. . . . SUBVERSIVE DREAMS

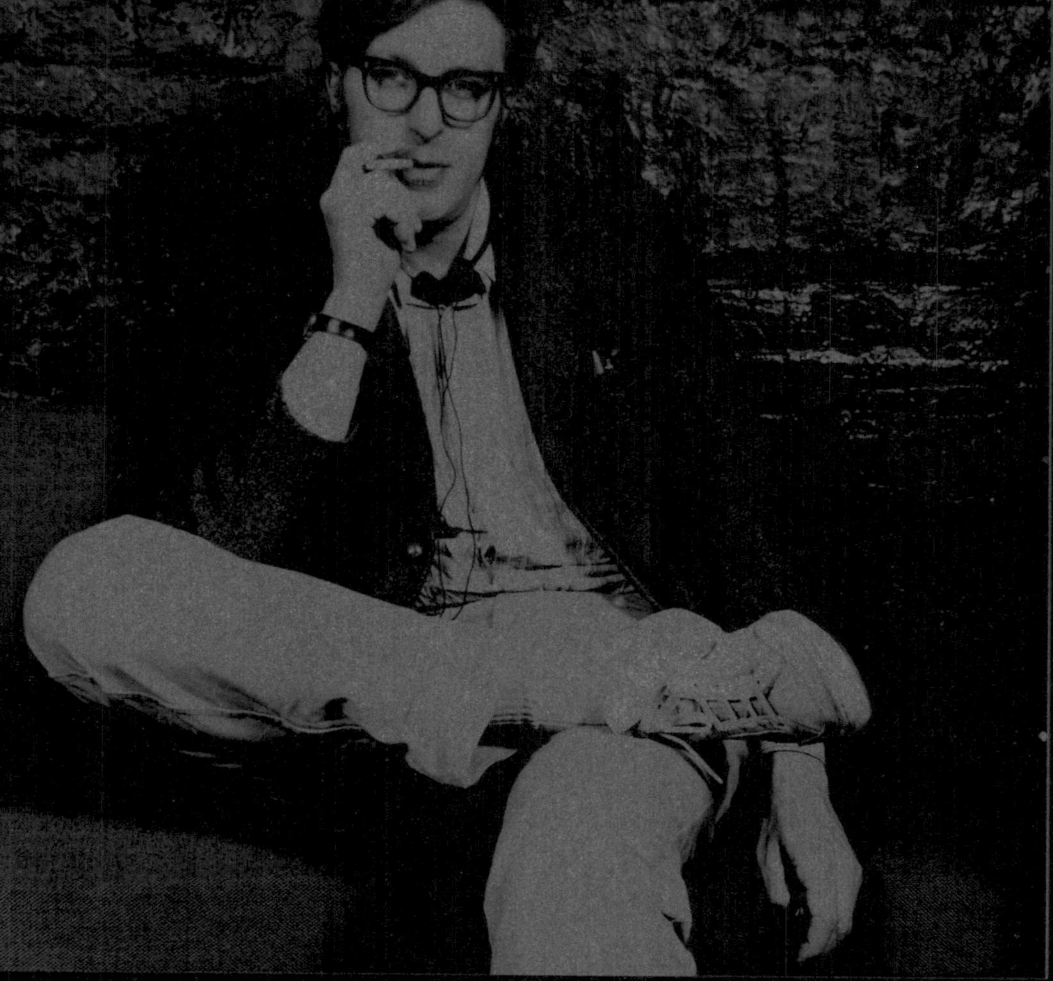

THE MALE LOOK

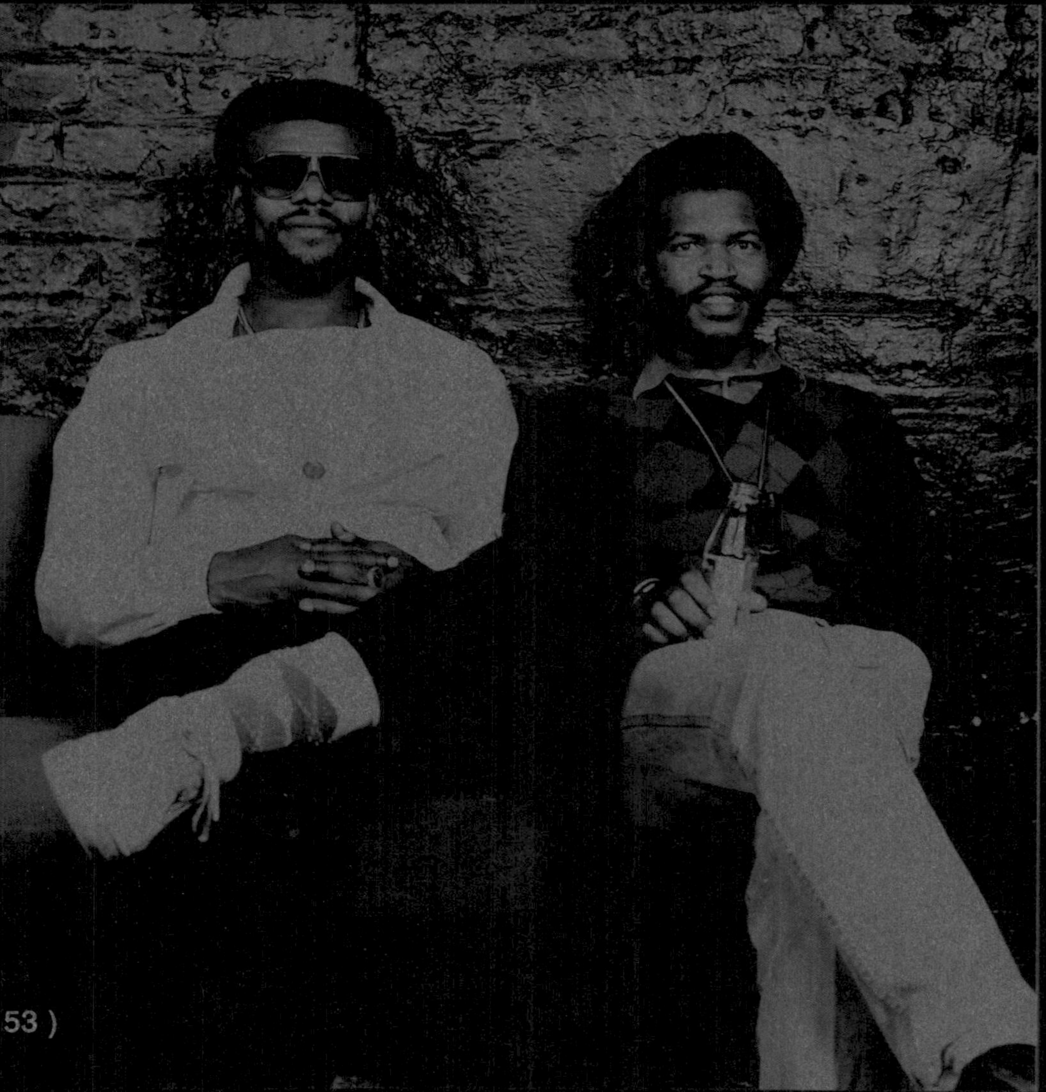

We are all constantly
surrounded by
stereotyped images of
men and women in
newspapers, magazines,
on billboards, on
television etc...
They set examples of
'the look' and 'the
pose' of the male and
the female, which are
learnt by most of us
from an early age,
and we 'show the
camera' what we
consequently believe
to be 'our best side'.

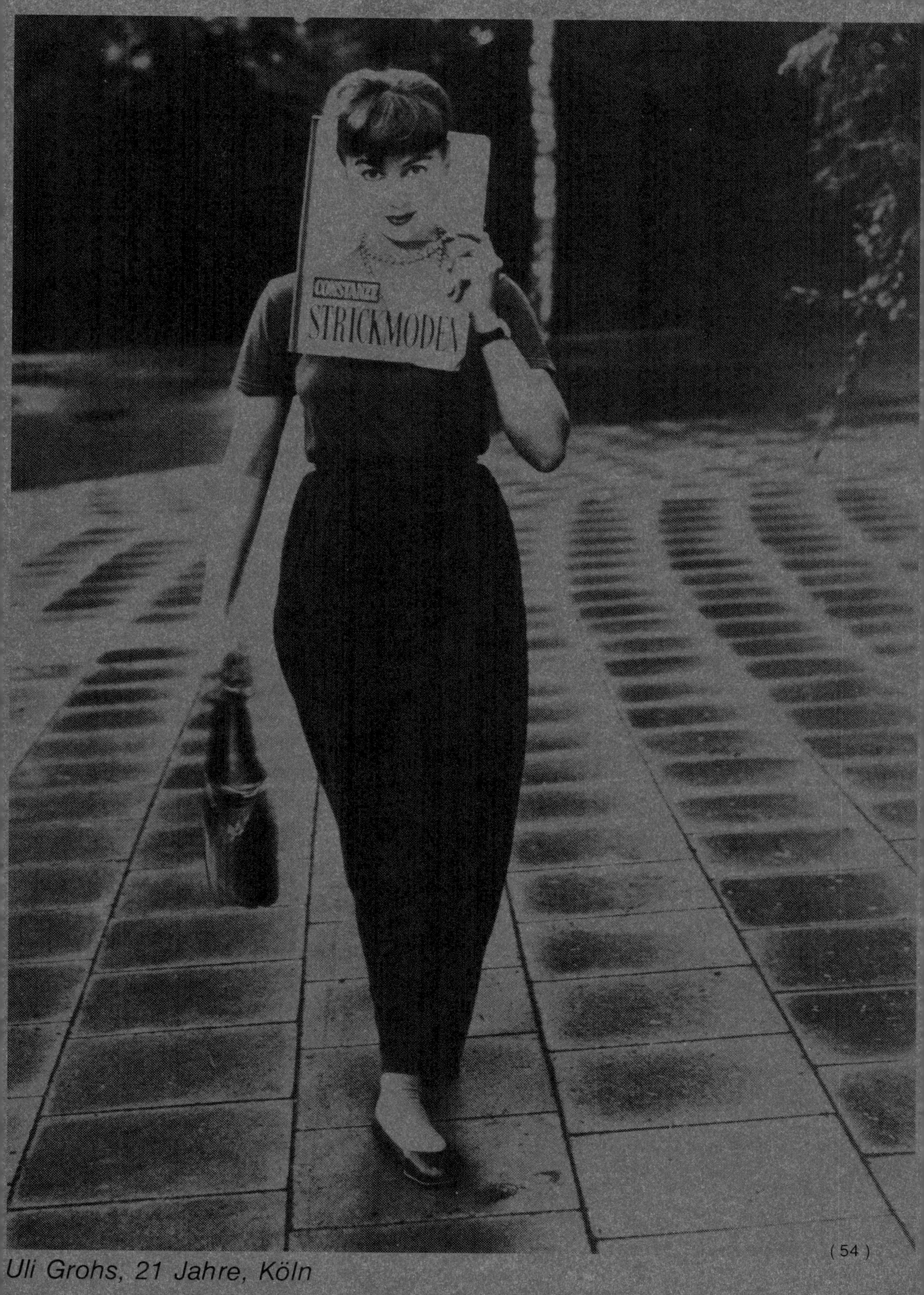

Uli Grohs, 21 Jahre, Köln

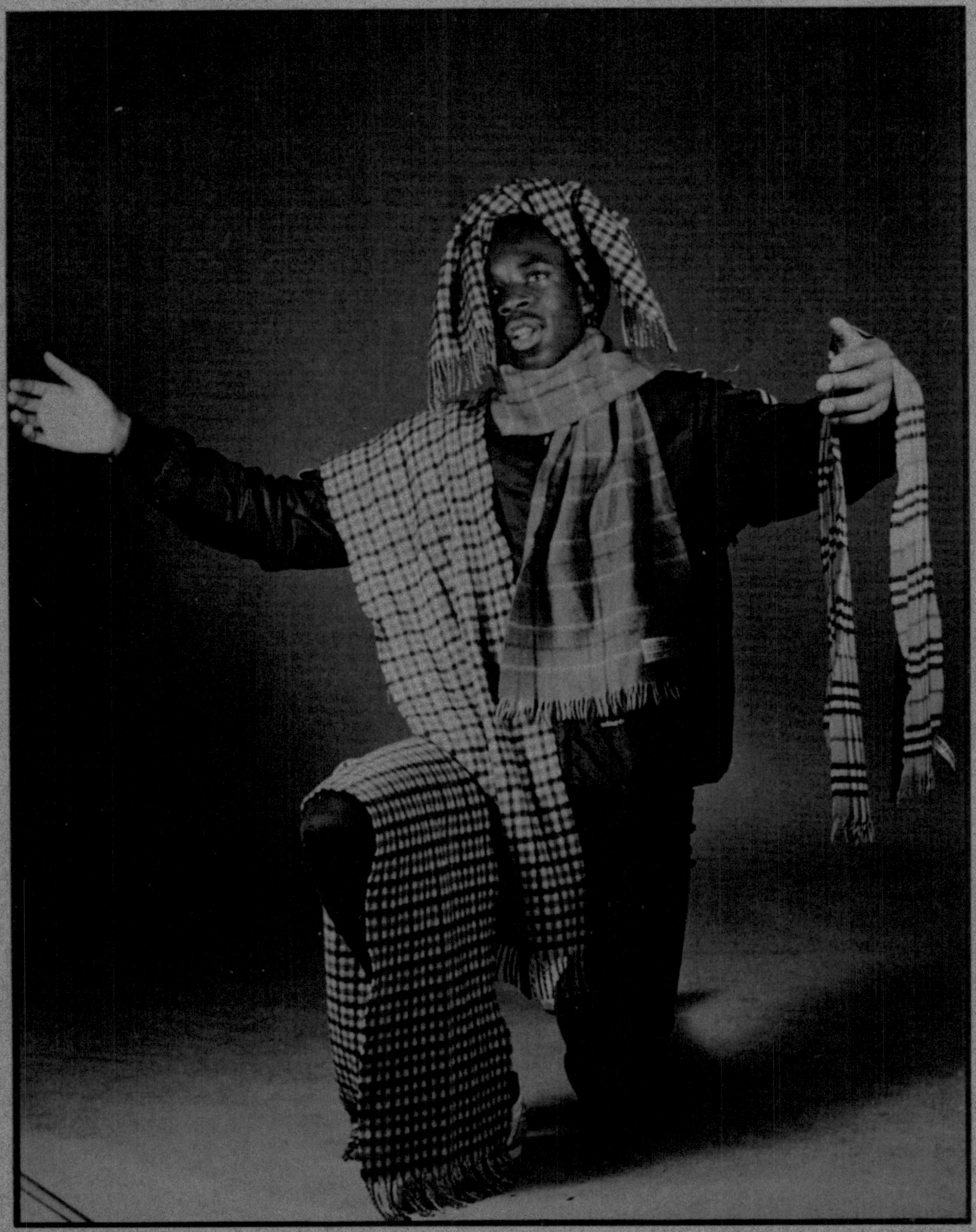

Studio photograph. 'Style' and having a laugh with the group members, Burberry scarves, which were virtually badges of membership

(55)

Мода входит в цех

«Шейте сами — это красиво, удобно, модно, практично» — эти слова были девизом конкурса, организованного на заводе впервые женсоветом металлургического производства. На участие в конкурсе заявки подали восемь цехов.

В день конкурса красный уголок цеха № 36 был оформлен специальными номерами стенгазет. В них было немало интересных и полезных советов по шитью, рукоделию, кулинарии. Красочное объявление приглашало всех тружениц принять участие в зрительском жюри и выбрать лучшие модели года.

По условиям конкурса его участницы должны были не только представить модель, но и сделать ее выкройку для зрителей. На вечере царила праздничная атмосфера. Открыла конкурс председатель женсовета металлургического производства Г. Г. Прокопенко. Всем болельщикам были выданы карточки членов зрительского жюри. Жюри специалистов возглавила модельер-консультант С. А. Вяткина. В его состав вошли представители женсоветов других производств и управлений.

Перед показом моделей, изготовленных руками самих участниц, председатель жюри С. А. Вяткина коротко рассказала об основных направлениях современной моды. А вот и начался сам показ. Под музыку на сцену выходят 30 нарядно одетых манекенщиц. Среди моделей платья и костюмы на любой вкус и любой с л у ч а й жизни: строгие деловые платья, вязаные изделия, модные юбки и комбинезоны. Самую большую коллекцию представил на конкурс цех № 36. В цехе вот уже несколько лет работает кружок рукоделия, которым руководит старший инженер-экономист Г. Г. Прокопенко.

Победительницей конкурса стала контролер ОТК цеха № 41 Т. А. Кудинова. Ее белое нарядное платье с кружевами и вышивкой получило самые высокие оценки и жюри, и болельщиков. В числе победителей: Л. М. Исакова, стерженщица цеха № 34, Т. В. Малкова, крановщица цеха № 38, Г. Г. Прокопенко, старший инженер-экономист цеха № 36, Е. Б. Голикова, электросварщица цеха № 52.

Как видим, победители — люди разных и очень трудных профессий, у большинства из них есть дети. И тем не менее они находят время на это чисто женское занятие — красиво, со вкусом одеваться.

Завершился этот необычный конкурс парадом победителей и участников. Всем им были вручены памятные призы.

С. ГУРЕВИЧ,
организатор
соцсоревнования
цеха № 36.

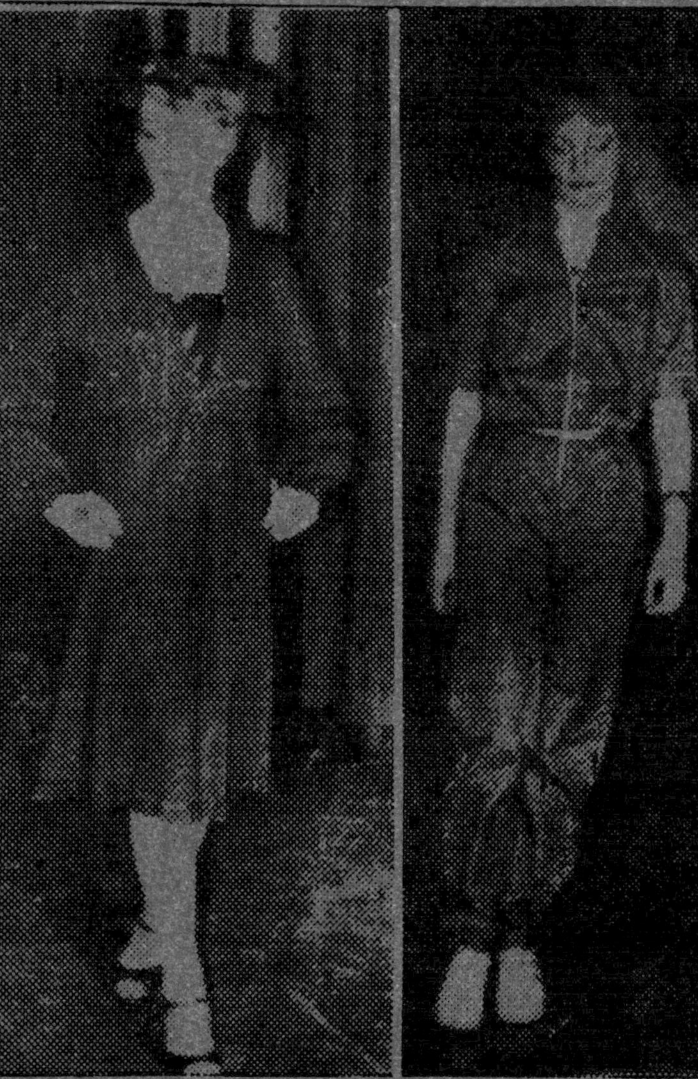

На снимках: идет конкурс.

Фото В. ЖДАНОВА,
Г. МЕЛЬЧАКОВА.

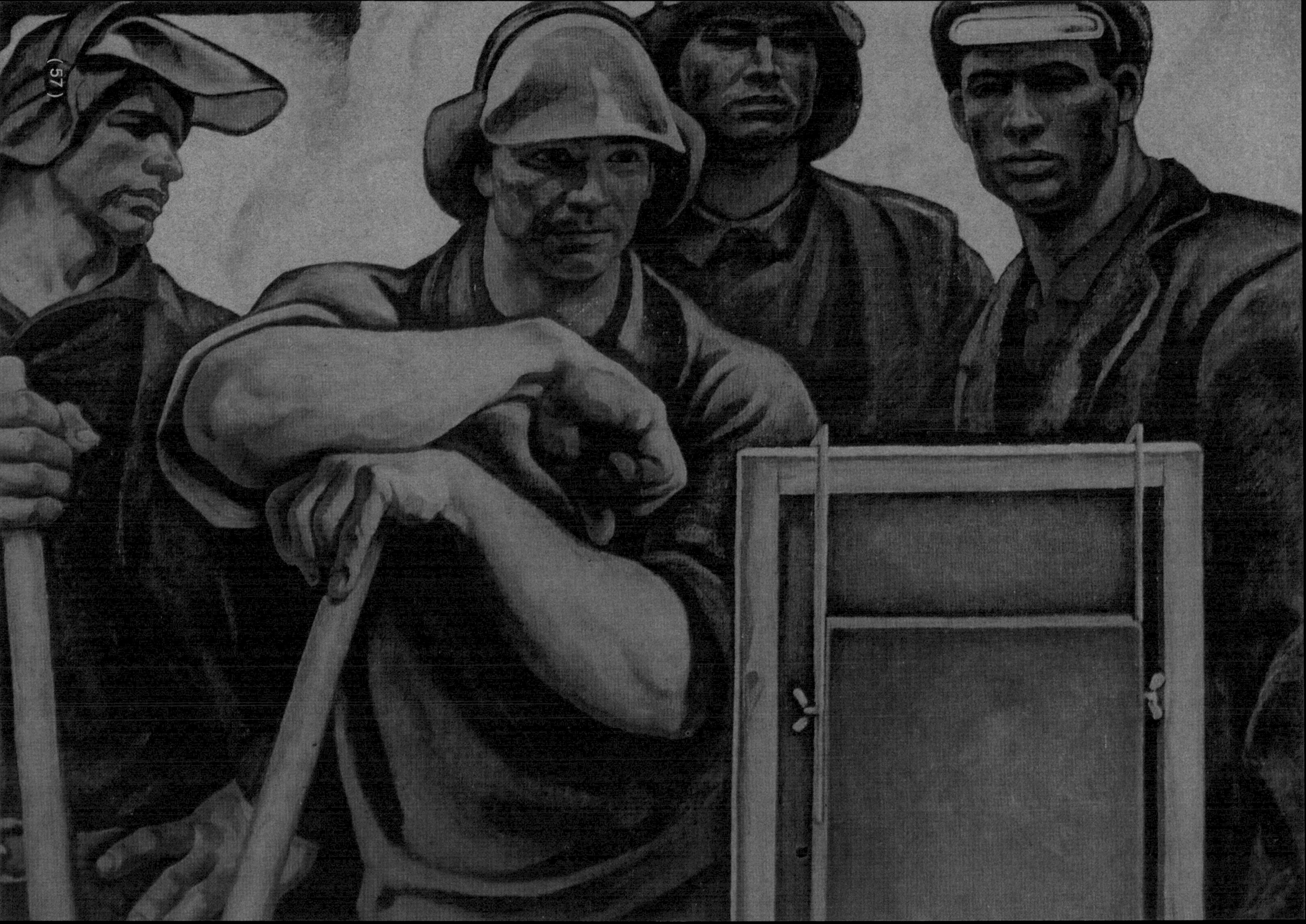

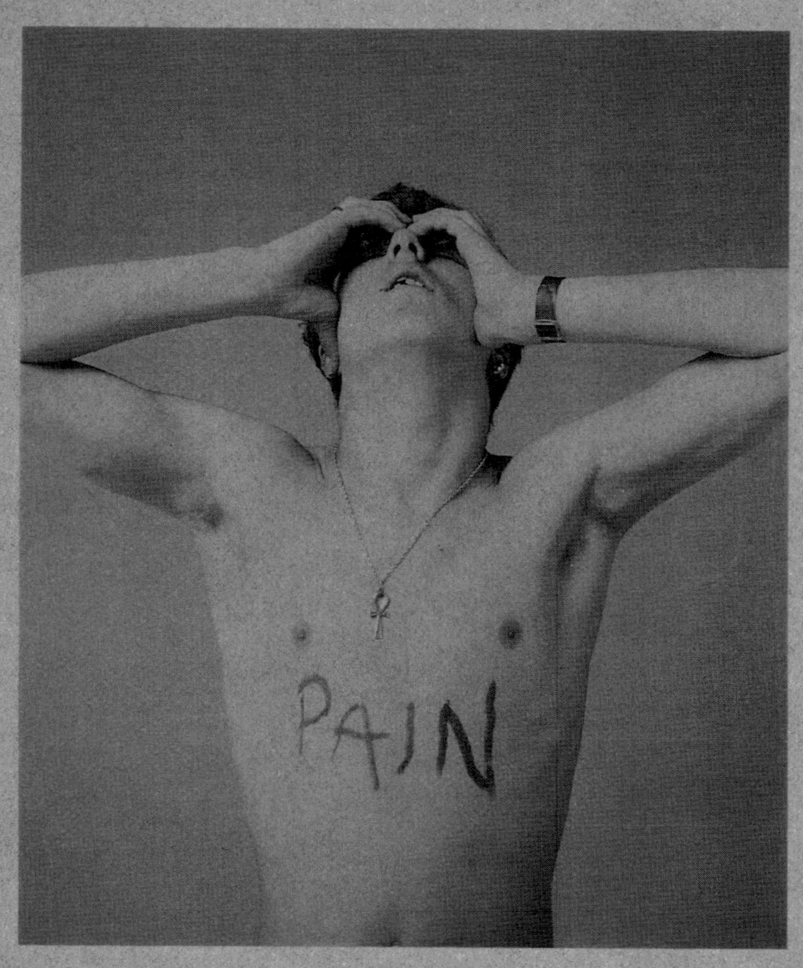
PAIN

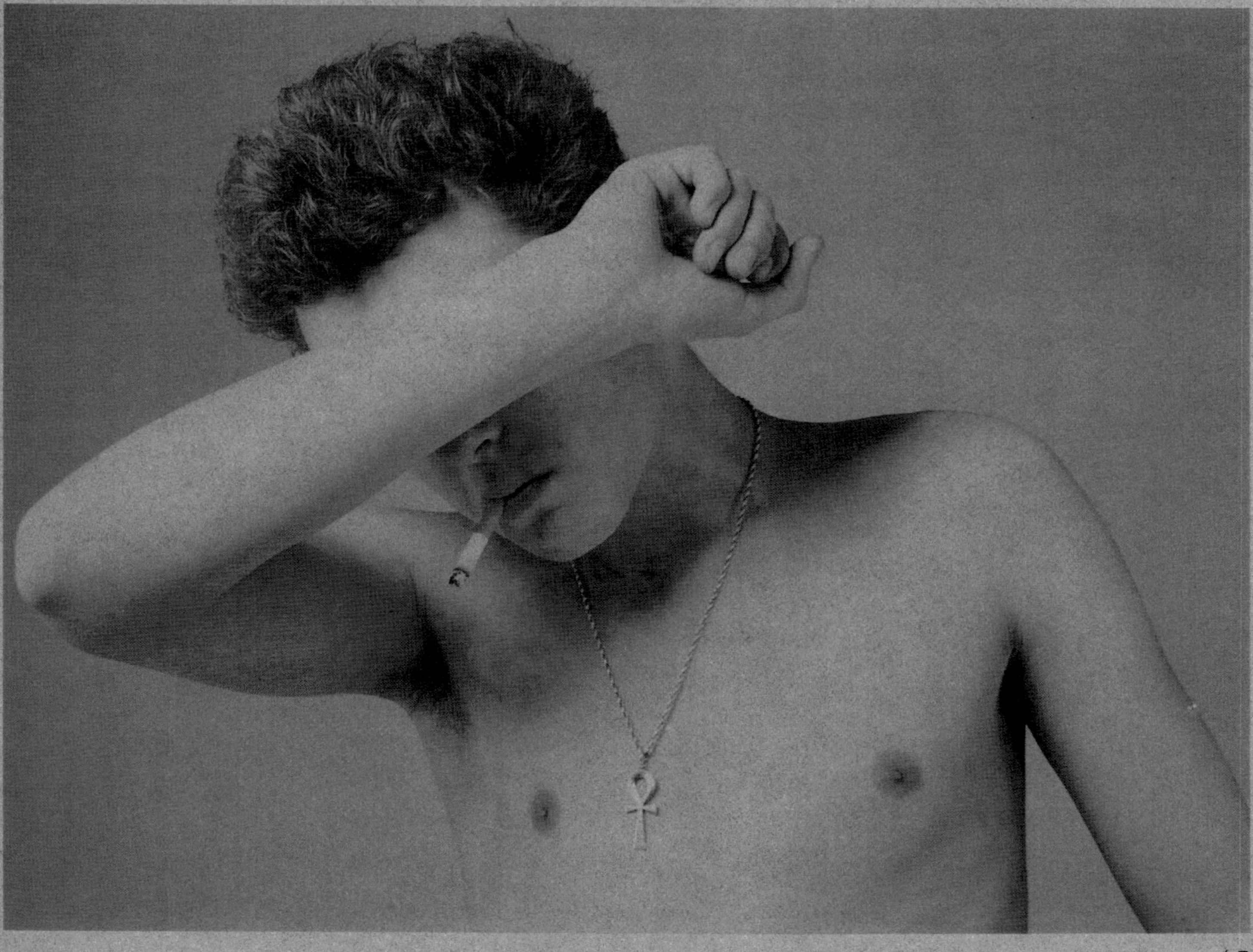

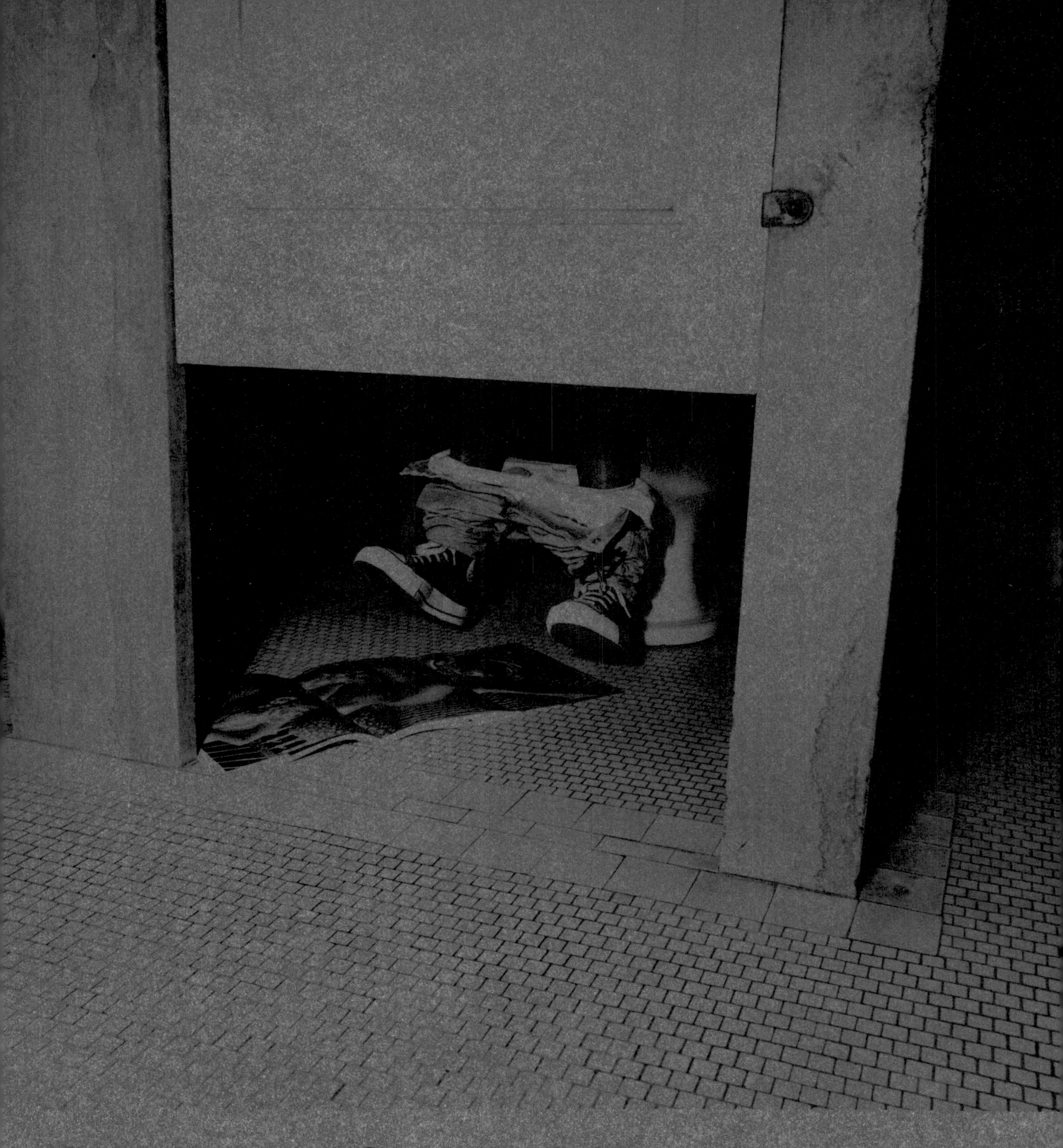

WHAT SORT OF MAN READS PL*YB*Y?

A young man in touch with himself and his own imagination. Self-reliant, and with an appreciation for his personal privacy, he keeps his hand close to his chest and an eye out for unexpected interruptions of his daily routines. With confidence in his ability to handle himself in tense situations, the PL*YB*Y reader wrings every last drop of satisfaction from his private pursuits. Helping him stand up to that challenge is his favorite magazine. Fact: PL*YB*Y is read by nearly half of all young men who eventually excell at tennis, handball, or arm wrestling, and spent at least $12 on fine spurting goods last year alone. To reach that young man, put yourself in PL*YB*Y. He does. (Source: 1973 TGIF.)

(59)

New York • Chicago • Detroit • Los Angeles • San Francisco • Midville • Atlanta • London • Tokyo

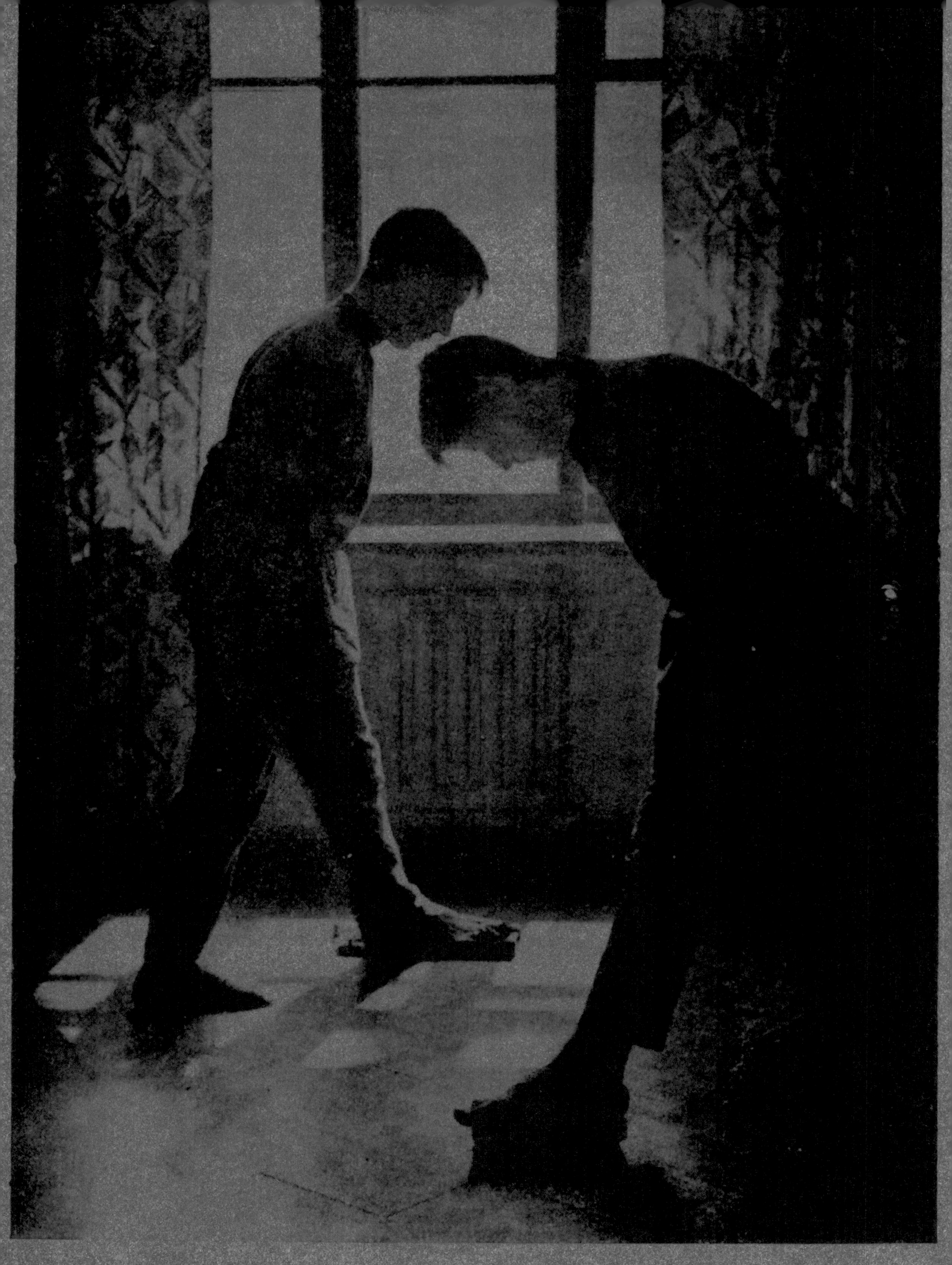

ПОЛОТЕРЫ

Е. С. М. (Москва)

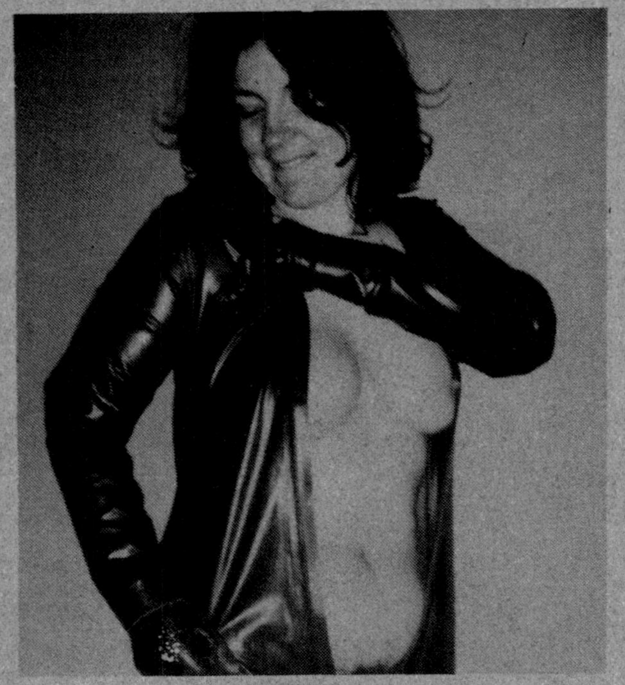

PULLING ON THE SUIT.
- - - - - - -
ZIPPING HERSELF IN TIGHT.

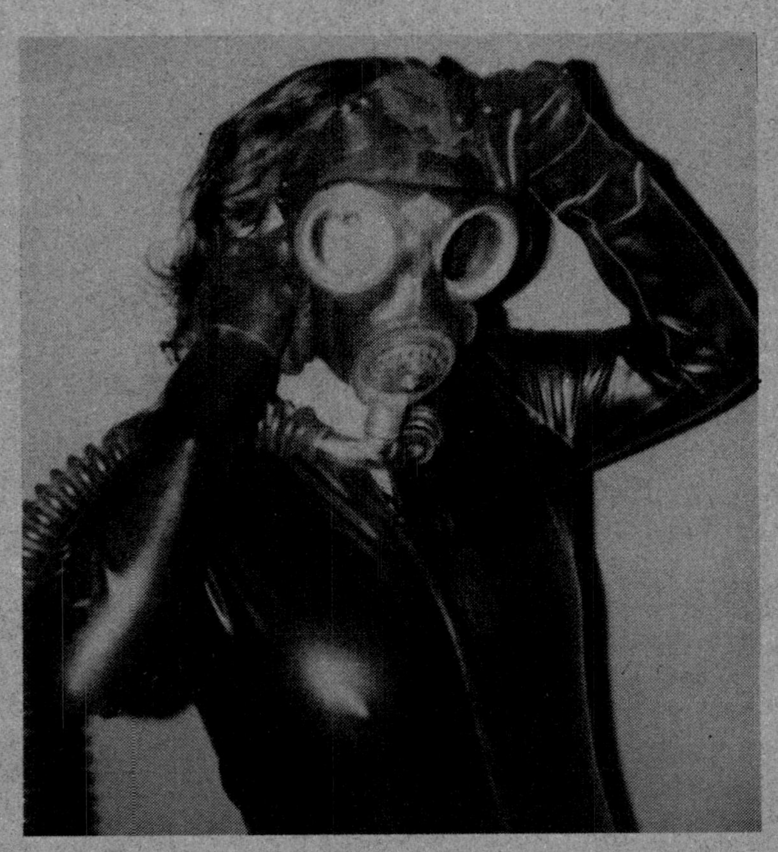

ON WITH THE MASK-THEN PULL IT
TIGHT TO THE HEAD.

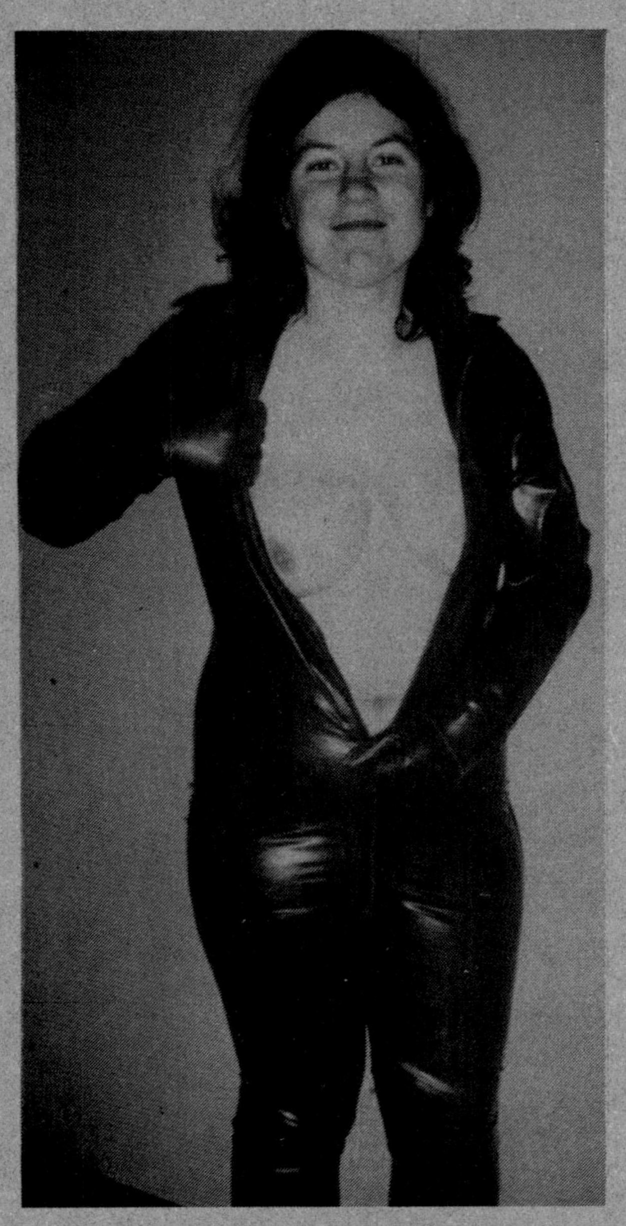

ANNE OF BRISTOL

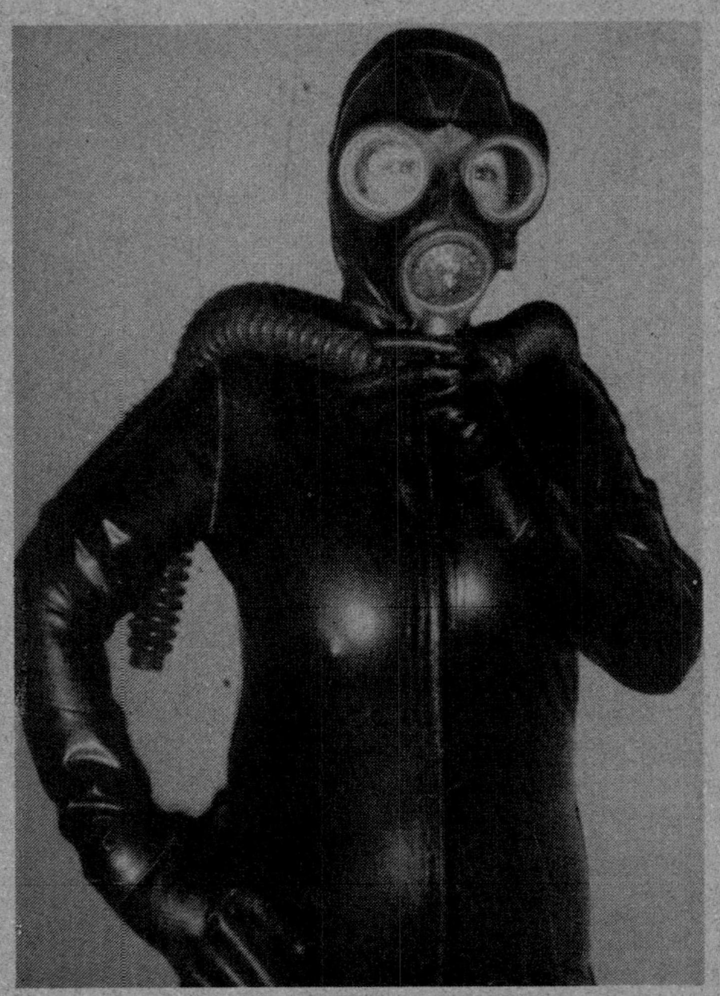

READY FOR GOOD FUN AND GAMES!

I CAN HARDLY WAIT TO SEE IF THE
CROTCH ZIP IS STILL IN WORKING
ORDER.
(P.S. It was - wow!)

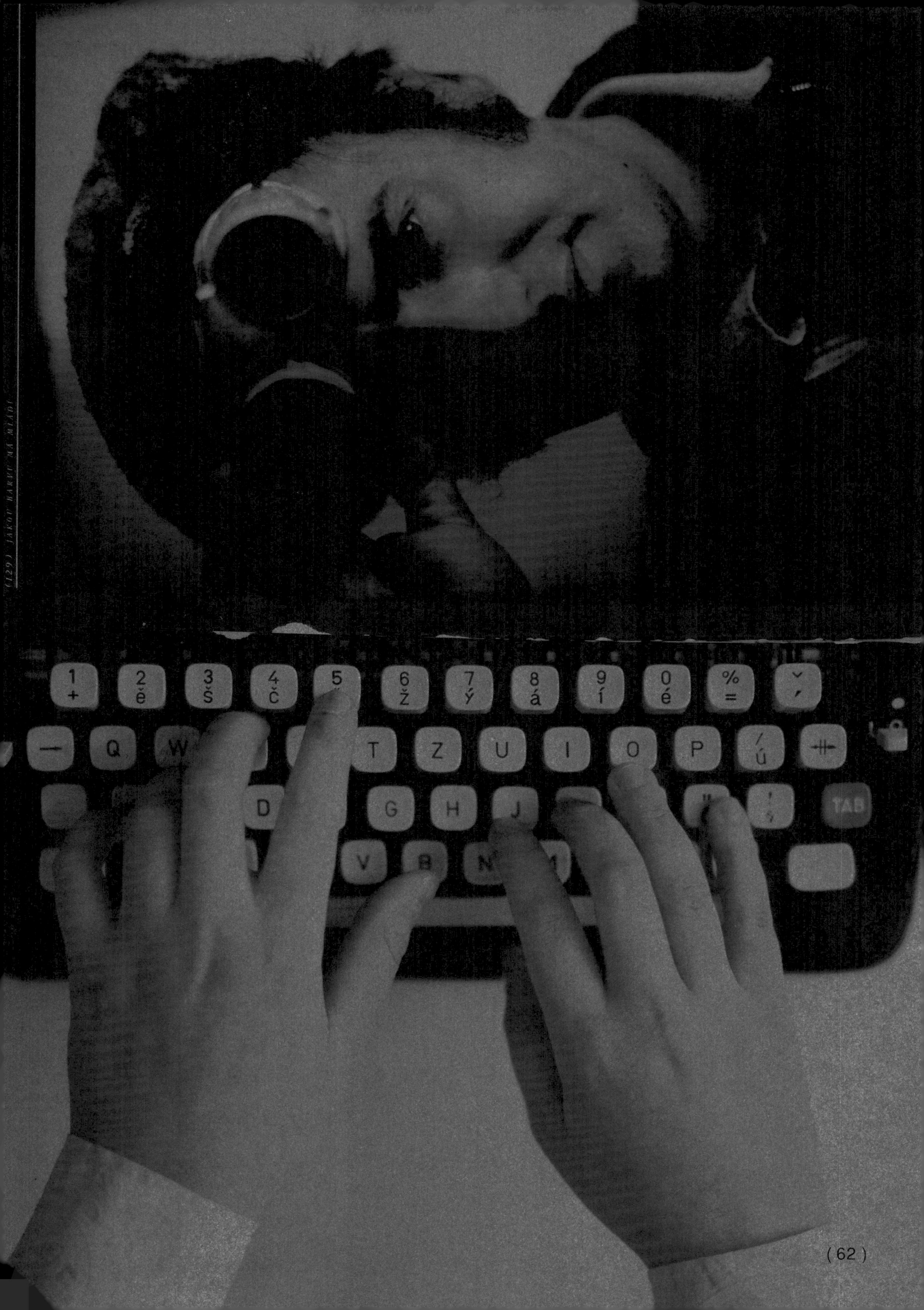

(129) JAKOU BARVU MÁ MLADÍ

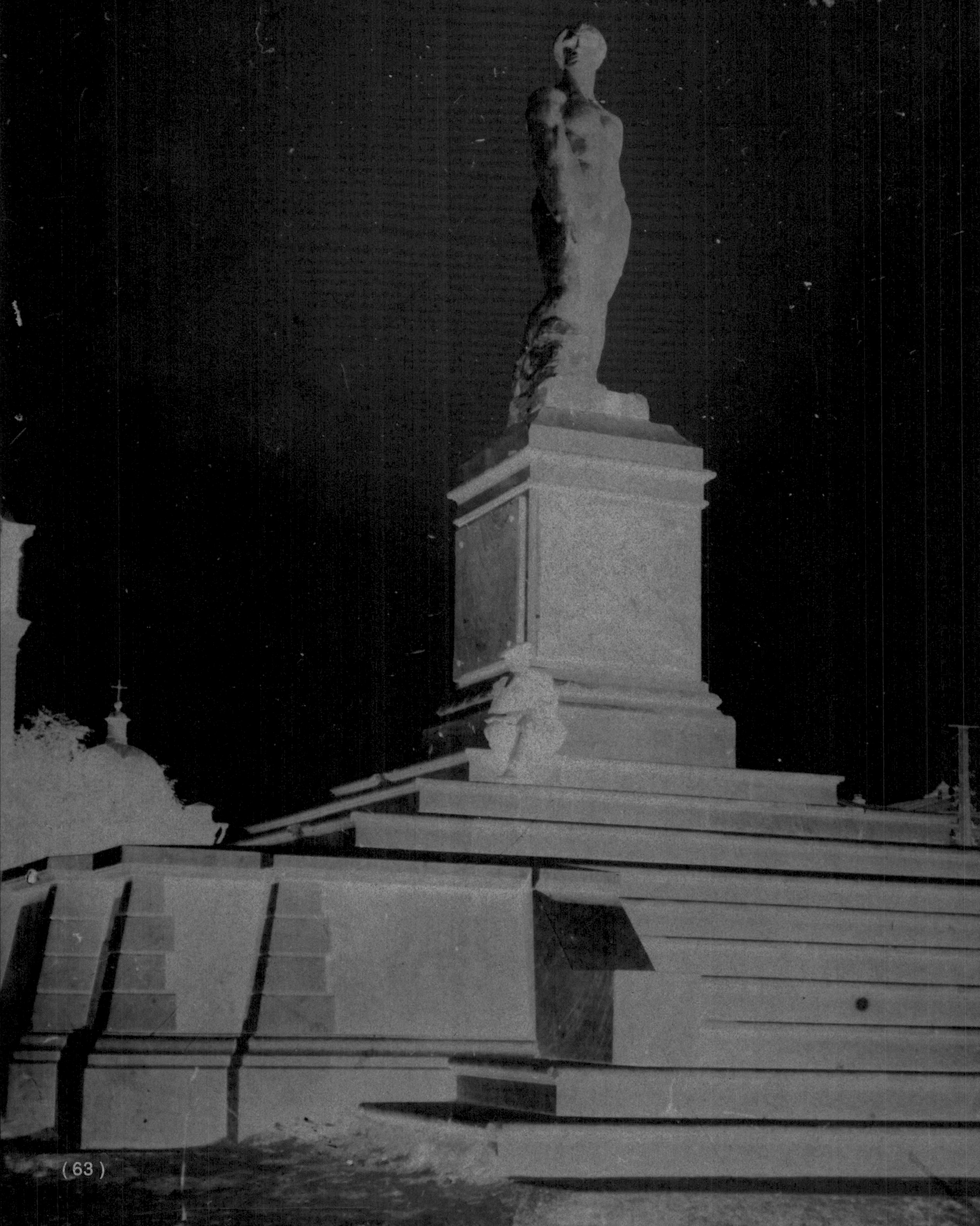

(63)

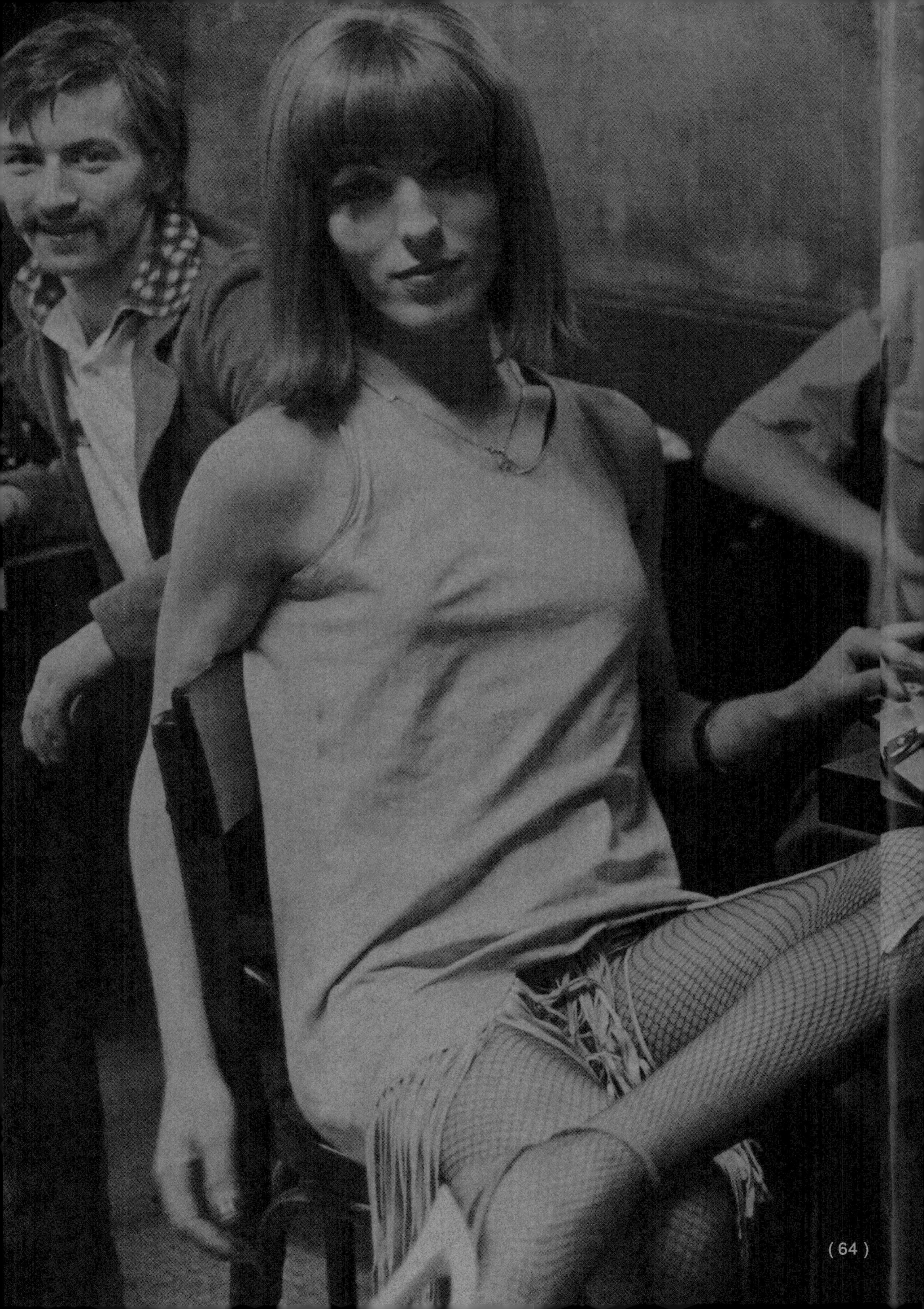

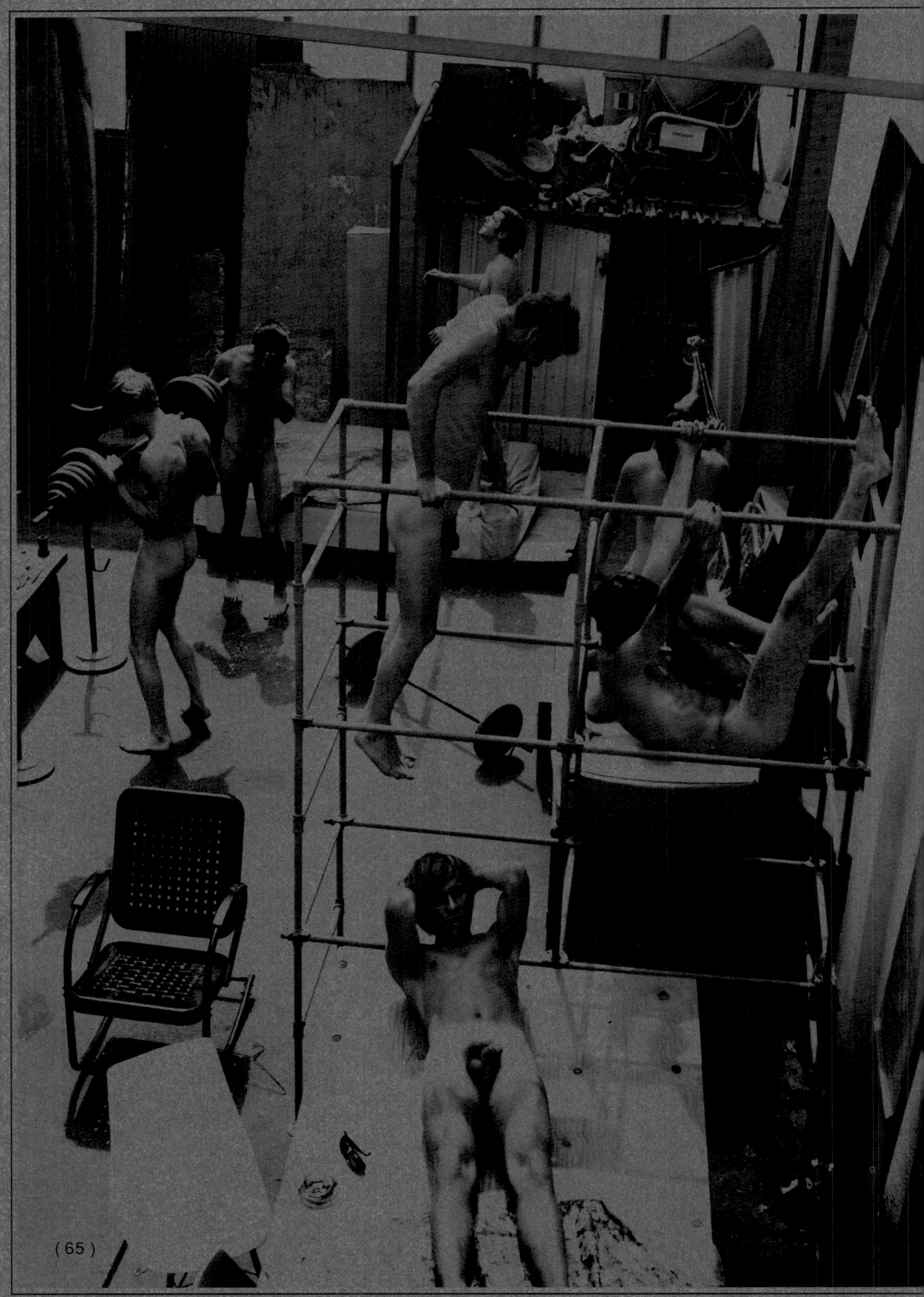

(65)

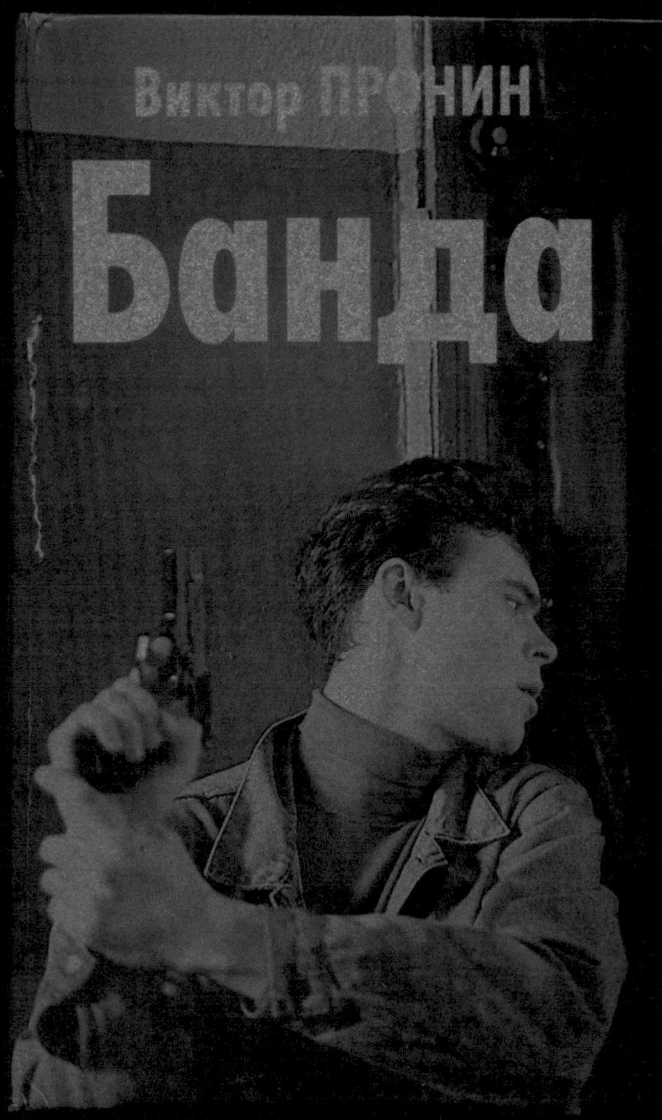

Виктор ПРОНИН
Банда

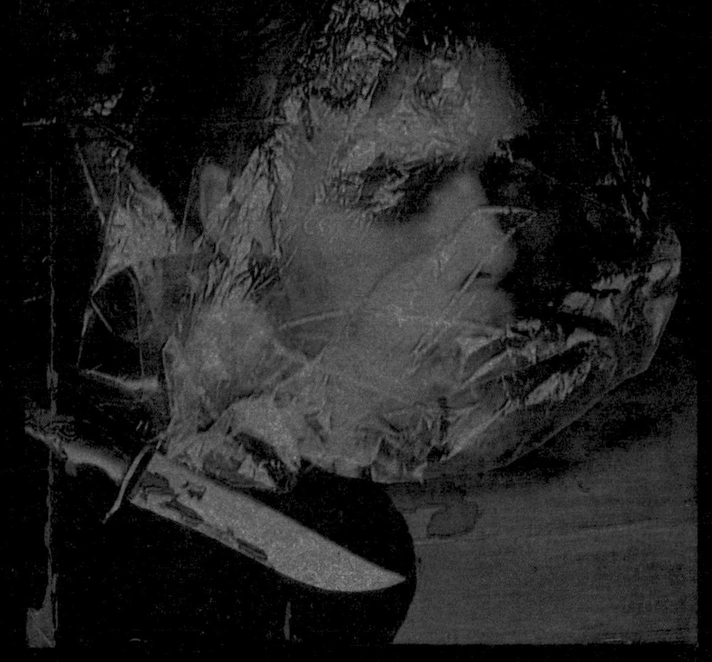

Виктор ПРОНИН
Банда 2

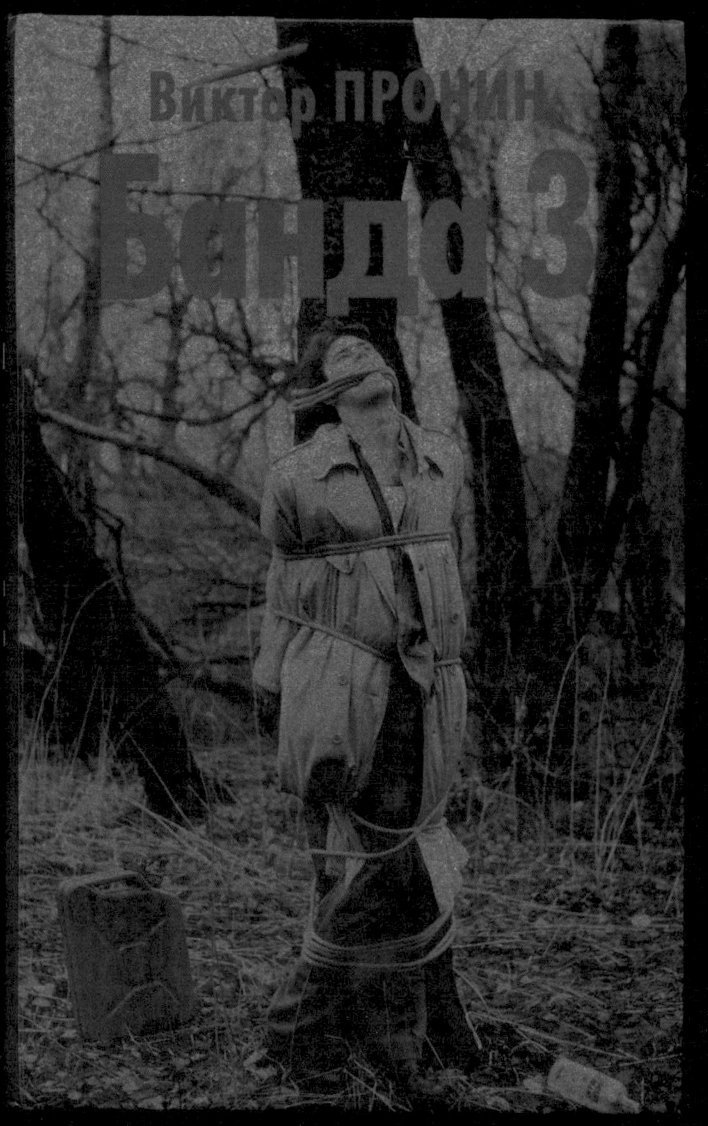

Виктор ПРОНИН
Банда 3

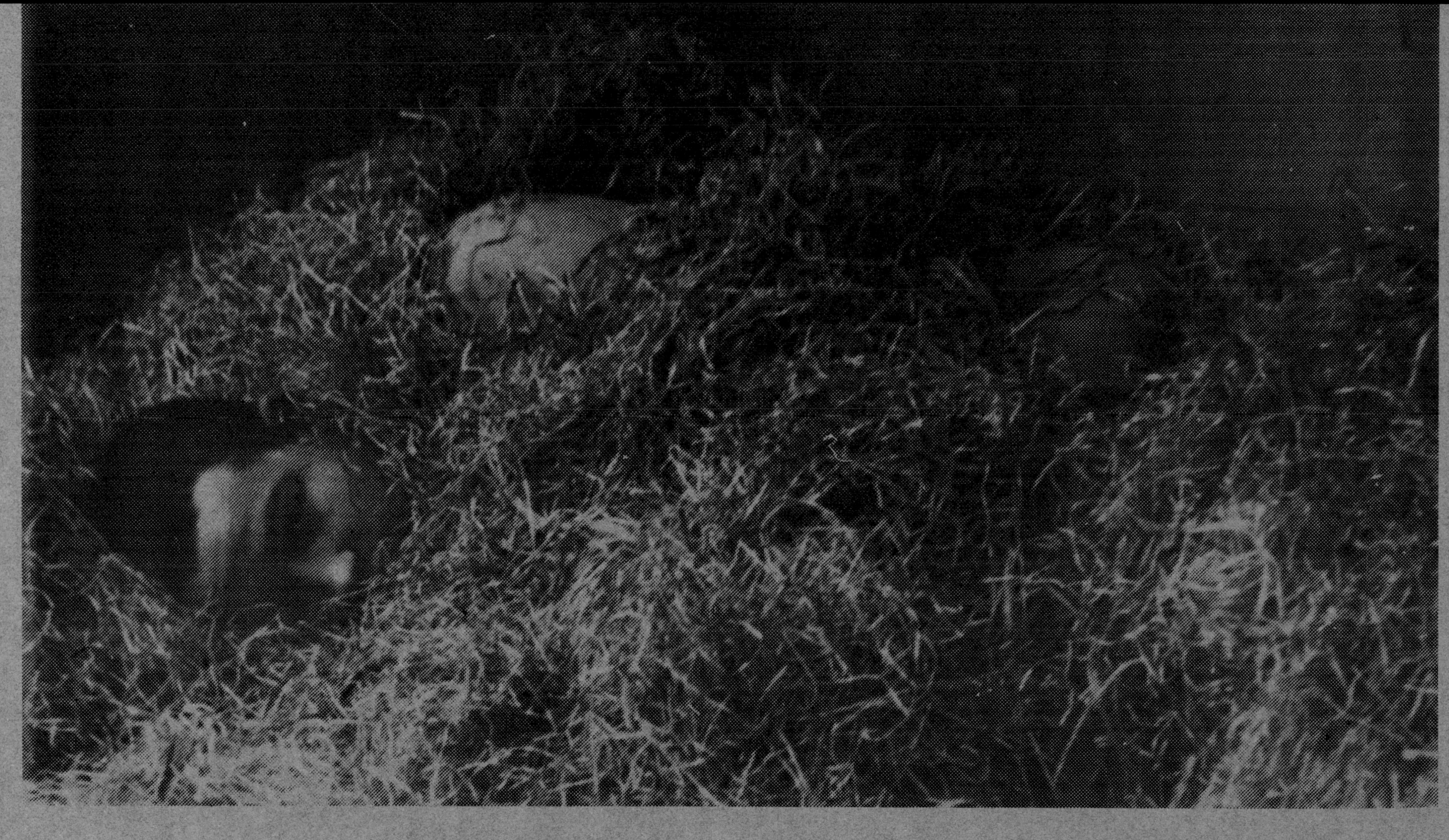

Een patiënt die naakt in zeegras wordt verpleegd, onder meer in verband met zijn neiging om kleding te verscheuren.

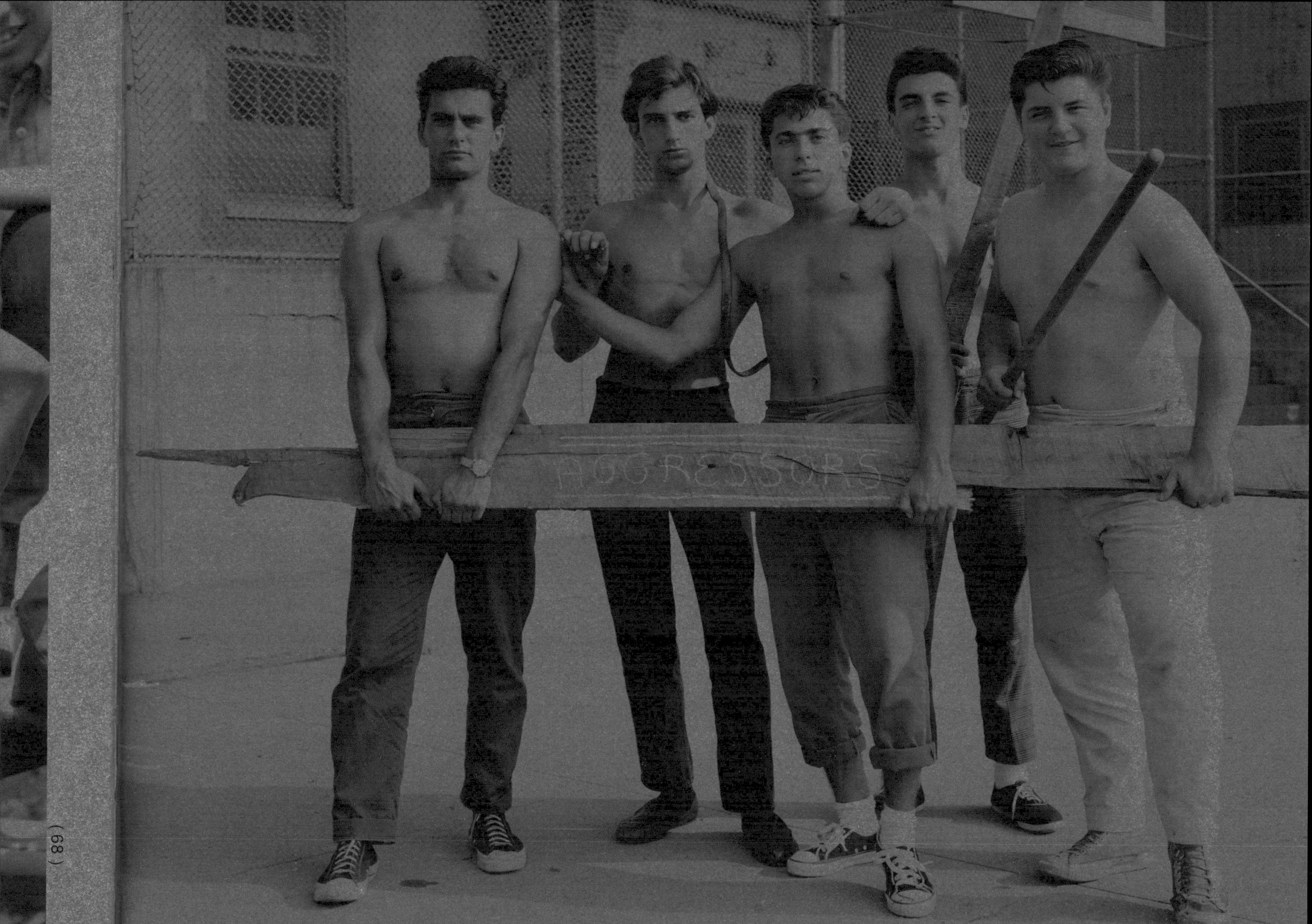
AGGRESSORS

victory
lected
 of the
r fans
ent, of

marks
ture in
of their
ly – as
coste,
on the
ubs at

f, in an
major
casual
on the
s and
opean
in this
orward
were
e best
(69)
opean

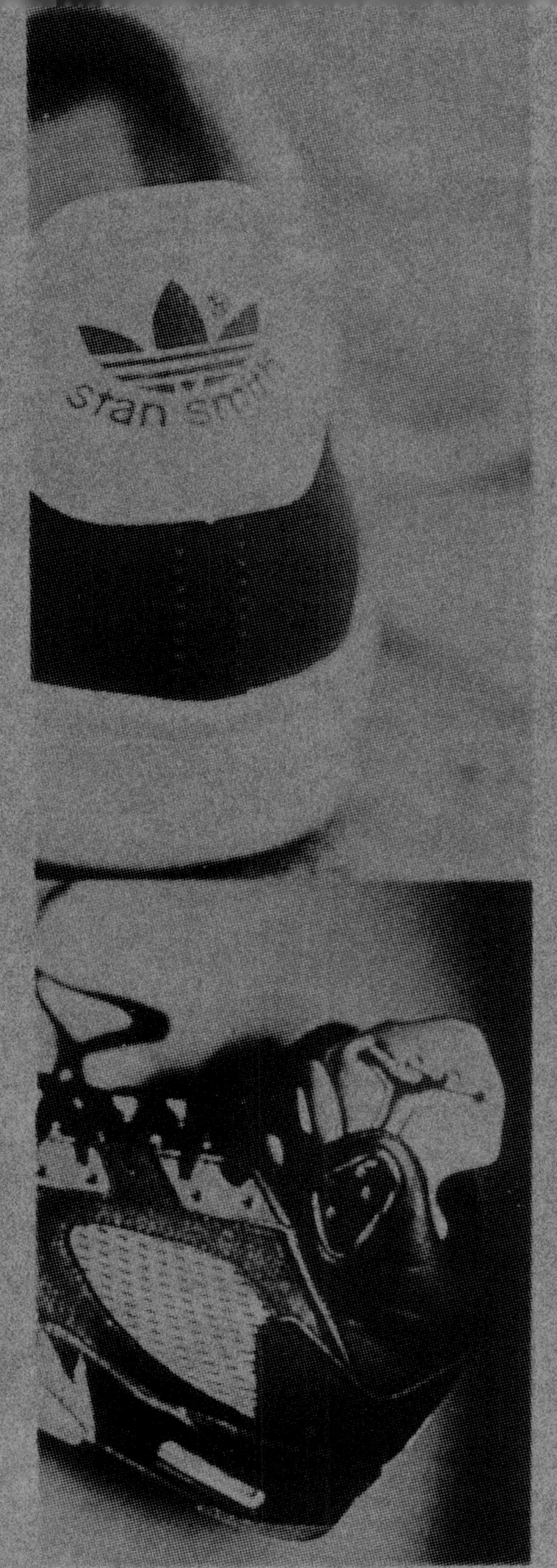

1. Travel Fox Bar
   (and all others
2. Nike Air Jorda
3. (Black) Fila To
4. Anything by T
5. British Knight
6. LA Gear (hilari
7. Reebok Pump
8. Nike Air Press
   (you've got to
   the bastards u
9. Hi-Tec (never
   pair yet)
10. Jordache (no

TOP TEN CLAS

1. Adidas Samba
2. Puma Argenti
3. Adidas S.L. 80
4. Adidas Stan S
5. Adidas Forest
6. Adidas Trim T
7. Adidas Shell-T
8. Diadora Borg
9. Adidas Gazell
10. Puma States

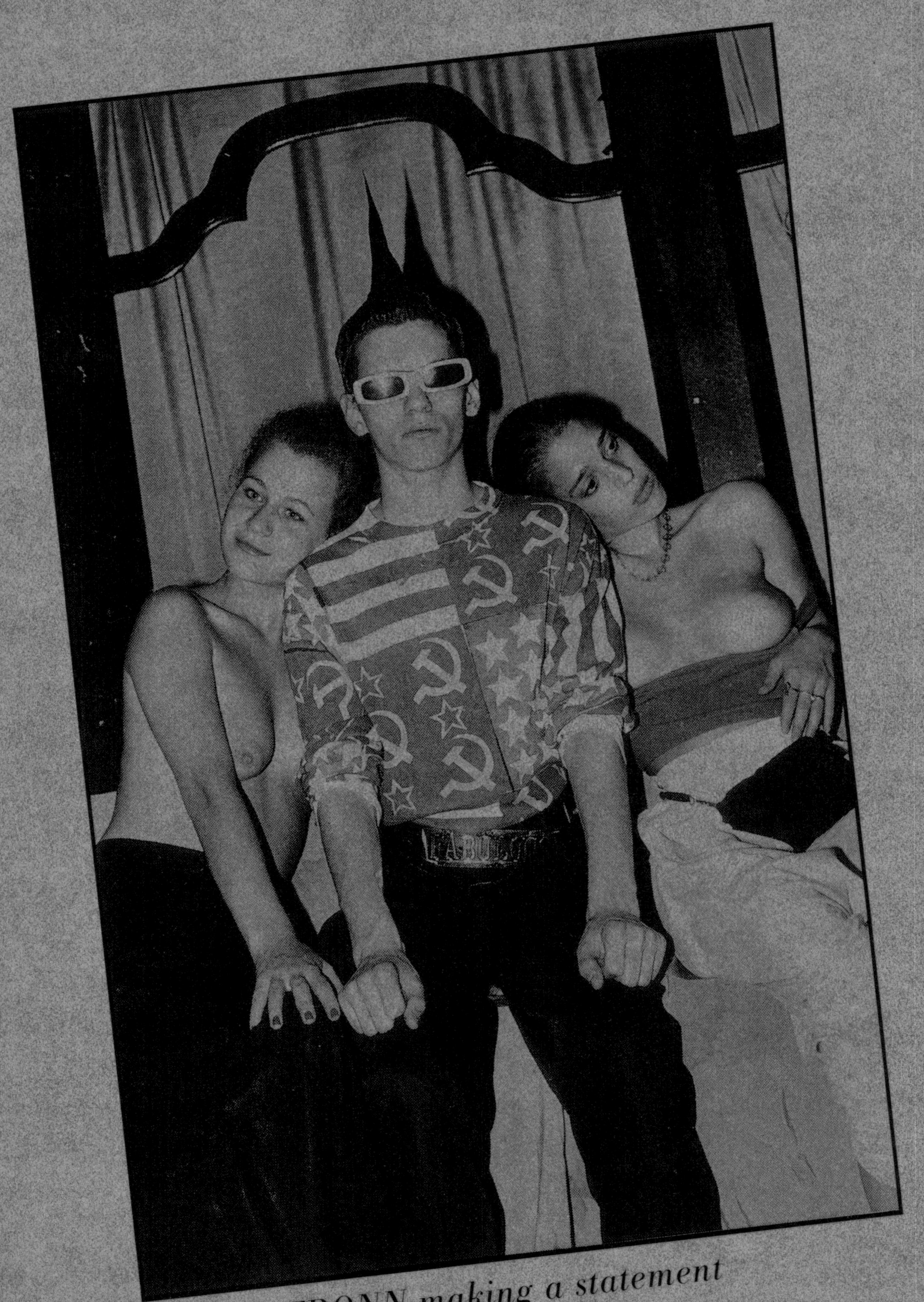

MYKUL TRONN *making a statement*
On the left, HOPE, very happy
On the right, STANA, quite tired

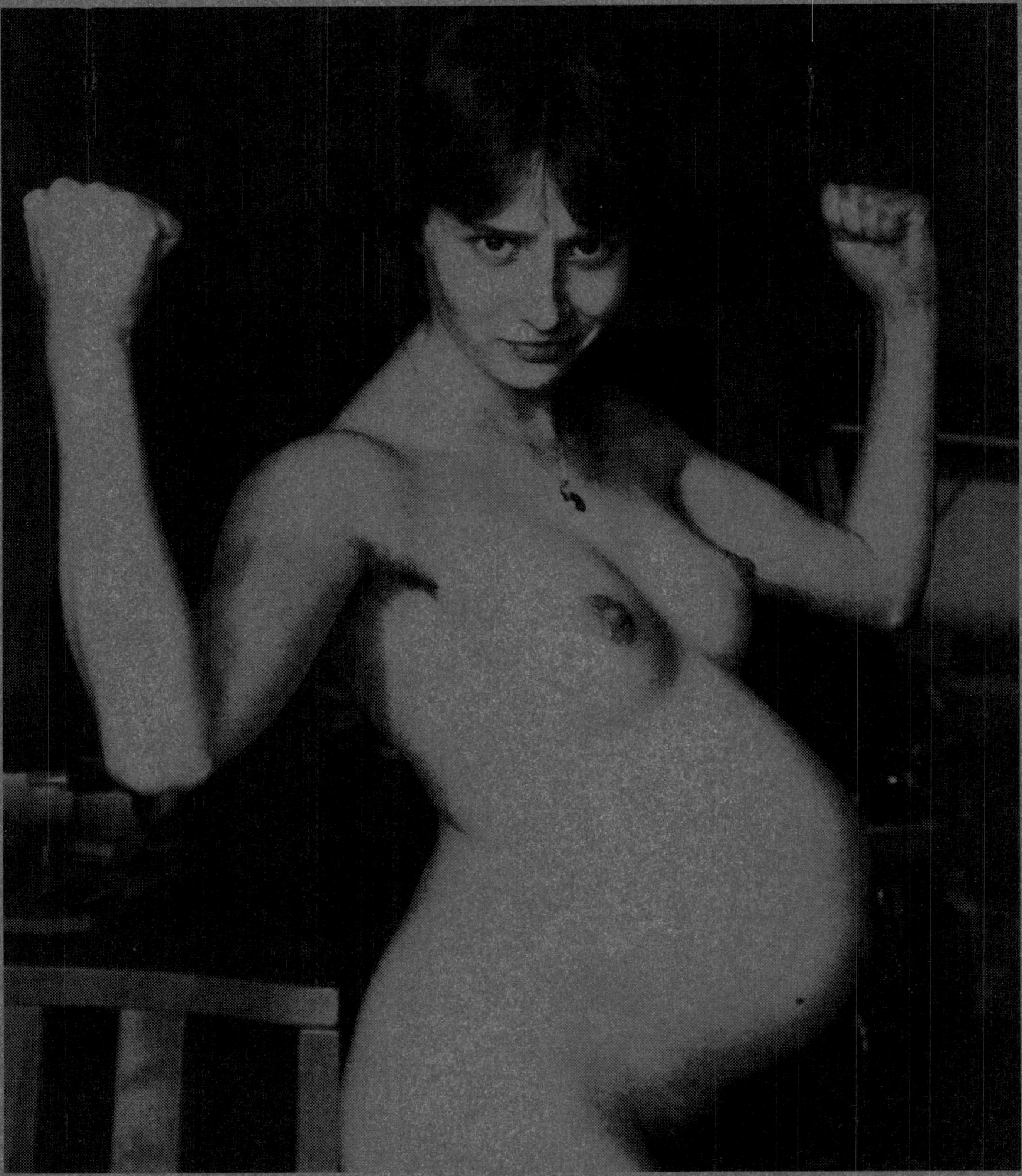

Günter Zint, Mackie mit Annalena im achten Monat, 1983

Künstlers E.J. Bellocq. Um das Jahr 1912 fotografiert er im Hurenviertel von New Orleans. Hierzu ist bei DuMont im Jahre 1978 nach der amerikanischen Original-

louse-Lautrec. Bellocq, den die Huren „Papa" nannten, muß von abschreckender Häßlichkeit gewesen sein. Ein wasserköpfiger Halbzwerg mit senkrechtstehenden Augen-

(71)

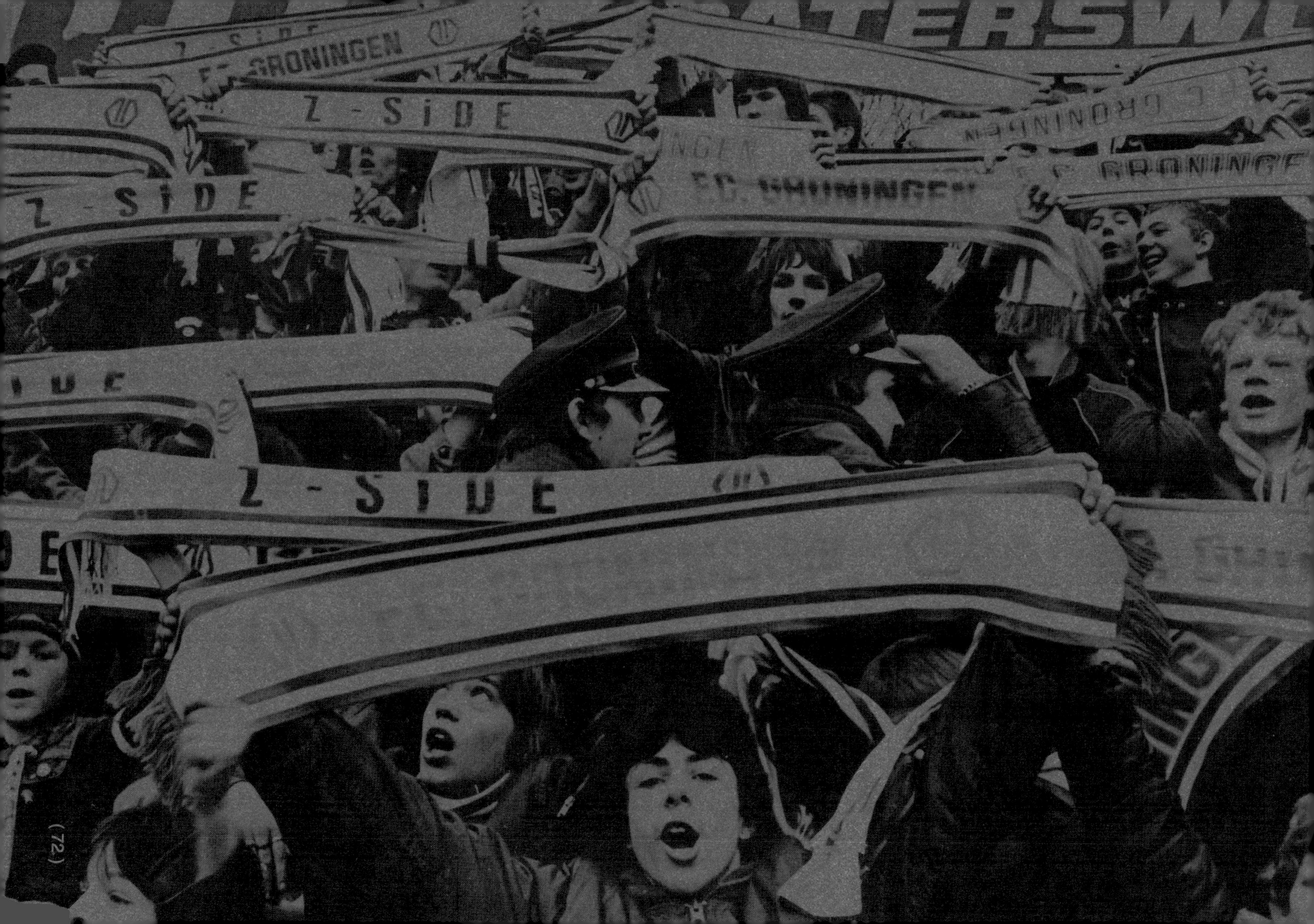
Z - SIDE
FC GRONINGEN
Z - SIDE
Z - SIDE
FC GRONINGEN
Z - SIDE
ATERSW

ПРЕЗЕРВАТИВЫ
У СТЕН МОССОВЕТА

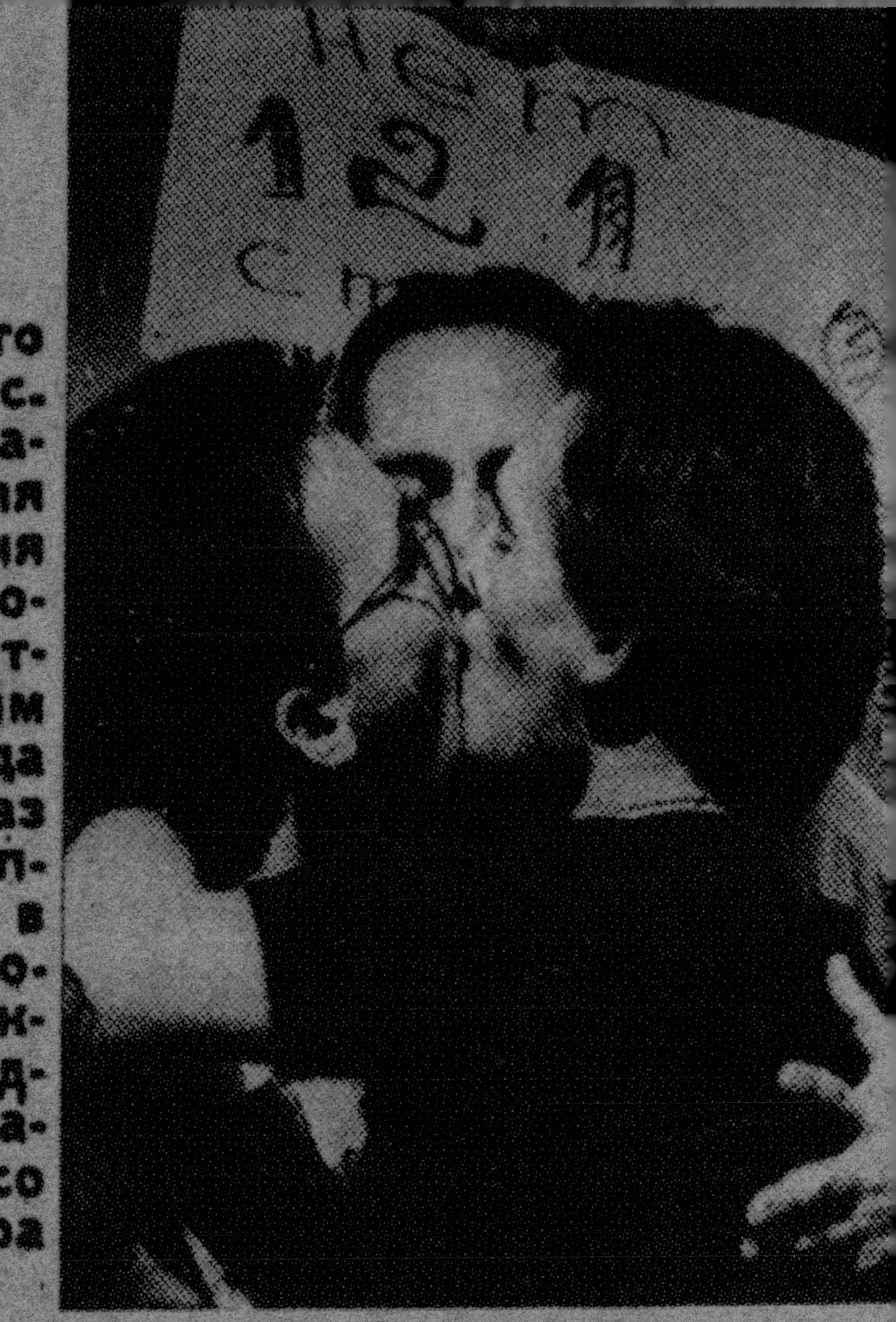

Похоже, в Москве это становится модой — бесплатная раздача презервативов. По крайней мере для голубо - розового движения это стало хорошим способом привлечения общественного внимания к своим проблемам. Кстати, когда вы видели в последний раз этот «предмет» любви в аптеке? А сколько он стоит в коммерческих ларьках, помните? То-то. Подобная акция в рамках Международного симпозиума по правам человека и борьбе со СПИДом состоялась вчера в 15.30